p. 342

p. 449

p. 372

p. 459

p. 357

p. 325

p. 377

p. 390

p. 396

p. 257

p. 386

p. 344

p. 447

p. 330

Mr. Food®
YES YOU CAN

Weight Loss Plan

**How I lost 35 pounds
and you CAN too!**

Oxmoor House®

Library of Congress Catalog Number: 2001-135890
ISBN: 0-8487-2484-4
Printed in the United States of America
First Printing 2001

Mr. Food®, the Logos, and OOH IT'S SO GOOD!! are registered marks owned by Ginsburg Enterprises Incorporated.

Be sure to check with your health-care provider before making any changes in your diet.

Ginsburg Enterprises Incorporated
    Chief Executive Officer: Art Ginsburg
    Chief Operating Officer: Steven Ginsburg
    Vice President, Publishing: Caryl Ginsburg Fantel
    Vice President, Creative Business Development: Howard Rosenthal
    Vice President, Sales and Licensing: Thomas R. Palombo
    Director of Finance and Administration: Chester Rosenbaum

Oxmoor House, Inc.
    Editor-in-Chief: Nancy Fitzpatrick Wyatt
    Executive Editor: Katherine M. Eakin
    Art Director: Cynthia R. Cooper

MR. FOOD® YES YOU CAN WEIGHT LOSS PLAN
    Editor: Anne Chappell Cain, M.S., M.P.H., R.D.
    Writer: Suzanne Henson, M.S., R.D.
    Assistant Foods Editor: Carolyn B. Land, R.D.
    Copy Editors: Donna Baldone, Catherine Ritter Scholl
    Editorial Assistant: Suzanne Powell
    Copy Assistant: Jane Lorberau Gentry
    Editorial Intern: Megan Graves
    Director, Test Kitchens: Elizabeth Tyler Luckett
    Assistant Director, Test Kitchens: Julie Christopher
    Recipe Editor: Gayle Hays Sadler
    Test Kitchens Staff: Jennifer A. Cofield,
        Gretchen Feldtman, R.D., David Gallent,
        Ana Price Kelly, Jan A. Smith
    Senior Photographer: Jim Bathie
    Publishing Systems Administrator: Rick Tucker
    Director, Production and Distribution: Phillip Lee
    Associate Production Manager: Theresa L. Beste
    Production Assistant: Faye Porter Bonner

    Contributors:
    Designer: Rita Yerby
    Copy Editor: Dolores Hydock
    Indexer: Keri Bradford Anderson

WE'RE HERE FOR YOU!
We at Oxmoor House are dedicated to serving you with reliable information that expands your imagination and enriches your life. We welcome your comments and suggestions. Please write to us at:
    Oxmoor House, Inc.
    Editor, MR. FOOD YES
    YOU CAN WEIGHT
    LOSS PLAN
    2100 Lakeshore Drive
    Birmingham, AL 35209

To order additional publications, call 1-205-445-6560.

For more books to enrich your life, visit oxmoorhouse.com

Contents

Preface

About a year ago, I realized that after years of surrounding myself with delicious foods, a few extra pounds had surrounded me! I needed to lose weight, but didn't want to go on one of those "fad" diets where you have to cut out all kinds of foods. I knew there had to be a way to eat things that I liked, but still lose weight. So I came up with my own plan and lost 35 pounds! I was so excited about my weight loss and wanted to share my success with other folks, knowing that there must be a lot of other people out there like me.

Well, I had been working with the book publishers at Oxmoor House on some other cookbook projects. They publish books for *Cooking Light* magazine and have a staff of dietitians and health editors. I went to them with the idea for a weight-loss book, and they said, "Let's do it!"

So we did. I worked with three registered dietitians to make sure that my plan got a "thumbs-up" from the nutrition professionals. They reviewed all the tips, tricks, and advice, and even added some of their own. Plus, they reviewed all of the recipes to make sure that they were acceptable for a weight-loss plan.

I'm telling you this to assure you that this is not some gimmicky diet plan. It's just a commonsense approach to healthful eating and physical activity that can work for anyone. I'm certainly no nutrition expert, but I sure have learned what it takes to lose weight!

As you know, one of my main interests is food, so food had to be a big part of my weight-loss plan. You'll get plenty of quick and easy recipes and menus that you can use to help you lose weight. Try them and see if you don't say "OOH IT'S SO GOOD!!"

I'm not claiming that everything about losing weight is easy, but I am telling you that it's not as hard as you might think. If I can do it, you can too. And this is the place to start. Good luck!

Mr. Food

Acknowledgments

I couldn't have created this book without a lot of help. Weight-loss books don't just happen; they are the result of a lot of team-work, and I want to thank all of the people on this book team.

First, I'd like to thank Suzanne Henson, M.S., R.D. She is the registered dietitian who helped me make sure that this plan was safe and on the right track, nutritionally speaking. I knew that the plan had worked for me, but before I started telling anyone else about it, I needed to make sure that the nutrition experts would approve. Suzanne advised me on all of the material in this book so that I could be sure the information I was giving you was sound.

I also want to thank my friends at Oxmoor House for coordi-nating the production of this book, and for reviewing my recipes and making sure that the nutrient numbers were just right. It was a pleasure to work with them.

As always, I am grateful to my Editor and Book Project Manager Caryl Ginsburg Fantel for making everything come together. Also, thanks to Howard Rosenthal for his creative input, to the other members of my management team, Steve Ginsburg, Tom Palombo, and Chet Rosenbaum and to my wonderful admin-istrative staff.

And I would be remiss if I did not thank a few others: The kind folks at Bill Blass clothing for helping me look so elegant in one of their dashing tuxedos; Bones and Ellen Long for being such great exercise models as well as models of good health; and Nancy McCracken, physical therapist, who reviewed the exercise program and the stretching exercises.

And, finally, thanks to my wife, Ethel, my children, and my six grandchildren who all have inspired me and given me so much sup-port in my weight-loss efforts. You are my reason for losing weight and getting in shape.

Yes You Can! Plan

CONGRATULATIONS! BY READING THIS BOOK, YOU'VE taken the first step toward losing weight and keeping it off for good. If you're like a lot of folks, you've probably tried the fad plans or popped diet pills and discovered that they just don't work!

Trust me, I know how it feels to look down at the scale one day and see a surprising number staring back at you. Or to pull on a favorite pair of pants only to discover that they're tight in all the wrong places!

Now, I've lost 35 pounds (and counting)! I'm so excited about my new, healthier lifestyle—and waist-line—that I can't wait to share my secrets with you!

In this section, I'll tell you a little more about my weight-loss plan and show you how you can get started. With help from a registered dietitian, I'll also answer some common questions about losing weight and learning a healthier way of living.

It's a simple plan, but it sure works for me! And I'll bet it will work for you, too!

8 Great Reasons to Lose Weight

1. Cut **risk factors**. Losing weight will help reduce your risk of heart disease, diabetes, stroke, and certain cancers. *2.* Increase **energy**. Incorporating regular physical activity into your day is a sure-fire way to increase your energy level. When you lose weight, you have less to carry around! *3.* Age **better**. Adopting healthy eating and activity habits will help you manage conditions associated with aging, such as arthritis and menopause. *4.* **Relax**. Exercise is a fantastic way to relieve tension and stress. *5.* **Breathe** better. Strengthen your lungs with regular exercise and a healthy diet. *6.* **Up** your **immunity**. The healthier you are, the better your body is able to fight off illness. *7.* **See** the next **generation**. Stay healthy so that you can live to see your children and grandchildren grow up—and be able to keep up with them. *8.* Feel **fabulous**. The better you take care of yourself, the better you're going to feel!

Chapter 1

The Secrets of My Success

Success Without Sacrifice

*Here's my strategy for success for everyone
who wants to lose weight, feel great,
and eat incredible food.*

Most people who try to diet see their resolve fizzle out quickly. Usually, that's because the weight doesn't come off as fast as they'd hoped or they're tempted by a barrage of mouthwatering foods their family and friends "can" eat but they can't because they're "dieting."

That's what I discovered when I tried to lose the 30-plus pounds I had gained over the past several years. I've been surrounded by rich food all my life, and for the past 20 years, I've cooked up yummy recipes for fans across the country every day during my segment on television news shows. But I noticed my attitude toward eating had changed. I had become a "second-helping eater." My motto was, "if a little is good, more is better."

Well, that attitude got me into plenty of trouble! When I was younger, I was a football jock and Navy boot camp graduate. But in recent years, my eating habits caught up with me. My belly was so

> I didn't give up my favorite foods, drink meal substitutes, or hire a personal trainer.

big that when I bent over to tie my shoes, I could barely reach the laces. I didn't sleep well, I got winded before I even teed off on the golf course, and my grandkids complained that I couldn't keep up anymore.

That's when I said, "Enough!" I took a look at some of the popular fad diets, but I knew they wouldn't work for me. After all, I'm Mr. Food! I can't cut all carbohydrates from my meals or survive on lettuce leaves and celery stalks!

So I came up with my own weight-loss plan. I lost 35 pounds by eating a little bit of everything—in moderation of course. That's right! I didn't give up my favorite foods, drink meal substitutes, or hire a personal trainer. I simply focused on eating commonsense portions of flavorful, satisfying foods made more nutritious with a few changes. I also found creative ways to fit easy exercises into my busy schedule.

It worked! Now I want to share my strategy for success with everyone who wants to lose weight, feel great, and eat incredible food.

"I've gone down two suit sizes, and didn't have to sacrifice to do it!"

A Plan For Success

It's my business to know a lot about food, but now I know a lot about weight control, too. After personally experiencing the extraordinary physical and emotional benefits weight loss brings, I decided to document my strategy so that other folks could experience the same kind of success.

My plan is based on the theory that if you eat moderate amounts of the good-for-you foods you love, you're less likely to overeat in order to feel satisfied. But I wanted to make sure that my plan was safe, realistic, and complete, so I asked the real weight-loss experts—registered dietitians and exercise physiologists—for input. These folks told me the truth about losing weight and keeping it off, and they gave me hundreds of tricks, tips, and techniques to help me stay on track. Check out the next page for a sampling of the tools the experts helped me come up with. I figure if these tools helped me lose weight, they'll help you, too! And I hope that you'll notice that not everything on the list is about food. To lose weight the right way you need to work on your attitude and your activity level.

> If you eat moderate amounts of foods you love, you're less likely to overeat in order to feel satisfied.

TOOLS YOU CAN USE

Portion size guide

Here's the best way to get a handle on what you eat! (See page 76.)

Attitude adjusters

Sometimes one slip-up can make you feel like a weight-loss loser, not winner. Instead of giving in to temptation, take advantage of the best binge busters! (See page 94.)

Grocery list of good-for-you foods

Shopping's a breeze! This list is all I need to stock up on the best basics! (See page 120.)

Step-by-step quick-cooking guide

I wouldn't be Mr. Food if I didn't give you the scoop on the latest (and healthiest!) "get-it-on-the-table-quick" cooking techniques! (See page 124.)

Top 10 superfoods

Eating an abundance of these foods every day helps keep the extra pounds away! (See pages 144 and 145.)

50 ways to break up exercise boredom

If you're bored to tears by the thought of a treadmill, this list offers the answers you've been looking for! And, I've included the experts' stay-fit secrets—even they don't want to crawl out of bed to run on a rainy morning! (See page 193.)

What's in the Plan?

Due to my own success, I know you can lose weight without feeling deprived or sacrificing your enjoyment of food. Here's a quick summary of what you'll get with the Mr. Food plan.

Easy Recipes

Being Mr. Food, I wanted to give you time-saving solutions for real food that tastes great. Like my television segments and previous books, my weight-loss program is built on that easy idea.

Great-Tasting Food

When I thought about what foods my plan would contain, I knew that the food had to be delicious. I know that if the food on a weight-loss program isn't satisfying, you won't stick with the program for long!

Family Favorites

I modified some of my favorite recipes to reduce my risk of heart disease and diabetes. I'm proud to say that I was able to decrease fat, cholesterol, and salt in these recipes and still satisfy my "OOH IT'S SO GOOD!!" standard. You'll recognize familiar comfort recipes such as creamy soups, chewy brownies, and cheese-topped casseroles.

Need-to-Know Nutrients

The recipes in this book are ideal for folks who are trying to lose weight or anyone who wants to begin a healthier lifestyle. Every recipe contains a complete nutritional analysis, as well as diabetic exchanges. That makes each recipe easy to include in diabetic meal plans or other specialized diets.

Fun with Fitness

Once I figured out how to make my favorite foods more nutritious, I found ways to incorporate more activity into my busy schedule. I firmly believe that being fit doesn't demand grueling hours in a gym. And I think it's important to find activities that are fun and simple so that you'll keep them up over the long haul.

It's important to find activities that are fun and simple.

That's why the exercise section of this book is different. There are no complicated moves or expensive pieces of equipment to buy. I think you'll love my simple walking guide and easy exercises to increase strength and flexibility. The best part is that these easy moves can be done around the house!

Motivation Made Easy

Every day I'm surrounded by 15 pounds of sugar, 8 pounds of butter, and 10 pounds of flour! I know it's not easy to stay on track. That's why I've gathered plenty of tips to keep you motivated.

It's ooh-so-simple!

My fans know that I like to keep everything super simple. So I tell folks who want to lose weight to remember these three simple steps:

1. **Keep a positive attitude.**
2. **Add activity to your day.**
3. **Eat good-for-you, great-tasting food.**

Sounds simple, right? Well, I can't wait to show you how easy and fun it is to look and feel better!

Are You Ready?

Before you get started on a weight-loss program, it's important to pinpoint your reasons for wanting to lose weight. First, set aside some quiet time away from all interruptions. Relax for a few minutes. Take some deep breaths, then answer the following statements and questions. Go ahead and write your answers in the book. By the time you've completed this exercise, you'll have a pretty good idea of whether or not you're ready to lose weight for yourself, or if there are hidden obstacles that could hamper your success.

1 List three specific areas where losing weight will benefit no one but you. (Consider physical, medical, and emotional benefits.)

1._____

2._____

3._____

2 What problems or stressful situations are you currently facing in your life?

_____

_____

_____

_____

_____

_____

_____

3 List those stressful situations that can be improved if you lose weight.

_____

_____

_____

_____

4 Which of the following health benefits can result from even moderate weight loss?

❏ better diabetes control

❏ lower blood pressure

❏ lower cholesterol

❏ decreased stress

❏ decreased risk of heart disease

❏ less stress on joints

answer: all of the above

5 Check all of the concerns you have about making changes in your eating and exercise habits.

❏ I'll have to give up all my favorite foods.

❏ I won't have any energy.

❏ I don't know how to cook healthy foods.

❏ I'm embarrassed to put on workout clothes.

❏ I just don't like to exercise!

❏ My family won't like it if I start cooking different foods.

❏ List others: _____

_____

_____

6 List obstacles you face to losing weight successfully (for example, lack of time or lack of support from family).

_____

_____

_____

_____

_____

7 Come up with solutions to overcoming those obstacles (for example, getting up 30 minutes earlier to walk).

_____

_____

_____

_____

8 Name the people you can count on to support you in your weight-loss effort.

_____

_____

_____

9 List some lifestyle changes that might be possible for you to make permanently (for example, daily exercise, drinking more water, watching serving sizes).

_____

_____

_____

_____

10 List some situations that might cause a setback in your weight-loss efforts.

_____

_____

_____

_____

11 How will you measure your success in losing weight?

❑ Number of pounds lost

❑ Better fitting clothes

❑ Smaller size of clothes

❑ Compliments from others

❑ More energy

❑ Lower blood pressure

❑ Other_____

12 In what time frame do you want to reach your desired weight?

❑ 1 week   ❑ One year

❑ 1 month   ❑ Other_____

❑ 6 months   _____

13 What is a healthy rate of weight loss?

❑ 1 pound per month   ❑ 10 pounds per week

❑ 1 to 2 pounds per week   **answer: 1 to 2 pounds per week**

6 Steps to Success

1. **Take small steps.** Approach weight loss as something you will accomplish in a series of small steps, not all at once. *2.* **Solve problems.** People who lose weight and keep it off are people who overcome obstacles by finding creative solutions. *3.* **Keep track.** When you write down everything you eat and how much you exercise, you can see where your slip-ups are, as well as your improvements.

4. **Reward yourself.** To keep yourself motivated, celebrate successes with nonfood treats. *5.* **Don't give up.** Slow and steady wins the race, and the healthiest kind of weight loss is the kind that happens gradually. *6.* **Plan to succeed.** And chances are, you will!

Chapter 2

Smart Steps

Getting There
Step-by-Step

Most projects seem more manageable when they're broken down into smaller tasks.

Think about a recent project you've worked on. Maybe it was a remodeling job at your house or a year-end report at work. Or you may have just planted a garden or coordinated a charity event.

Now think about how those projects were completed. You didn't do it all at once—instead, you did it in a series of small steps. Whether you're installing new kitchen cabinets or pulling weeds in your garden, most projects are more manageable when they're broken down into smaller tasks. That's just common sense! When you tackle a challenge at work or home, you're going through the same commonsense steps it takes to lose weight.

I've met many folks who believe that losing weight is an "all-or-nothing" proposition that requires a complete overhaul of your lifestyle all at once. There may be a lot of areas that need improvement, but the best way to make changes permanently is to work on one or two at a time. Breaking weight loss down into a series of small changes makes the effort seem less overwhelming.

"I try to find ways to get a little exercise anywhere I can...lifting cans is a great way to work your biceps."

Beyond Willpower

Stop counting the failed diets, unused gym memberships, and dust-covered workout machines. Don't throw in the towel because you think it's too difficult. You're not destined to be overweight because you "have no willpower." Successful weight loss isn't driven by willpower alone. Dietitians and personal trainers say that the people most likely to lose weight are people who are problem solvers and planners. For example, weight-loss winners come up with creative solutions to fit workouts into their busy schedules or plan meals in advance. That's right. Plan to succeed, and chances are you will. Fail to plan, however, and you're planning to fail!

Mr. Food's Fun Trip

A lot of folks ask how I stick with my new eating and exercise routine, especially since I'm surrounded every day by incredible food. I tell them I'm having so much fun, I can't imagine falling back into my old habits!

I make losing weight fun by thinking of it as a vacation I plan to stay on forever. In fact, when you lose weight, you are taking a vacation—a permanent vacation from feeling lousy! Think about what you do before you take a vacation. First, you decide where you want to go and how you want to get there. If you're driving, you look at a map to figure out the best route.

Next, you pack the things you'll need while you're gone, and you might even buy some new clothes before you leave. Once you get to your destination, you live it up, sampling new foods and trying new activities.

Well, I think losing weight is a fabulous fat-busting expedition. This trip is different from a quick summer getaway, though, because you'll have so much more than souvenirs or snapshots for your efforts. Besides your ooh-so-slim profile, you'll be able to show a healthier body and new self-confidence.

"I have so much energy now, I feel like I'm 20 years younger."

Here's my step-by-step guide to help you reach your ultimate destination—great health:

1. Know Your Goal

Why do you want to lose weight? In the "Are You Ready?" exercise on page 18, you wrote down some areas in your life that would improve if you lost weight. Remember, when temptation strikes, it's not enough that someone else wants you to lose weight. So pinpoint your reasons for wanting to change and how doing so will improve your health and quality of life. You may find it helpful to write your reasons on a card that you can refer to when your motivation dwindles.

2. Map out Your Plan

How are you going to make it happen? When will you work in a little extra activity? What type of activity will you do? Do you have time to cook meals? Do you eat out often? Come up with a plan and write it out!

I find it helpful to break my plan down into specific goals that I can accomplish quickly. Taking small, consistent steps toward a healthier lifestyle keeps me focused on my long-term goals. For example, when I realized I needed to lose weight, I first set out to do just a few sit-ups and push-ups every morning. That eased me into the exercise groove again, and I stayed motivated by my success. Later I increased the number of each exercise I did, started walking, and added back-strengthening stretches.

> I make losing weight fun by thinking of it as a vacation I plan to stay on forever.

As I adopted new eating and exercise habits, one of my greatest fears was burnout—you know, when the fitness fire fizzles? I asked the diet and exercise experts for some stick-with-it strategies. First, they told me to **schedule exercise just as I would a doctor's appointment or business meeting.** That helps me a lot! By treating my daily walks as can't-miss meetings, I squeeze in my workout even on days when fatigue or a spur-of-the-moment dinner invitation tempts me to skip it.

Another tip that helps me curb the burnout blues is **trying a new food or recipe every week**. Okay, I know you're thinking, "How is anything new to Mr. Food?" Well, believe me, there are a lot of different products out there that even I haven't tried! So I have fun in the kitchen. I whip up fruit-based smoothies for snacks, and change some of my favorite recipes to reduce my risk of high cholesterol, high blood pressure, and heart disease. During my weekly supermarket sweep, I go on a hunting expedition for the latest reduced-fat foods. When I eat out, I

> I'm having so much fun, I can't imagine falling back into my old habits!

experiment with portion control strategies. This way I can sample new menu items and even enjoy dessert while staying on track!

I've also learned how important it is to **reward yourself for small victories**. Sure, feeling and looking better is your long-term goal, but it helps to work for bonus incentives along the way! Many fellow weight-loss winners swear by the reward system to sustain their motivation. Do this for yourself by drawing up a list of indulgences that range from small and inexpensive to major investments. Then choose one to celebrate meeting your weekly or monthly goals.

One weight-loss counselor I spoke with keeps such a reward list for herself. She includes cost-free gifts of time or inexpensive treats. She includes such items as curling up with a book from the best-seller list or taking in the latest box-office thriller. She selects more costly gifts, such as a magazine subscription or a new pair of tennis shoes, after reaching major milestones. If the experts rely on such secrets to stay motivated, you can be sure they'll work for you!

3. Watch out for Roadblocks

A close friend confessed recently that she's a closet cookie addict. If she brings home a box of cookies, particularly reduced-fat ones, there'll be nothing but crumbs left within a day. Another friend finishes off a pint of ice cream faster than it melts in the summer sun! But both friends recognize their weakness and know not to keep diet traps lurking in the kitchen. Stop splurges where they start—at the grocery store. You won't be forced to test your willpower if you don't bring temptation home. I'm not suggesting you deprive yourself of foods you love—occasionally indulging your weakness is not off-limits!

Here's a temptation-proof trick from those friends I told you about: When you crave a particular food, simply buy a small portion and enjoy every last bite! For example, buy a snack- or travel-sized package of cookies, or purchase only one special item from the bakery. If you're an ice cream lover, it's smarter to buy one scoop at an ice cream stand, rather than pick up even a pint at the store. Torture-free tactics like these will help you lose weight and build better food habits without giving up your favorite foods.

To be a weight-loss winner, you've got to plan ahead.

In addition to food temptations, what bumps in the road could hinder your success? Is your life unusually stressful right now? Do you have health problems that make exercising difficult? Do work deadlines and family commitments keep your schedule stretched thin? To be a weight-loss winner, you've got to plan ahead, and identify the main obstacles to your success. Once you recognize those obstacles, do some creative problem solving and come up with several strategic solutions.

4. Track your Progress

Many weight-loss winners swear by record-keeping to track what they eat and how much they exercise. That serves a two-fold purpose because you see where your slip-ups are and how you've improved. A variety of journals can energize your weight-loss efforts. Here are several to try:

Fat-Friendly Album: If you're motivated by visual incentives, try this tactic. Document your progress through pictures, starting with a photo at your heavier weight. Then, commemorate milestones with shots of your slimmer profile. Some folks sustain their motivation with older photos picturing themselves at their desired weight. They post these shots in high-traffic areas such as on the bathroom mirror or refrigerator door. That visual reminder of leaner days bolsters sagging spirits when the scale won't budge.

Food and Mood Diary: Many weight-loss experts strongly suggest keeping a food diary to discover moods or stressful situations that trigger binges. This tool is especially important if you eat on the run or turn to food for emotional comfort. (Turn to chapter 7 for ways to control emotional eating.)

Pick up a pocket- or purse-sized notebook and record what you eat, the amount or serving size, where you are and how you feel. Look at my example on page 32 to see how a food diary can reveal important information about your eating habits. You

"Here are just a couple of the pictures I look at when I am really tempted to go back to my old habits. Do you see the size of that belly?"

may be shocked to see how few fruits and vegetables you eat! The diary can help you get a glimpse of one thing you could easily change about your eating habits. For example, say you eat a giant cinnamon bun as you dash off to work every morning. The fat-gram count in that high-fat breakfast (about 12 grams) might add an extra half-pound to your frame every week! Switch to a cinnamon-raisin bagel spread with a tablespoon of reduced-fat cream cheese (about 2.5 grams of fat), and you'll likely notice a difference on your own buns!

FOOD DIARY—Tuesday

FOOD	AMOUNT	WHERE EATEN	MOOD
cereal bar	2	car	stressed
bacon cheeseburger fries milkshake	1 reg lg X-lg	desk	busy
candy bar	king-size	breakroom	tired
spaghetti garlic toast tossed salad w/ ranch dressing cheesecake wine	plateful 2 slices small bowl 1 Tbsp 1 slice 2 glasses	front of TV	bored
ice cream	soup bowl full	front of TV	tired

Workout Log: If you think exercise logs are only for extreme athletes, think again! Even mall walkers benefit from recording their progress. Not only is it terrific to see how far you've come, but you'll also notice when you've reached a plateau and need to push yourself a little harder.

5. Assess and Adjust

If the scales start to tilt back toward your old weight or your waistband begins to get a little snug again, take a look at what's changed in your life and make adjustments. You may discover you've eaten out more, or that carting the kids to after-school activities has left little time to walk. Or maybe it's the ups and downs of life that interfere with reaching your fitness goals. If your routine gets interrupted, be creative and think of some new weight-loss activities so that you can get back on track.

"My wife and I love to get out on the dance floor together. Dancing is a blast—and you can burn 153 calories by jitterbugging for just 30 minutes!"

6. Have Fun!

Nothing's quite as much fun as receiving a compliment from a member of the opposite sex. (My wife of 40-plus years agrees with that one!) And while flattery is definitely a terrific motivator, you need to stay creative in order to keep weight loss fun over the long haul! Enjoy new taste sensations by sampling healthy new recipes. Reward your success with nonfood pleasures. Keep your energy up by tuning in to funky music during your next workout and trying different activities. (I know several grandmothers who swear by rollerblading!) When you get creative and make healthy eating and fat-burning activity fun, it's easier to keep the weight off!

5 Health Facts About Weight

Did you know... **1.** More than **half** of **American** adults are **overweight?** **2.** About **20%** of **teenagers** have **weight problems?**

3. About **300,000 deaths** in the United States each year can be **linked** to **obesity?** **4.** Almost **$70 billion** a year is spent by our **healthcare system** to treat problems related to being **seriously overweight?**

5. Americans spend more than **$33 billion** a year on **weight-loss** products and services**?**

Chapter 3

Health
Matters

Healthy Weight Loss

A sound weight-loss plan helps you understand how your body works and why you gain weight.

Every time I pick up a magazine or turn on the TV, there's yet another headline or ad promising a quick fix for permanent weight loss. Those sensationalized stories are usually just gimmicks and confuse those of us who want to learn commonsense lifestyle habits. It certainly isn't easy to separate fact from fiction when you're bombarded by misinformation that's marketed as "miracle science."

I believe a sound weight-loss plan helps you understand how your body works and why you gain weight. I also think it's important to identify key health habits that make it easier to keep the weight off in the long run.

Unfortunately, we're all looking for a magic bullet. And there are plenty of fad plans out there that tell us it's possible to lose weight without changing our eating or exercise habits. But the way you lose weight is to eat fewer calories than you use. This fact really doesn't change, regardless of so-called "diet discoveries."

Eating less and moving more sounds like a simple equation. The equation is simple, but I'll admit that putting that equation into action can seem quite complicated! But if you talk to the right people—the real weight-loss experts—they can help you understand what it takes to drop those pounds. I spent some time with Suzanne Henson, a registered dietitian who's had a lot of experience helping people like me lose weight. She set a lot of things straight for me about weight loss, so I thought I'd share a bit of our conversation.

MY WEIGHT-LOSS EXPERT

Suzanne Henson, M.S., R.D. is a registered dietitian with Oxmoor House, the book publishing division of Southern Progress Corporation. Suzanne is the editor of *Weight Watchers Annual Recipes for Success 2000, Weight Watchers Simple & Classic Homecooking*, and *Weight Watchers Miracle Foods: More Fruits, More Veggies*.

In addition to editing weight-loss cookbooks, Suzanne has taught weight-control classes and has worked extensively with clients on an individual basis to help them develop personal weight-loss plans.

She has a degree in journalism and a master's degree in nutrition from The University of Alabama. Suzanne will soon be assuming the position of coordinator for the popular EatRight weight-loss program in the Department of Nutrition Sciences at the University of Alabama at Birmingham. This is one of the longest running and most successful weight-loss programs in the United States.

Talking with the Expert

MR. FOOD (MR. F.): Suzanne, how does someone lose weight?

SUZANNE HENSON, R.D. (SH): There are many factors that can affect your weight, but the fact is that most overweight people simply eat too much and exercise too little. Sorry, but that's the truth. You really have to eat fewer calories than you expend through exercise or any other activity that gets you moving.

MR. F.: That sounds simple enough. But I know a lot of people who sign up for pricey weight-loss programs or vow to shed the extra pounds once and for all, and they never lose the weight. What are they doing wrong?

SH: The trick is how an individual approaches weight loss. Each year in this country, we spend about $33 billion on weight-loss products and programs. That's a lot of money for little success.

People need to understand why they really want to lose weight. Often they just want to improve their appearance, but I think they'd be more successful if they focused on improving their health, with the trimmer profile being a bonus.

It's important for people who want to lose weight to pinpoint their weaknesses. I know my own roadblocks, which may differ from yours. There are certain situations, like parties and holidays, that stop my good habits dead in their tracks, so I have preplanned strategies to deal with them. (See "Help for the Holidays," page 91.)

MR. F.: But you're a registered dietitian, Suzanne! You know what to do!

SH: I promise you, most people, myself included, have to do a daily willpower check. The important thing is to figure out what your personal obstacles are, and come up with a way to work around them. For example, I can't turn my grocery cart down the cookie aisle. I know I'll be tempted to pick up a package of cookies, and I've learned that my resolve melts with the first bite. So for me, it's a smarter idea to buy one cookie from the bakery. That way, I satisfy my craving without splurging. Someone else might keep the package of cookies out of sight in the kitchen, or buy a single-serving package.

MR. F.: I hear a lot of people claim that their weight problem is due to a medical condition. How common is that?

SH: You're probably thinking about thyroid problems or other hormonal imbalances, which can contribute to weight gain or cause someone to have difficulty losing weight. However, less than 2 percent of weight problems are related to a thyroid or other hormonal disorder.

Sometimes people say they've never had success with any weight-loss plan. They need to make sure that their eating and exercise habits are not preventing them from losing weight. If they've cut their food intake and upped their exercise without success, then they need to visit a physician and ask for a thyroid test. That'll help determine if there is an underlying medical problem that can be treated and increase the individual's ability to successfully lose weight.

MR. F.: What about a family tendency toward weight gain? Doesn't that account for a lot of problems?

SH: There are definitely genetic traits that set someone up for weight gain. Take a look at some families. Many times, you'll notice that family members carry their excess weight in the same place.

You've probably seen the ads in which a woman jokingly refers to "having my mother's thighs."

While genetics may make us susceptible to gaining weight, it's our lifestyle habits that determine if that weight gain actually occurs. Families typically have the same health habits. You learn your food habits at the family table (or in the fast food drive-thru, in some families). That's why parents who make changes to improve their own health are also setting a terrific example for their children.

MR. F.: What else besides weight gain tends to run in the family?

SH: Heredity plays a role in making some people more likely to get Type 1 (insulin-dependent) diabetes, but often people with no family history of diabetes are diagnosed with the disease. You also might inherit a tendency to get Type 2 (non-insulin-dependent) diabetes. But again, you might have just "inherited" your family's habits of overeating and not exercising.

High cholesterol, heart disease, and some kinds of cancer also have family links. So it's a good idea to know something about your family's health history and do something to decrease your chances of developing one of these conditions.

MR. F.: If we learn a lot of our habits in childhood, isn't it a little unrealistic to expect grownups to make major changes in their eating and exercise habits?

SH: You'd be surprised at the difference even a small change can make. I recommend that you make just one change in your eating or activity habits. For example, if you drink a sugary soft drink every day, try to cut out that one thing, or switch to a calorie-free soda. That saves close to 1,200 calories a week, or about one-third of a pound!

It's also easier to make permanent changes in your health habits when you make them gradually. That's why you need to set small goals and ease into new lifestyle patterns. If you do that, you'll stay motivated by your success.

MR. F.: How do the folks who lose weight keep the weight off over the long haul?

SH: Well, you really have to take responsibility for your weight, and realize that only you can control it. That goes back to viewing weight as a health issue, rather than related primarily to your appearance. Maintaining good eating and exercise habits is one positive thing you can do for yourself.

There are so many people who take care of everyone else, but never themselves. This a common problem for women who think they're being selfish by taking time to exercise. Or they feel guilty for serving healthy meals when the kids want fast food or their husband wants rich desserts. It's amazing to see the change in someone who regains control of their eating and exercise habits. I've worked with women who say taking control of their weight gave them an incredible feeling of power—and they love it!

MR. F.: At food shows I've met plenty of folks, particularly women, who sacrifice their own health for others. I always tell 'em: You've taken care of everybody else, now it's time to take care of yourself!

SH: Exactly! In addition to taking responsibility for their health, people who control their weight long-term have four things in common, according to the National Weight Control Registry.

MR. F.: Wait a minute! I've heard of bridal and baby registries, but a weight registry?

SH: Obesity researchers started the National Weight Control Registry to determine what works long-term to control weight. They polled people who lost 30 or more pounds and kept it off for a year or more. So far, people who successfully lost weight and kept it off share most of the following habits: they keep track of their weight, eat breakfast, eat a low-fat diet, and exercise regularly.

---

4 HABITS OF SUCCESSFUL "LOSERS"

1. Keep track of weight.
2. Eat breakfast.
3. Eat a low-fat diet.
4. Exercise regularly.

MR. F.: Sounds like common sense, not miracle science! But I've heard a lot of hype about some fad "low-carb" diets. Do they really work?

SH: You can lose weight on some of these diets, but there's no evidence that these plans are effective for long-term weight control. Cutting out an entire food group is never a good idea. I'm concerned about diet plans that eliminate starches but encourage eating plenty of foods that are chock-full of cholesterol and saturated fat, such as eggs, butter, and high-fat meats. Consuming an excess amount of those types of foods can set someone up for heart disease or other serious health conditions.

MR. F.: What other health conditions are related to being overweight? From my own experience, I can tell you that the extra pounds aggravate arthritis!

SH: There are many. About 300,000 people die each year from conditions related to obesity. In addition to heart attack and stroke, excess weight increases the risk for Type 2 diabetes, some cancers, and gallbladder disease. And as you mentioned, extra weight puts a lot of pressure on arthritic joints.

MR. F.: Sounds like being overweight can be as dangerous as smoking!

SH: I think it is. Almost half of American adults are overweight, and about one in four is considered clinically obese. Those are pretty scary numbers. Even a moderate weight loss of 5 to 10 pounds can have tremendous health benefits.

MR. F.: Okay, let's talk about some specific diet stuff.

SH: What do you want to know?

MR. F.: I heard that drinking a lot of water helps you lose weight. Is that right?

SH: Almost everybody needs to drink more water, whether you are trying to lose weight or not. You need to drink at least 8 (8-ounce) glasses a day. But if you are exercising, especially if you're sweating a lot, you need to drink more than 8 glasses.

Sometimes if you think you're hungry, it may just be that you are thirsty, and after you drink water, you feel satisfied. I like to drink a lot of water before I go to a party where there will be a lot of food. The water makes me feel full, so I'm not as likely to overeat.

MR. F.: Do diet soft drinks count?

SH: Even though diet drinks do have some water, they often have caffeine, which actually causes your body to lose water. So if you drink a lot of caffeinated beverages, you need to drink more than 8 glasses of water each day.

MR. F.: Do I need to cut back on caffeine when I'm trying to lose weight?

SH: A moderate amount of caffeine (equivalent to about 2 cups of coffee) won't hurt you, and actually might help you lose weight. Since caffeine is a stimulant, drinking a cup of coffee or tea before exercising speeds up your metabolism so you burn a few extra calories.

People who have high blood pressure, migraine headaches, insomnia, and anxiety probably need to limit their caffeine intake.

MR. F.: When I first started checking into losing weight, I kept hearing, "Just give up pasta, and you'll lose weight." Why is that?

SH: I think the reason people lose weight if they quit eating pasta is because when they were eating pasta, they were eating a lot of it, and it was topped with a creamy sauce.

Pasta itself has almost no fat—but it's often served with a rich, creamy sauce. And the portions, especially at restaurants, are huge, so you're eating a lot of calories when you eat a big platter of pasta. There's really no reason to give up the noodles if you pay attention to the portions and go for tomato-based or light cream sauces.

MR. F.: It seems like the reason a lot of people don't even try to lose weight is because they think they have to give up desserts. That's not quite true, is it?

SH: No. A lot of people think that a sweet tooth is their downfall in losing weight. But no foods are really "good" or "bad," so there's no reason you should have to completely give up desserts. Sure, desserts are often loaded with sugar and fat and calories, but if you only eat rich desserts every now and then, and eat just a small portion, then eating desserts shouldn't keep you from losing weight. You can also satisfy your sweet tooth with low-fat sweet things like fruit and low-fat ice creams.

MR. F.: So sugar is okay?

SH: There's nothing wrong with sugar. Table sugar has only 16 calories per teaspoon and no fat at all. The problem with sugar is that we usually eat it in rich desserts that have a lot of sugar, not to mention a lot of fat. And if you're getting all your calories from sugary desserts, you're not getting all the other nutrients you need.

Your new dessert recipes are good examples of using small amounts of sugar for flavor, but not going overboard.

MR. F.: Do you recommend using sugar substitutes?

SH: I think that's a personal choice. Sugar substitutes can give you a sweet flavor with fewer calories than sugar, so if you like them, that's fine. Some people dislike the taste of substitutes and would rather just use a small amount of sugar. That's fine, too.

MR. F.: You've told me I need to eat more fiber. What does that have to do with losing weight?

SH: Well, Mr. Food, you've certainly lost weight since you started eating more fresh fruit and vegetables! You get fiber in fruit, vegetables, and whole-grain breads and cereals. High-fiber foods are important in a weight-loss plan because they make you feel full, plus they're usually low in calories and fat.

MR. F.: I know alcohol has a lot of calories. Is it best just to give that up?

SH: You get more calories from an alcoholic beverage than you might think, especially when the alcohol is combined with a sugary mixer. Also, alcohol stimulates the appetite, so people often eat extra food when they drink.

If you choose to drink alcohol, your best bets in terms of calories are a glass of wine, light beer, or a liquor mixed with water or club soda.

WHAT'S IN THE GLASS?

BEVERAGE	SERVING	CALORIES
Light beer	(12 fluid ounces)	99
Bourbon and soda	(8 fluid ounces)	110
White wine	(6 fluid ounces)	120
Red wine	(6 fluid ounces)	127
Beer	(12 fluid ounces)	146
Piña Colada	(8 fluid ounces)	466
Daiquiri	(8 fluid ounces)	448

MR. F.: Do I need to take vitamins?

SH: The best way to get vitamins and minerals is in the foods you eat. Food gives you some things that pills don't, like fiber and disease-preventing antioxidants. But sometimes it's hard to get 100 percent of the nutrients you need each day. It's especially hard for women to get enough iron and calcium.

It's not a bad idea to take a multi-vitamin supplement once a day, but talk to your doctor before you start taking any kind of supplement. And don't skimp on eating good-for-you foods just because you took your vitamin. Think of the supplement as extra insurance on the days you don't get everything you need from food.

MR. F.: Well, you know if I have the choice between eating and popping a pill, I'm going with the food!

SH: And with recipes like yours, why not? Dietitians like to eat, too, you know.

It's All in Your Mind

WHAT WORRIES YOU ABOUT BEGINNING A WEIGHT-loss program? Don't know where to start? Or are you afraid you can't make it over the long haul?

Those are understandable concerns. But, my friend, not believing in yourself undermines the most genuine weight-loss efforts. When I realized I was the boss—that's when I started seeing results!

I want you to know that YOU CAN DO IT! In the following four chapters, you're gonna learn how you can lose weight and become a stronger, more self-confident person. I'll share my secrets for staying motivated and tell you about some folks who changed their eating and exercising habits for good, and transformed their lives as a result!

No matter what your weight-loss obstacles are, I've got some suggestions for replacing "I can't!" with "Yes I Can!" I've got attitude adjusters, motivation makers, portion-control tricks, and binge busters. It's all about taking charge of your health and your life. I believe you can do it. Do you?

8 Attitude Adjusters

1. **Wake up in a new world** each day. How do you see the world? It's all in your attitude. Each day is a fresh start and a time for new beginnings. ***2.*** **Act happy.** Most people are about as happy as they make up their minds to be. (Abraham Lincoln) ***3.*** **You have the power** to change a situation simply by changing your attitude about the situation. ***4.*** **Hold up your head!** **You were not made for failure.** You were made for victory. Go forward with joyful confidence. (George Eliot) ***5.*** **Declare your freedom** from anxiety, from fear, and from any belief in lack or limitation. ***6.*** **Stay the course.** Weight control is about perseverance, not perfection. ***7.*** **If it is to be, it is up to me.** (Shirley Hutton) ***8.*** **Laughter** is the best medicine.

Chapter 4

You're the Boss

Yes I Can! Attitude

Do you want to know a key secret to successful weight loss?
I can sum it up in one word: attitude.

Do you remember the last time you decided to lose weight, get in shape, and permanently change your eating and exercise habits? Maybe it was a New Year's resolution that fizzled by early February. Or a birthday wish that flickered out before the candles did.

For many people who are constantly "going on a diet," it doesn't take much to override good intentions. Before they realize it, they've lapsed into old eating patterns. Other folks want to lose weight, but aren't sure if they can stay motivated.

Do you want to know a key secret to successful weight loss? I can sum it up in one word: attitude. You have to believe you can do it! I mean really believe it. Not a mousy "Well, I'm going to try." No, I'm talking about a determined "Yes, I AM going to look and feel better!"

I call this the "Yes I Can!" attitude. With this attitude, you take charge of your body and your health. Ask anyone who lives with a challenging medical condition such as diabetes or arthritis. They'll agree that a can-do attitude gives you greater control over your life. You're primed to tackle any obstacle, whether it's managing a difficult medical problem or losing weight.

You have to believe you can do it!

I know what you're thinking: "Sure, it's easy for him to say that. He's won the battle of the bulge. But how am I supposed to take control when I've dieted over and over again, only to fail every time?"

Trust me, I know what it's like to feel trapped in a cycle of "on-again, off-again" dieting. Over the years, my indulgences caught up with me. Whenever I noticed my waistband was a little snug, I'd try the latest popular diet. I lost weight, only to regain what I lost and then some! And as I tipped the scales, my spirits sagged.

Do It For You

Getting over that hopeless feeling isn't easy. The first step may be the most challenging for you. It was for me. You'll need to understand why you have difficulty sticking with a weight-loss plan. Many times, underlying issues are the problem. Sometimes folks who struggle with weight issues aren't completely honest with themselves.

The last time you set out to lose weight, did you assure yourself that you were doing it for all the right reasons?

- To live longer.
- To look better.
- To feel better.
- To have more energy.

Or did you decide to drop a few pounds to please your spouse or impress a new companion? Perhaps you believed shedding fat would help you fit into a particular social circle. Or did you convince yourself that you'd have better luck landing a new job minus some extra weight?

Unfortunately, a lot of people jump into a weight-loss program to please someone else—their spouse, children, parents, or boss. Others believe losing weight will resolve difficulties they're facing.

Too often I hear folks say, "If only I were thin, everything would be so much better . . ."

It's important to realize that losing weight won't fix problems in your life. It won't rescue a troubled marriage, better your relationship with your family, or secure the dream job you've wished for.

Be honest with yourself about why you want to lose weight.

Of course, continuing with your current lifestyle habits won't solve your problems, either. I'll admit the chocolate-chunk ice cream seems to make the problems go away. Truthfully, though, it doesn't. Taking control of your health and gaining the incredible self-confidence that this control brings is the real solution.

In some cases, however, losing weight appears to be the answer. We are judged by others, and, unfortunately, weight affects their assessment of us. Some research on weight issues in the workplace suggests that overweight individuals earn less than their thinner counterparts. And larger-sized employees may not be promoted as quickly as trimmer coworkers.

Discrimination is a shameful fact in our world, but the real issue is whether you are comfortable with yourself. If an unkind comment triggered your desire to get in shape or you believe being overweight limits your career advancement and *you* want a change, then I say go for it!

Be honest with yourself about why you want to lose weight. If you don't, you're setting yourself up to fail. And that, my friend, will only cause you to lose faith in yourself.

Selfish Success

You have to want to lose weight for yourself and not for anyone else. It may sound selfish, but it's really not.

Let me explain. I can't tell you how many people I see everyday who are so focused on caring for others that they never stop to take care of themselves. Women are especially vulnerable to this deceptive trap. At cooking demonstrations, I'm often visited by moms who juggle so many roles, I wonder when they have time to sleep!

Listen to a success story that I heard at a recent cooking demo. I think this busy woman's lifestyle makeover is an example of how taking care of yourself benefits you as well as your loved ones.

When you take control of your health, you'll gain a greater quality of life.

Jackie's Story

Newly divorced and exhausted from her demanding job, Jackie needed healthy meal ideas. But her criteria were strict. She worked full-time, so meals had to be quick and easy. Most importantly, they had to satisfy her teenage son's picky palate!

Here's a typical day for Jackie. (Boy, I needed a nap after hearing this schedule!) She rolled out of bed before dawn to cook her son's breakfast, pack his lunch, do the dishes, wash laundry, and pay the household bills. All that before heading out the door to her full-time job! As soon as she got home from the office and stepped out of her work shoes, the cycle started again. She made supper, cleaned the kitchen, made sure her son did his homework, and returned a few phone calls.

When Jackie joined a weight-loss program at the community center, she was physically out of shape and emotionally drained. First, the dietitian leading the group discussion provided ideas for quick, healthy meals. Then she suggested to Jackie that she get her son in the kitchen to help cook. By doing that, eating healthfully became a habit for him early in life. This single mom also got her son involved in the household chores. That freed up more time for her to walk in the morning or evening.

> Jackie lost weight and discovered a renewed gusto for life.

Jackie lost weight and discovered a renewed gusto for life. As a bonus, her son learned the importance of balancing work and household chores with good health habits. And he loved seeing his mom happy again!

When you take control of your health, you'll gain a greater quality of life. Don't get me wrong. I'm not saying you need to forget your responsibilities at work or home in order to hit the gym. But I like to caution folks, particularly parents, who think they don't have time to take care of themselves. Remember, your kids learn their health habits by watching you! For all of you out there who've spent your life caring for others, now's the time to take care of yourself!

My Success Story

Since I lost 35 pounds (and counting!), I get a kick out of the smaller number I see when I step on the scales now. I sure love the comments I get on my new, slimmer profile. Plus, I feel better and have more energy. Don't tell my golfing buddies, but I'm barely

"My grandchildren love it that I now have so much more energy to play with them!"

winded after playing 18 holes of golf. Most of 'em can't keep up with me!

What I love most, however, is the fact that I now have plenty of energy for my six incredible grandkids! I sure don't want to miss a minute with them. They love it that I have more energy to join their games and swim at the beach. So call my motivation selfish if you want, but I think it's a pretty strong reason to stay fit.

Motivation Magic

It's important to think about how you'll maintain your motivation—before temptation strikes.

Okay, we've talked about recognizing why you want to lose weight, and we've agreed that you're doing it for yourself. Knowing why you want to do it is one thing; following through is another. It's important to think about how you'll maintain your motivation—before temptation strikes.

On the following five pages, you'll discover my bag of tricks, as I like to call it. These are 20 tips I use any time I feel my willpower slipping. Some are concrete ideas for the long haul and others are last-ditch efforts to use on tough days. I assure you, every idea is a sure-fire solution to those occasional slip-ups every dieter faces. So, try several of my tricks until you find what works for you. Then, in Chapter 7, we'll talk about how to put the brakes on binges.

20 STAY-ON-TRACK MAGIC TRICKS

1 **TAKE A PICTURE.** Either find a current picture of yourself or have a friend or family member take one. Keep this snapshot of a larger-size you on your refrigerator door, the bathroom mirror, or in your wallet.

2 **FIND A PHOTO.** Pull out a picture of yourself before the weight gain and hang that image in a spot where you'll be sure to see it.

3 **DRINK UP.** Feeling hungry? You may just be thirsty. A lot of folks mistake thirst for hunger. So drink a minimum of 8 (8-ounce) glasses of water daily. (I like to shoot for 10 to 12!) Add flavor with juice from a lemon, lime, or orange if you don't like the taste of plain water.

4 **GO AT A SNAIL'S PACE.** It can be overwhelming to think of losing 30 to 40 pounds. Instead, set small goals, like one to five pounds at a time. When you accomplish these small goals, you'll stay motivated by your success over the long haul.

5 **MARK MILESTONES.** Do you have an anniversary, reunion, landmark birthday, or other significant event coming up? Use that day as a kickoff to your lifestyle makeover to achieve the new, slimmer you.

6 **PLOT YOUR PROGRESS.** Track your weight loss on a chart or graph, starting with either your current weight or picture, and document your success along the way.

7 **LIFT SOME WEIGHT.** Want to feel the difference a few (or plenty of) pounds can make? On your next trip to the grocery store, pick up a 5-pound bag of sugar or a 10-pound package of dog food. Think about how much better you'll feel when you're not carrying that much extra weight on your body!

8 REWARD YOURSELF. Sure, you're losing weight to look and feel better, but wouldn't it be fun to reward yourself along the way? Come up with a list of nonfood treats to celebrate your success. Your list might include some fitness items, such as a subscription to a health magazine, a new pair of sneakers, or a gym bag. It could also include gifts for yourself, such as a professional manicure or massage, a CD or movie you've wanted, or an expensive item that seems self-indulgent.

9 CHEW ON IT. Chew sugarless gum while cooking, clearing the table, driving, or any time you're tempted to munch.

10 DRAW A FORTUNE. Write "fortunes," or mood-lifters, on small strips of paper. Include activities such as calling a friend or family member, writing a letter, taking a long bath, going for a walk, or browsing the nearest bookstore. Keep these fortunes in a jar in your kitchen. Pull one to redirect your thoughts whenever you're tempted to overeat.

11 PACK YOUR BAGS.
If you'll be traveling, remember to pack your tennis shoes, shorts, and a T-shirt so you can squeeze in a walk or exercise in the hotel's health club.

12 FLY LIGHT. Airline
food can be high in fat and calories, so pack a healthy sandwich, fruit, snack, and bottled water for your next flight. Or call the airline (before your flight) and request a low-fat meal.

13 PLAN AHEAD. If your
motivation to exercise drops when you head home after work, keep your workout gear in your car or office. Then you can exercise on your lunch break or immediately after work.

14 TAKE THE STAIRS. If
you're traveling and your hotel doesn't have a fitness room, simply find some stairs and go up and down as many flights as possible!

15 SHOP SMART. Make
your supermarket run at a time when you're not likely to be stressed and hungry. For example, if you work weekdays, instead of shopping on your way home from work, wait until Saturday or Sunday afternoon.

18 **PULL THE LAST STRAW.** What triggered your decision to lose weight once and for all? Keep some reminder of that "last straw," whether it was a comment, event, or article of clothing. It will always remind you of how you felt before committing to lose weight.

16 **SPLIT A SNACK.** Can't avoid the vending machine's call? Find a buddy at work to split a candy bar, package of cookies, or bag of chips when you've simply got to have a not-so-healthy snack.

19 **NAIL IT.** If you're tempted to binge, do your nails instead. You'll keep your hands busy long enough for the urge to go away.

20 **TAKE A LEFT.** Feel like you could inhale food? Try slowing down by eating with your left hand. (Southpaws, you get the picture.)

17 **POLISH UP.** Before you reach for an unplanned snack, try polishing your shoes.

8 Tips from the Winner's Circle

1. **Make changes** for you. Know that you are losing weight for your own health and well-being, not simply to please others.

2. **Get the support** of your family and friends. Let them help you make the changes and cheer you on. *3.* **What's up, Doc?** Talk to your doctor before starting any kind of weight-loss or exercise program. *4.* **Be consistent.** Try to stick to a regular schedule for meals and snacks. *5.* **Prioritize** time and activities. Move exercise and eating right to the top of your "to-do" list.

6. **Past** perfect. Don't get stuck in the past and feel resigned to the way things have always been. There's no time like the present to start new habits. *7.* Get **cooking.** Have fun in the kitchen as you learn to prepare some tasty new low-fat dishes and try brand-new techniques. *8.* Be **patient.** Healthy weight loss is often slow and gradual. But when it comes off slowly, it's usually off for good.

Chapter 5

Weight-Loss Winners

Mr. Food's Hall of Fame

When these people took charge of their health, they
achieved more than a slimmer figure.

I love to meet people who make good things happen in their lives! I think you'll agree with me that the following folks did just that when they regained control of their eating and activity habits.

These individuals are winners not simply because they lost weight. When these people took charge of their health, they achieved so much more than a slimmer figure. Some individuals took control of challenging medical conditions such as diabetes. Others rebuilt sagging self-esteems, while some warded off future health problems. One woman not only improved her own health, but helped her daughter get healthier, too! You may recognize a little of yourself in these folks, and I know you'll learn a thing or two from their stories.

If you've got a success story to share, I'd love to add your name to my Hall of Fame! There's nothing that makes me happier than knowing that others are sharing my success. Tell me about the tips that worked for you or the recipes that you and your family enjoyed the most. And what has been the best thing for you about losing weight? I want to hear from you!

Write to me at:

Mr. Food Weight Loss Plan
P.O. Box 9227
Coral Springs, FL 33075-9227

Manic Mom

Liz B. is a 40-year-old mother of three. This busy mom says her weight problem began after she had children and started taking insulin to control her diabetes. When Liz set out to lose about 40 pounds, she realized her weight problem didn't stem from a lack of good food know-how. She admitted that she bought and prepared healthy foods whenever possible, and usually ate regular portion sizes.

The problem, she said, was her family. "It was difficult for me to follow a regular eating pattern because of the kids' after-school activities. I usually just picked up fast food in the evening," she

> "I wanted to feel better about myself. That meant making some changes for me."

explained. "Plus, I didn't really get a lot of support for my needs from my husband or children. It seemed like I was just there to take care of everyone else."

Her hectic schedule and stressful home life spurred frequent binges on sweets and snack foods. That, in turn, caused Liz's blood sugar and weight to soar while her self-esteem spiraled downward. She took a hard look at her health habits and knew something had to change.

"I was going to have complications from my diabetes if I didn't take charge. Plus, I wanted to feel better about myself. That meant making some changes for me."

Liz did make changes. She cut back on her kids' after-school activities so that she had time to walk in the afternoon and prepare a healthy dinner. She also sat her family down and explained to them what might happen if she didn't get her diabetes under control.

Now, Liz is about 30 pounds lighter ("I'm working on those last 10 pounds," she says), and she's feeling a lot better about herself.

"I love the fact that I finally did something for me!"

Weighty Workaholics

Dan P. and his wife Mary both have demanding careers, he as a financial planner and she as a public relations manager at a large company. This early-30s couple said their weight gain resulted from sitting behind computers all day before moving on to lengthy business dinners.

I know what she means about having a hectic schedule! You've just gotta figure out a way to carve out a little time for yourself.

"The working world really takes a toll on your health—and your waistline," Dan explains. "Mary and I've both noticed that we have gained a lot of weight since college."

Dan says the extra weight crept up on them until both needed to lose about 20-plus pounds.

"I've heard that's pretty common with people our age—all of a sudden, you've packed on the weight and you never noticed it.

Although we're pretty young, neither of us felt good anymore, and we kept 'outgrowing' our clothes. We had to get in shape before we started a family so we'd have enough energy to keep up with a baby!"

These busy professionals committed to scaling back on their working dinners so they could go to a gym together, then head home to prepare a quick, healthy meal.

> "Although we're pretty young, neither of us felt good anymore, and we kept outgrowing our clothes."

"We both worked to arrange meetings at work or during lunch, rather than over dinner, whenever possible," Mary explains. "It's easier to control what you eat and drink during a lunch meeting because everyone has to get back to the office."

Dan says they brushed up on their cooking skills with the extra time they have in the evening. "We both love cooking now," he says. "We don't do anything elaborate, we'll usually just grill, roast, or stir-fry. But we've discovered that you can have home-cooked meals in a matter of minutes rather than hours!"

Mary agrees, "I always thought cooking meals from scratch would be difficult and time-consuming, but boy, was I wrong! Your Marmalade Pork Chops (page 374) are my favorite because they're so easy and take less than 15 minutes to cook!"

Surprising Diagnosis

Like Dan and Mary, George L. logged so many hours as a truck driver that he never noticed the numbers on the scale inching up over the years. He realized he had gotten out of shape, however, when arthritis prevented him from doing the things he loved, such as bike riding with his three kids.

"My doctor told me the extra weight was putting a lot of pressure on my knees, which were already damaged due to the arthritis. He said losing weight would make a big difference in how I felt."

> "I had been so busy working to take care of my family that I let my own health slip."

In his late-30s, George decided he had too many good years left to let arthritis rule his life. He decided it was time to make some changes.

"I had been so busy working to take care of my family that I let my own health slip," he explains. "I talked with my wife about adjusting our budget so that I could cut back on the hours I drove."

George did just that, and he lost about 30 extra pounds. In addition to easing his arthritis pain, the weight loss eased another medical problem, obstructive sleep apnea.

"Losing weight made a big difference! I sleep so much better now, and my wife appreciates that I don't snore so loudly anymore!"

Attitude Adjustment

Marie F. battled her weight for much of her 42 years. In fact, she really was so accustomed to being overweight that she simply accepted it.

"I stopped thinking about it much," she explains. "I had been overweight as a teenager and all through adulthood. Despite the fact that I'd tried many diets, I could never stick with anything. I just decided I'd be overweight and eat whatever I wanted—until I found out I had Type 2 diabetes!"

That news meant Marie had to lose weight or risk her health.

"My doctor told me losing weight would really make me less dependent on medication and improve my blood sugar control. She said it would also decrease my risk for complications like amputations and blindness. I couldn't think of one reason not to lose weight!"

> "I had been overweight as a teenager and all through adulthood."

Marie admits, however, that she was a little nervous about making changes in her eating and activity habits. After all, when she tried other weight-loss plans, she could never stay motivated.

"I would start a weight-loss program, join a gym, and promise myself I wouldn't eat anything fattening ever again," she remembers. "Of course, I usually binged by the end of the first week and was so upset with myself that I just gave up!"

After talking with her doctor, Marie realized that in the past, she made a lot of changes too quickly. This time, she decided to make moderate changes, with the help of a registered dietitian and certified diabetes educator.

"I took baby steps and gradually worked new activities, such as a walking program, into my daily routine. It made a big difference!"

Marie has lost 40 pounds since learning she had diabetes. She's almost off the oral medication she takes to control the condition.

"I had given up hope that I'd be thin. And while you wouldn't call me skinny, I promise you I'm a lot healthier than I used to be!"

> I've gotta agree with Marie! Losing the 35 extra pounds I was carrying around made a big difference.

Like Mother, Like Daughter

Faye G. was 49 when she started noticing that her weight was a problem. She had always stayed steady at about 150 pounds, until family problems prompted her to turn to food for comfort. When the scales hit 210, Faye knew she had to make a change. Unfortunately, her first attempts to lose weight were unsuccessful —and dangerous.

"I tried a liquid diet, and I took several diet pills, some of which were later pulled off the market," Faye explained. "I lost weight initially, but if I went back to eating solid foods or stopped taking the pills, it came right back! And I was pretty scared that I could have seriously damaged my health." Faye admitted that she isn't patient and wanted the extra weight to come off quickly. And when it didn't, she got depressed and gained more weight.

So, after watching her weight seesaw for about five years, Faye decided to get serious about making healthy changes in her eating and exercising habits. While she wanted to lose weight the right way, she also wanted to set a good example for her teenage daughter Donna.

"I saw her starting to gain a lot of weight, and I wanted to see her get a handle on it now, especially since she's going off to college soon," she explained.

> "I finally realized that it's better to lose the weight slowly, because then I'm more likely to keep it off."

Faye started meeting her daughter right after school at the high school's track and walking several laps daily. Faye also started planning the family's meals, rather than relying on fast food or frozen dinners in the evening. Donna helped her mom out and learned the basics of healthy meal planning. She also lost about 10 pounds, which thrilled this upcoming college freshman. Faye's pretty pleased with her own success, as well.

"We've been making changes for about three months now, and I've lost about 12 pounds," she said. "I've finally realized that it's better to lose the weight slowly, because then I'm more likely to keep it off! And I'm happy that I could set my daughter on the right track for the future."

8 Ways to Right-Size Your Portions

1. Quit the **clean-plate** club. Try to leave behind about one-third of your meal (or save it for later). *2.* Be a **kid again.** Ask for a child's portion as your main course, both at sit-down and fast-food restaurants. *3.* Move your **mouth.** Chew each mouthful of food about 10 times before you swallow. You'll spend a longer time eating a smaller amount of food. *4.* Fill up on **fruit** and **veggies.** If you munch on whole fruit and vegetables rather than drinking fruit or vegetable juices, you'll feel full faster. *5.* **Brown bag** it. Deli sandwiches can be loaded with calories, so pack a lunch with whole wheat bread, lean lunch meats, and veggies. *6.* **Bag** your **bun.** Bakery and deli-style buns and bagels can equal as many as four bread servings. Save calories by wrapping your sandwich fixings in a flour tortilla instead. *7.* Turn off the **tube.** Don't watch TV while you eat so you can pay attention to your food and savor every bite. *8.* Serve **yourself.** Serve your plate in the kitchen, rather than setting food out on the table. That way, you'll be less tempted to take seconds.

Chapter 6

Picture This!

Portion Pointers

Keeping a keen eye on portion size is the best way to control what you eat.

Boy, have I got a secret for you! I don't count calories, carry around a fat-gram counter, or weigh my food to stay in great shape! You wanna know my secret? I've become portion savvy.

That's right, portion control is my secret weapon for counting calories without actually having to do the math! Many folks who are trying to lose weight take portion size for granted. Remember, it's the portion on your plate—and how much of it you eat—that determines the number of calories you'll consume. Keeping a keen eye on portion size is the best way to control what you eat. You may have switched to healthful low-fat foods, but your weight-loss efforts might not work if you're eating the wrong amounts! Well-meaning folks wanting to lose weight overdo their calorie intake because they innocently misjudge their portion size. Sometimes when people have lost weight but see it return, it's because their portion sizes have crept back up.

> Portion control is my secret weapon to count calories without actually having to do the math!

Sizing Up Portions

I'll be the first to say that portion size can be deceptive. When I talk with friends about losing weight, most are amazed that I caution them about "healthy" foods such as packs of trail mix or granola bars. Don't assume that a package equals one serving. Check the label for the real serving size, because usually just one granola bar equals a serving. And if you measure out an actual serving of trail mix, I'll bet you'll be pretty shocked at how small one serving is! For that reason, it's important to read the food label carefully.

I asked Suzanne Henson, a registered dietitian, for tips on portion control. She first pointed me to the U.S. Department of Agriculture's Food Guide Pyramid. Serving sizes—and number of servings—are the foundation of the Food Guide Pyramid, which is the standard for healthy eating. (Turn to page 79 for the Food Guide Pyramid and page 80 for a serving size guide.)

The next time you reach for a bagel, weigh it first and compare it to the serving size guide. A big, chewy bagel can tip the scales at 5 ounces. According to the guide, that bagel equals five servings of bread!

Keeping track of portion size is challenging when you're served a mixed dish, such as spaghetti and meatballs. For example, ½ cup of spaghetti with meatballs and tomato sauce counts as one serving of grain, one vegetable, and one meat serving.

> **Three ounces of meat is about the size of the palm of an average woman's hand.**

I'm a big steakhouse fan, so I double-checked my favorite restaurant's portion size for meats. I discovered that a steak as large as half of your dinner plate (a typical serving in a lot of restaurants), is much larger than the recommended 3 ounces. Three ounces of meat is about the size of the palm of an average woman's hand. When I learned that fact, I took action. Now, I ask that half my steak be boxed up before it ever arrives at the table. That way, I control my portions, and take home an extra meal!

Portion-Control Tricks

Think small when you set the table. Buy 4-ounce juice glasses and small bowls that hold 1 cup of soup.

Serve meals on luncheon plates. Since luncheon plates are smaller than dinner plates, you won't be able to put as much food on the plate. But it will look like you've really piled it on!

Order appetizers in restaurants. You can have a varied meal—in smaller, more appropriate portions—by ordering starters rather than full-sized (or oversized) entrées.

Fork it. Instead of pouring on salad dressings and sauces, save loads of fat and calories by using this trick: Simply dunk your fork in the dressing or sauce, shake it, and then spear the salad greens or food item.

Bag the bun. A lot of bakery buns are loaded with calories because they're two times a normal portion size. So when you crave a hearty sandwich, wrap your fixings in a tortilla or pita instead.

THE FOOD GUIDE PYRAMID

The Food Guide Pyramid was developed by the U.S. Department of Agriculture (USDA) to be a visual guide to healthful eating. It outlines the number of servings needed each day from each food group. Healthier foods form the base of the pyramid, so center your focus there.

FOOD GUIDE PYRAMID
A Guide to Daily Food Choices

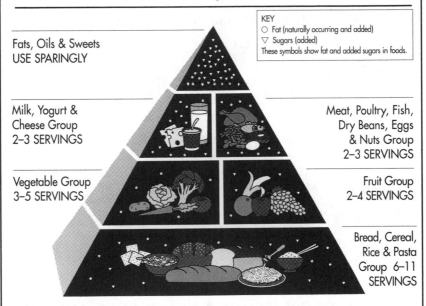

KEY
○ Fat (naturally occurring and added)
▽ Sugars (added)
These symbols show fat and added sugars in foods.

Fats, Oils & Sweets
USE SPARINGLY

Milk, Yogurt &
Cheese Group
2–3 SERVINGS

Meat, Poultry, Fish,
Dry Beans, Eggs
& Nuts Group
2–3 SERVINGS

Vegetable Group
3–5 SERVINGS

Fruit Group
2–4 SERVINGS

Bread, Cereal,
Rice & Pasta
Group 6–11
SERVINGS

Source: U.S. Department of Agriculture/U.S. Department of Health and Human Services

The placement of food groups in the pyramid corresponds with the recommended number of daily servings. For example, you should try to eat the most servings from the group at the base of the pyramid—breads, cereal, rice, and pasta. These foods supply vitamins, minerals, complex carbohydrates, and dietary fiber—all important nutrition components that contribute to overall health. Eat the fewest servings from the group at the top: fats, oils, and sweets.

What Counts as a Serving?

Here are the standard serving sizes that are recommended on the Food Guide Pyramid.

BREAD, CEREAL, RICE, AND PASTA

- 1 slice bread (approximately 1 ounce)
- 1 ounce ready-to-eat cereal
- ½ cup cooked cereal, rice, or pasta

VEGETABLES AND FRUIT

- 1 cup raw leafy vegetables or other raw vegetables
- ½ cup cooked vegetables
- ½ cup vegetable juice
- 1 medium apple, banana, or orange
- ½ cup chopped, cooked, or canned fruit
- ½ cup fruit juice

MILK, YOGURT, AND CHEESE

- 1 cup milk or yogurt
- 1½ ounces natural cheese
- 2 ounces processed cheese

MEAT, POULTRY, FISH, DRY BEANS, EGGS, AND NUTS

- 2 to 3 ounces cooked lean meat, poultry, or fish
- ½ cup cooked dry beans
- 1 large egg = 1 ounce lean meat
- 2 tablespoons peanut butter = 1 ounce meat
- ⅓ cup nuts = 1 ounce meat

Measure Up

Suzanne and other dietitians recommend that you occasionally take out your measuring cups to check portion sizes. You might want to buy an inexpensive set of kitchen scales. This is particularly helpful when you're starting to regain control of your eating habits because it gives you a visual guide to follow. You might be surprised at the size of your servings. "Servings tend to get bigger and bigger when we're not paying attention," one expert told me.

When I decided to lose weight, I took out my measuring cups and started checking how much I had scooped onto my plate. I kept this up until I got an idea of how much I was eating. You know what? It worked! Now I'm great at judging servings when I'm at home and when I eat out.

"Once you start measuring, you might be surprised at the size of your typical servings."

PICTURE THE PORTION

Use these visual examples to make quick
estimates of serving sizes.

3 ounces cooked meat, poultry, or fish	=	Deck of playing cards, cassette tape, or palm of a woman's hand
1 ounce cooked meat, poultry, or fish	=	Matchbook
1 ounce cheese	=	4 dice or a lipstick tube
2 tablespoons peanut butter	=	Golf ball
½ cup cooked vegetables	=	6 asparagus spears, 7 to 8 baby carrots or carrot sticks, 1 ear of corn, or 3 spears of broccoli
½ cup chopped fresh vegetables	=	3 regular ice cubes
1 cup chopped fresh leafy greens	=	4 lettuce leaves
1 medium apple or orange or 1 cup fruit or yogurt	=	Baseball
1 standard bagel	=	Hockey puck or 6-ounce can of tuna
1 cup potatoes, rice, or pasta	=	A woman's fist or a tennis ball
1 medium potato	=	Computer mouse or 1 small bar of soap

Source: National Center for Nutrition and Dietetics of The American Dietetic Association and its Foundation, ADAF copyright 1998

"Now I'm great at judging servings when I eat out."

What "Right" Looks Like

Use the guide at left to help you "see in your mind's eye" the appropriate serving size for a variety of foods.

My dietitian, Suzanne, recommends visualizing portions in ways that you can relate to. For example, if you're a tennis player, it's helpful to know that 1 cup is roughly the size of a tennis ball.

Try some of my tricks to get an idea of the amounts you're eating. Pretty soon, I'll bet you can look at your plate and say, "My serving's not too big and not too small; it's just right!"

10 Ways to Beat a Binge

1. Satisfy your **sweet tooth**. When you're craving something sweet, go ahead and have a **small** treat. **2.** Drink **less**. Alcohol, that is. Alcohol weakens your willpower, so you're more likely to overeat. **3.** Slow **down**. Eat slowly so your body can feel full before you overeat. **4.** Quench your **thirst**. Reach for water or another noncaffeinated beverage first when you feel hungry. **5.** Order à la **carte**. When you eat out, choose individual dishes or appetizer portions instead of an entrée.

6. **Halve** it all. If you order an entrée, ask the waiter to box up half of your order before it reaches the table. **7.** Shop **smart**. Do your grocery shopping when you're not tired or hungry. **8.** Brush **up**. Brush your teeth right after you eat, and you'll be less likely to keep eating. **9.** Keep **candy** close by. If you crave something sweet between meals, eat a lollipop. It's low-calorie and will get rid of the taste of food in your mouth.

10. Eat **breakfast**. A morning meal will help you avoid a raid on the vending machine at 10 a.m. and help you burn calories more efficiently during the day.

Chapter 7

Beat Binge Attacks

Binge Triggers

I've figured out what causes me to overeat and how to put the brakes on binge attacks.

In the past, a crisis at work or home sometimes drove me to seek comfort in large amounts of snack foods or rich desserts. But as I've adopted healthier habits, I've figured out what causes me to overeat and how to put the brakes on binge attacks. Managing binges is one of the keys to long-term weight control.

Weight-loss experts say emotions play a major, but often overlooked, role in eating patterns. For many people, emotions are responsible for many late-night refrigerator raids and stress-eating episodes. If you don't believe me, ask the chocolate lovers you know what they reach for when the going gets tough!

Emotions aren't the only cause of binge eating, however. Here are the 4 most common binge triggers:

1. emotions
2. fatigue
3. lack of fluids
4. holidays and celebrations

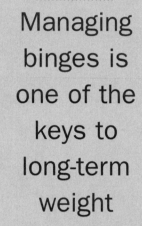

Managing binges is one of the keys to long-term weight control.

Second That Emotion

I'd like to give you some damage-control tips in the event of a binge attack. But first I think it's important to recognize how you react to stressful situations. This will help you redirect your emotions and curb your desire to seek solace in fattening foods. To discover triggers, I want you to take your "emotional temperature."

You can gauge your emotional temperature by asking yourself how you react in particular circumstances. There are several situations that often prompt negative emotions:

- social pressure
- friction at work or home
- a negative mood (brought on by being angry, upset, depressed, or nervous)

If you have a fight with a family member, do you talk through the problem, or do you turn to food to ease the stress building in your shoulders? If you're out to dinner with friends and they insist you order a decadent dessert, what is your response? Do you get defensive and feel pressured into eating the high-fat treat? Or do you politely offer to split the sweet?

Although maintaining weight loss does get easier with time, it's crucial to learn what causes your lapses in willpower and come up with strategies to overcome them. For me, eating out was always a problem. When I visit restaurants, I feel as though it's an

I've learned to taste the treat with just a couple of bites and then share with the entire table!

insult to the chef if I don't sample the ultracreamy soup or rich dessert that's sent to my table. In the past, I would feel pressured to eat the entire dish, but I've learned to taste the treat with just a couple of bites and then share with the entire table! Ooh-so-simple, right? Well that trick is just one idea I've used to tame my fat tooth. It's saved me countless calories!

Take a look at my complete list of binge-busting tips on pages 94-95. I promise you, these strategies will help you control cravings and curb binge attacks.

Get Some Zzzzs

Stress, excess work, and even medications can make quality sleep difficult to achieve. Although a few folks function well on as little as four or five hours of sleep, most adults need a minimum of eight hours sleep each night. Lack of sleep has many negative health effects. Fatigue impairs memory, diminishes concentration, and weakens the immune system.

For anyone trying to lose weight, fatigue often sets up a vicious cycle of overeating in order to recoup sagging energy. I know I have to be careful when I haven't slept enough. When I'm tired, I want to reach for sweets to recharge my batteries. Those sweets, however, offer only a temporary "sugar high" and don't really boost energy. I've started keeping healthy snacks such as dried fruits, apples and pears with a little peanut butter, and low-fat cheese on hand for those times when I need a boost.

If you want to wake up healthy (and avoid binge attacks), you've got to set some good sleep habits. If you're always counting sheep, try my tips to get some shut-eye.

Secrets to Better Sleep

Have a timetable. Go to bed and get up about the same time every day (even weekends) to set your body's internal "clock."

Don't toss and turn. While you should stick to a regular bedtime as much as possible, go to bed only when you're sleepy. If you're unable to fall asleep within 15 to 20 minutes, try reading a book or magazine, or some other relaxing activity. Also, establish bedtime rituals, such as reading or taking a warm shower or bath. A light bedtime snack is also a good idea, but avoid heavy meals.

Don't drink. Both caffeinated and alcoholic beverages can cause you to stay awake during the night. So save tea, coffee, and caffeinated sodas for morning or early afternoon.

Don't smoke. Not only does smoking do serious harm to your overall health, it can disrupt sleep habits as well. Like caffeine, nicotine in cigarettes works as a stimulant.

Exercise early. Working out right before your head hits the pillow can disrupt your sleep schedule. Time your workouts early in the day or no later than six hours before going to bed.

Cool down. Keep the temperature in your bedroom cool, and don't use heavy blankets. If your body temperature rises, you're likely to wake up.

Drink Up

When you don't get enough water, you suffer from more than simple thirst. Fatigue and headaches often result from inadequate hydration. And according to the weight-loss experts, a lot of folks overeat not because they're hungry, but because they're thirsty!

You've probably heard that most everyone needs 8 (8-ounce) glasses of water each day. That's a good rule of thumb, but your fluid needs really depend on your weight, activity level, and age, as well as the climate you live in. Use the general 8-glass guide as a minimum, and add on extra glasses from there.

If you drink a lot of caffeinated beverages, however, you'll need more water. Caffeine acts as a diuretic and robs the body of water. And if you work out, you'll need to replenish the fluids you lose through perspiration. It's usually a good idea to shoot for far more than your minimum. I like to drink at least 10 to 12 glasses of water a day!

HOW MUCH WATER DO YOU NEED?

To find the ounces of water you need based on your weight, divide your weight in pounds by 2. For example, a woman who weighs 140 pounds needs about 70 ounces of water daily. That translates to roughly 8½ (8-ounce) glasses.

Help For The Holidays

For a lot of folks, gaining weight between Thanksgiving and New Year's is as much a holiday tradition as giving gifts. But some pre-planning can help you keep your weight-loss goals on track during the holiday season.

Here are my five strategies to greet the new year with only fond memories, not an extra 5 or 10 pounds.

Mr. Food's Holiday Helpers

1. Stay steady. If you're not losing weight during the holidays, focus on at least maintaining your current weight. Simply try to stick with your new and improved eating habits, and remember that you can do it!

2. Plan ahead. You can have chips and dip anytime during the year, so save calories for seasonal treats. For example, if you look forward to pumpkin pie every Thanksgiving, bypass the spinach dip and ask a relative to split a slice of pie with you. Plan ahead for problem situations. If you know your mother gets offended when you don't take seconds, practice ahead of time what you'll say, or take a very small portion the first time.

3. Remember to eat. That's right, you need to eat—regular meals, that is. Don't skip meals in order to splurge. If you arrive at a get-together hungry, you're far more likely to overeat. Enjoy a reasonable breakfast and lunch—you'll hit the buffet with a better chance of success.

4. Savor the first bite. I always say the first few bites of any food are the best because they're the most satisfying to your taste buds.

So, instead of piling your plate high with mashed potatoes, stuffing, and pecan pie, savor the flavor of your favorites in small servings.

5. Save the spirits. The more you drink, the less control you'll have over what you eat. Alcohol can increase your appetite, is high in calories, and lacks nutritional value. The occasional glass of wine with dinner is generally fine, thanks to its heart-healthy benefits. Holiday spirits such as eggnog or hot buttered rum, however, can pack a big calorie punch. So cut back on your alcohol consumption by mixing drinks with low-calorie mixers such as water, club soda, or diet soft drinks, or alternate an alcoholic beverage with a calorie-free soda, club soda, or flavored water. (See "What's in the Glass" on page 46 for the caloric content of several common beverages.)

Damage Control

If your willpower lapses and you overindulge, don't give up! One episode of overeating won't destroy your chances of reaching your weight-loss goal. Too often, folks start a weight-loss plan with good intentions, but quickly cast aside those goals in the wake of a binge.

If you do binge, don't starve yourself for the next few days. Just make sure your other meals and snacks are low-fat and nutritious. There's no need to feel like you have to go work out at the gym for 3 hours, but do

An occasional indulgence isn't a problem. So don't beat yourself up.

find some time for moderate physical activity. Don't beat yourself up over an occasional indulgence. Simply put it in perspective, recognize what triggered the binge, and come up with strategies for the future.

Balancing Act

Keep in mind that living a healthy lifestyle isn't—and shouldn't—be dull. Balance and moderation are the keys to ensuring life-long weight control. The occasional binge isn't the end of the world. Simply recognize your weaknesses and develop strategies to enjoy your favorite foods and control your weight!

TOP 10 BINGE BUSTERS

1. Curb your cravings.

If it's a fudge brownie or other rich sweet that tempts you, indulge just a little. Buy one small treat or split it with a friend. You'll skimp on calories and satisfy your craving. If chocolate is your temptation, see my guide to the top 20 chocolate snacks on page 96. These snacks quell a craving without blowing your calorie budget.

2. Plan to indulge.

That's right, it's okay to enjoy high-fat foods now and then. Cutting certain foods completely from your diet only makes you want them more. So enjoy a treat occasionally.

3. Know your limits.

It's important to recognize what triggers your overeating. If you know you can't stop with just a few potato chips, don't buy a whole bag! Or buy an individual serving bag rather than the super-size bag.

4. Shop smart.

If the food's not in your pantry, you can't reach for it when a crisis strikes. Before you head into the grocery store, decide what you are—and aren't—going to buy.

5. Drink up.

Too often, folks mistake thirst for hunger. Aim for a minimum of 8 (8-ounce) glasses of water daily. Sugar-free, non-caffeinated beverages count toward that goal.

6. Make a move.

Folks who are more physically active are less likely to overindulge a craving. Who wants to spoil a fantastic workout by blowing it on a slice of cake?

7. Eat everything.

You've probably heard the buzz about cutting out carbs to lose weight. But I won't totally cut out carbs or anything else I love! There's no such thing as an unhealthy food—just unhealthy portions. Eat a variety of foods, and think moderation, not deprivation. Try my tricks on page 82 to keep an eye on portion size.

> Eat a variety of foods, and think moderation, not deprivation.

8. Open wide.

Tempted to keep eating after a meal? Try this secret: Brush your teeth or gargle with mouthwash as soon as you finish eating. That's a mental cue that you've finished eating, and you'll wash away your taste for food.

9. Get soupy.

Here's my sure-fire solution to avoid overeating: Choose a yummy broth-based soup for your first course, and you'll fill up fast with very few calories.

10. Eat air.

I find that air-filled foods fill me up faster, so I eat less. See page 234 for my secret snack that'll satisfy your sweet tooth and tame your appetite.

TOP 20 CHOCOLATE TREATS

Satisfy your sweet tooth with one of these guilt-free chocolate snacks. They're all under 200 calories!

1. 1 diet chocolate soda: **0 calories**

2. 1 chocolate-flavored rice cake with 1 tablespoon reduced-calorie whipped topping: **86 calories**

3. 2 tablespoons chocolate-covered raisins: **95 calories**

4. 4 bite-sized chocolate-coated caramel and creamy nougat bars: **97 calories**

5. 1 chocolate fudge popsicle: **100 calories**

6. 1 individual fat-free pudding cup: **100 calories**

7. 4 milk chocolate kisses: **104 calories**

8. 2 cream-filled chocolate sandwich cookies: **107 calories**

9. 1 packet hot chocolate mix (prepared with water): **112 calories**

10. 1 cup chocolate chip cookie-flavored dry cereal: **120 calories**

11. 3 miniature peanut butter cups: **126 calories**

12. 24 chocolate-flavored bear-shaped graham crackers: **130 calories**

13. Ooh-so-good s'more: **132 calories.** Top 1 graham cracker square with 1 tablespoon semisweet chocolate chips, 1 large marshmallow, and another graham cracker square. Microwave 10 to 15 seconds or until marshmallow is heated and chocolate melts.

14. 5 mini chocolate fudge chewy candy pieces: **133 calories**

15. Slim chocolate shake: **137 calories.** Combine 1 cup fat-free milk, 1 tablespoon fat-free chocolate syrup, and 3 ice cubes in a blender; process until smooth.

16. Chocolate oatmeal: **140 calories.** Stir 2 teaspoons semisweet mini chocolate chips into ½ cup cooked oatmeal (prepared with water)

17. 3 small chocolate-covered peppermint patties: **150 calories**

18. 14 malted milk balls: **154 calories**

"If these don't hit the spot, try my Mocha Ice Cream Squares on page 266. At 197 calories per serving, it's one of my favorite chocolate treats."

19. 1 cup fat-free chocolate milk: **160 calories**

20. Chocolate-covered fruit: **195 calories.** Dip 10 medium strawberries, 1 sliced small Golden Delicious apple, or 1 sliced small banana into 2 tablespoons fat-free chocolate syrup. Freeze 10 minutes or until chocolate sets.

In the Kitchen
with Mr. Food

IS YOUR PANTRY STOCKED WITH FLAVORFUL FOODS that you can combine easily for healthy meals? Or are you unsure which foods to buy and how to prepare them?

Making good-for-you food choices and planning simple, nutritious meals are the keys to losing weight without feeling deprived. That's why I want to give you time-saving solutions for real food that tastes great. Here's a sampling of what you can learn in this section:

- How to navigate the supermarket aisles and stock up on healthy foods
- Five ways to cook smart
- How to slash saturated fat, cholesterol, and sodium in recipes
- Ways to get a meal on the table in less than 30 minutes

Okay, get out some paper and a pen! We're gonna make a shopping list and get cooking!

6 Super Shopping Secrets

1. **Fuel up.** Make your grocery list and do your grocery shopping on a full stomach so that you won't be tempted to buy sweets and snack foods. *2.* **Go on-line.** If you usually go into the grocery store planning to buy just one item but come out with several, try shopping from some of the on-line grocers. You can submit your order and either have it delivered or drive by and pick it up. *3.* **Out of sight, out of mind.** As you unpack your groceries, reduce temptation by storing food behind closed doors. *4.* **Read labels.** Compare the Nutrition Facts labels on convenience items for calorie savings. *5.* **Save time at the salad bar.** Your supermarket's salad bar is a fantastic place to load up on precut fruits and vegetables. *6.* **Try something new.** The next time you shop, pick up one new fruit or vegetable to try. You won't invest much with just one new purchase, and you can slowly incorporate new foods into your diet.

Chapter 8

Take Stock

Smart Shopping

The supermarket offers unlimited choices of wonderful foods that can help you lose weight without feeling deprived or bored.

Every day I meet someone who says they walk around the grocery store overwhelmed by the maze of boxes, packages, cartons, and cans. That feeling is not unusual and is especially common for folks who are trying to lose weight. I agree that it's often difficult to know which foods are healthy for you and which aren't.

If you look carefully, though, the supermarket offers unlimited choices of wonderful foods that can help you lose weight without feeling deprived or bored. So let's maneuver that maze together. We'll start with some **supermarket strategies** that'll help you lose weight while keeping your shopping hassle-free. Then I'll decipher the **nutrition information** on food product labels. To clear up the confusion over grocery shopping, check out "My Can't-Miss Shopping List" on page 120. It's an **aisle-by-aisle** overview of products to look for. And don't go to the store before you read my **insider secrets on buying and preparing fresh fruit and vegetables**.

And to help you find your way completely through the maze, I'll share what I've learned about "good fats" and "bad fats" and what type of fat to look for on the ingredients list when you're choosing products.

Supermarket Strategies

Before you clip even one coupon, let's talk about how to shop. That's simple, right? Who needs to be taught how to buy groceries? Well, let me share some secrets I learned about shopping smart.

Unhealthy food habits often start with the weekly supermarket sweep. Folks frequently stop by the grocery store after work when they're tired and hungry and walk out with sugary treats and high-fat snacks. Or coupon clippers stock up on supposed bargains, only to discover that they really didn't buy anything for healthy meals. And a lot of people keep buying the same items they've always bought because they know their families will eat familiar items. Maybe now is the time to introduce yourself and your family to some of my new favorite foods!

> Unhealthy food habits often start with the weekly supermarket sweep.

Use the "10 Savvy Shopping Tips" on the next page to make your grocery trips more efficient and economical (and easier on your waistline). Once you've stocked your kitchen with good-for-you foods, it's a lot easier to stick with a sensible eating plan.

1. Make a list. Plan meals ahead for the week. Then make a list before you shop and stick to it! A list jogs your memory and helps you avoid buying items on impulse. Make your list on a full stomach so that you'll avoid the temptation to add not-so-healthy foods.

2. Shop on the weekend. Instead of shopping at the end of a busy workday, do your grocery shopping on Saturday or Sunday morning, or another time when you're less likely to be tired and hungry. Occasionally, I like to grocery shop when I have plenty of time so that I can walk the aisles, read and compare labels, and check out new products.

3. Be coupon conscious. Clip coupons for healthy foods and compare costs. Some foods with coupons aren't always the best bargain moneywise or healthwise.

4. Shop the outside aisles first. You may not realize it, but most grocery stores are organized in basically the same way. Usually, you'll find the most nutritious foods located along the outside aisles of the store: fresh fruits and vegetables, lean meats, fish and poultry, and low-fat dairy products. If you fill your shopping cart with healthy items first, you'll have more willpower to skip the cookie and chip aisles.

5. Beware of sales traps. Stores often place sale items such as high-fat snack foods and sugary soft drinks at the end of aisles.

6. Scan the top (and bottom) shelves. Stores frequently place sugary cereals and snack foods at eye level to attract children riding in grocery carts. So look up and down when you shop. You'll often discover the more nutritious foods lining the top and bottom shelves.

7. Shop for convenience. If you notice that fresh fruit and vegetables go bad before you can eat them, frozen or canned fruit and vegetables are your best choices. Plus, they help you keep your freezer or pantry stocked with healthy foods for those times when you need to fix a meal fast.

8. Don't succumb to a sweet tooth. If you're tempted by rows of cookies and candies, avoid those aisles altogether. If salty snacks are your weakness, steer clear of the chip aisle, or at least buy a single-serving snack food package instead of a family-sized bag.

9. Read food labels. See pages 106-108 for my tips on reading food labels. Once you start comparing products, you may be surprised by what you find. Reduced-fat peanut butter, for example, has approximately the same number of calories as its original counterpart. That's due to the sugar that's added to replace the lost fat. The same goes for some reduced-fat cookies. So if you prefer the taste of regular foods over the reduced-fat versions, compare the labels and see if you're really saving calories by eating the reduced-fat food. You may be okay staying with the regular food.

10. Don't be snared by the checkout trap. Grocery stores always stock candy and other snack items along the checkout aisles. If you're particularly tempted by these sweets, move to a candy-free aisle, or flip through a magazine while you're waiting in line.

I didn't pay much attention to the Nutrition Facts panel printed on most packaged foods until I became more aware of what I was eating. Now reading the label has become part of my shopping routine. The most important thing I've learned: If you know how to read this label, you can fit any food into a healthy eating plan. Here's a guide to help you understand the food label.

1 Serving Size

Values are for one serving of the food, which is a typical portion. A portion may be more or less than what you expect, so pay attention to the amount given.

Calories from Fat

2 Choose foods with a big difference between total calories and calories from fat.

g = grams
mg = milligrams

Nutrition Facts

1 Serving Size: 1 cup (228g)
Servings Per Container: 2

Amounts Per Serving

Calories 250   **2** Calories from Fat 110

3 **% Daily Value**

Total Fat 12g **4**	**18%**
Saturated Fat 3g **5**	**15%**
Cholesterol 30mg **6**	**10%**
Sodium 470mg **7**	**20%**
Total Carbohydrate 31g **8**	**10%**
Dietary Fiber 0g **9**	**0%**
Sugars 5g **10**	
Protein 5g	

11

Vitamin A	4%	Vitamin C	2%
Calcium	20%	Iron	4%

* Percent Daily Values are based on a 2,000 calorie diet. Your daily values may be higher or lower depending on your calorie needs:

Calories		2,000	2,500
Total Fat	Less than	65g	80g
Sat Fat	Less than	20g	25g
Cholesterol	Less than	300mg	300mg
Sodium	Less than	2,400mg	2,400mg
Total Carbohydrate		300g	375g
Dietary Fiber		25g	30g

Calories per gram:

Fat 9   •   Carbohydrate 4   •   Protein 4

3 **% Daily Value (DV)** This percentage indicates how much of your daily requirement for the nutrient you get from one serving of the food. For fat, saturated fat, cholesterol, and sodium, choose foods with a low % DV. For fiber, vitamins, and minerals, the goal is 100 percent each day.

4 **Total Fat** Try to keep fat intake at 30 percent or less of total calories. If you're eating about 2,000 calories a day, that's 65 grams of fat per day (1 gram of fat = 9 calories).

5 **Saturated Fat** The value for saturated fat is included in Total Fat. A high intake of saturated fat is associated with the risk of heart disease and certain cancers.

6 **Cholesterol** Try to keep cholesterol intake to less than 300 milligrams per day.

7 **Sodium** You call it salt, the label says sodium. Try to keep your sodium intake to no more than 2,400 milligrams per day.

8 **Total Carbohydrate** The value for total carbohydrate includes the starches, sugars, and dietary fiber in a serving. If you have diabetes, the total carbohydrate in your diet is an important part of blood sugar control.

9 **Dietary Fiber** This value is included in and listed under Total Carbohydrate. Try to eat at least 25 grams of fiber every day.

10 **Sugars** This value refers to both natural sugars and added sugar, but you need to look on the ingredients list panel to determine the type of sugar. The sugar value is included in Total Carbohydrate.

11 **Vitamins and Minerals** These are essential nutrients needed for disease prevention and to promote good health. The goal is 100 percent each day for each nutrient.

Coming to Terms with Labels

Food manufacturers have to meet specific requirements if they want to use terms such as "light," "lean," and "low-fat" on their product labels. Once you understand what these terms mean, you'll be able to make wiser choices at the supermarket.

Fat Free: The food must either be absolutely free of fat, or the amount of fat must be trivial and insignificant (less than 0.5 grams of fat per serving). Fat free does not mean calorie free.

Low Fat: A food meets the definition of "low fat" if the consumer can eat a large amount of the food without exceeding the Daily Value.

Lean and Extra Lean: These two terms can be used to describe the fat content of meat, poultry, seafood, and game meats. "Lean" means the food has less than 10 grams of fat, less than 4 grams of saturated fat, and less than 95 milligrams of cholesterol per 3½-ounce serving. "Extra lean" refers to food that has less than 5 grams of fat, less than 2 grams of saturated fat, and less than 95 milligrams of cholesterol per 3½-ounce serving.

High: A product with this claim for a nutrient such as vitamin C or fiber must contain 20 percent or more of the Daily Value for that nutrient in a serving. Other words that manufacturers might use for "high" are "rich in" or "excellent source of."

Light or Lite: These terms can mean one of two things: (1) The product contains one-third fewer calories or half the fat of the reference food; or (2) The sodium content of a low-calorie, low-fat food has been reduced by 50 percent.

Figuring Out Fats

A friend heard about my 35-pound weight loss and wanted to know my "secret." When I told her about my plan, which included foods with a moderate amount of fat, she balked. "But that's not a diet! If you're on a diet, fatty foods are bad!"

"Wrong," I said.

If you include a little fat in your diet, you'll feel full and stay satisfied longer. And that means fewer trips to the vending machine shortly after lunch! Rather than slash all the fat in your diet, focus on the amount and type of fat you're eating.

Good Fat, Bad Fat

The good-fat, bad-fat debate is due to the fact that various types of fat can either increase or reduce your risk of developing heart disease and possibly some forms of cancer.

> If you include a little fat in your diet, you'll feel full and stay satisfied longer.

Eating a large amount of one kind of fat (saturated) causes cholesterol to build up in your blood vessels. Cholesterol, a white, sticky kind of fat in blood vessels, slows blood traveling to your heart and brain. That, my friend, leads to a heart attack or stroke! But it appears that another type of fat (monounsaturated) may actually help reduce cholesterol! So you see what all the hoopla is about.

Eating a moderate amount of heart-friendly fats is a sure-fire step toward living a healthy lifestyle. It's a little confusing, however, to figure out what is and isn't considered a "good" fat. Here's my primer on the fats.

There are three basic types of dietary fat: **saturated, polyunsaturated,** and **monounsaturated**. The fat in most foods is a mixture of those three. But foods usually contain a greater amount of one fat than the others. That's how the food is classified.

Saturated fats are usually firm at room temperature. Common sources are animal products, such as butter, lard, and meat. **Polyunsaturated fats** are usually liquid at room temperature and come from fish and plant foods like nuts and corn, safflower, and sunflower oils. **Monounsaturated fats** also come from plant-based foods and are the fats that are healthiest for you. You'll find monounsaturated fats in peanut, olive, and canola oils, as well as avocados.

In addition to the three basic types, there's another fat hiding in some foods that's as harmful to your heart as saturated fat. It's called **trans fat**. Unlike other fats, trans fats don't occur naturally in foods, but are created in processing when foods are "partially hydrogenated." Vegetable shortening is an example of a food that has been partially hydrogenated and is full of trans fat. Fast-food fried items and many commercial cookies, cakes, and snacks also have trans fats. Right now, trans fat does not have to be included on food labels, but that might change.

Cholesterol Concern

Why should we be worried about how these fats affect cholesterol? Cholesterol is a white waxy fat that your body produces, and when it builds up in your blood vessels, you're at risk for heart disease. You add to your natural supply of cholesterol when you eat foods that are high in cholesterol, or foods high in saturated or trans fat. Dietary cholesterol is found only in animal products such as meats and dairy products.

The Truth about Fat-Free Products

Unfortunately, fat has gotten a bad rap in recent years. That's due in part to the slew of fat-free products that flooded store shelves a few years back. Let me explain why fat-free treats can be a weight-loss obstacle.

Many people who bought fat-free cookies and chips fell into a psychological trap and believed that the fat-free label equaled freedom to devour the entire package. Bags of chips and boxes of cookies later, those folks wondered why they gained weight.

Even though those foods are fat-free, they're sometimes loaded with calories. That's because food manufacturers often replace the fat with extra sugar. If you compare the nutrition facts labels of many foods and their fat-free counterparts, you'll notice that the "new and improved" versions may have more calories than the originals!

> Unfortunately, fat has gotten a bad rap in recent years.

Sure, the fat's gone, but those extra calories add up quickly, so dieters can easily consume more calories than they realize. Remember the weight-loss equation: You have to eat fewer calories than you burn if you're going to lose weight.

Fat-free products seriously hamper weight-loss efforts for some folks, whose good intentions to eat a sensible amount disappear with the first bite. For others, just one fat-free cookie tempers an out-of-control sweet tooth. So think twice before you buy. Shop smart by comparing labels and thinking about your typical eating behaviors.

Cut Fat, Not Flavor

So what should you do? Here are a few simple steps to keep in mind for weight loss and good health:

- Cut back on the amount of saturated and trans fats you eat.
- Increase monounsaturated fats.
- Choose polyunsaturated fats in moderation.
- Choose soft, pourable fats most often, and shop around for new products that have the claim "No Trans Fat" on the package.
- Eat a balance of reduced-fat and reduced-calorie foods along with moderate amounts of heart-healthy fats.

When I modified recipes to fit into my healthy lifestyle, I cut calories, fat, saturated fat, and cholesterol. But I kept the flavor. In my recipes, you'll find that I often substitute reduced-fat or low-fat products for their traditional counterparts.

I've also found some fat-free products that give fantastic results, so don't be surprised if you see those occasionally. I'm constantly experimenting with new products and different brands. If you're like me, you'll find new favorites every time you visit the store!

Fresh Produce Facts

Fresh produce puzzles many folks. I'm frequently asked, "How much do I need to buy?" or "What do I do with it?" Although I encourage shoppers to purchase fresh, frozen, and canned fruit and vegetables, I've often discovered that fresh produce is sometimes more economical when it's in season. And you have more varieties to choose from when you buy fresh produce. But the bottom line is that whether you buy them fresh, frozen, or canned, fruit and vegetables are staples in a successful weight-loss plan. So make sure you load up on plenty of these good-for-you foods.

On the next six pages, I've included guides for buying and preparing fresh fruit and vegetables.

FRESH FRUIT PREPARATION GUIDE

FRUIT	APPROXIMATE SERVINGS	PREPARATION*
Apples	3 to 4 servings per pound	Wash; peel and core as required, and cut as desired.
Apricots	3 to 4 servings per pound	Wash; cut in half, remove pit, and slice as desired.
Bananas	3 to 4 servings per pound	Peel, and cut as desired.
Blackberries	4 servings per pound	Rinse lightly just before serving.
Blueberries	4 servings per pound	Wash and drain; sort and remove stems.
Cherries	4 servings per pound	Wash; sort and remove stems and pits.
Cranberries	8 servings per pound	Sort, wash, and drain.
Grapefruit	2 servings per pound	Peel and section, or cut into halves and cut out sections.
Grapes	4 servings per pound	Wash thoroughly. Remove stems; leave whole or halve.

FRUIT	APPROXIMATE SERVINGS	PREPARATION*
Kiwifruit	3 to 4 servings per pound	Peel and slice, or cut off top and use a spoon to scoop out flesh.
Lemons	4 lemons per pound	Wash; slice or cut into wedges. Grate rind, if desired.
Oranges	2 servings per pound	Cut into halves, peel and section, or slice.
Peaches	4 servings per pound	Blanch to remove skin. Cut to remove seed. Chop or slice.
Pears	4 servings per pound	Wash; peel and core as required, and cut as desired.
Pineapple	3 servings per pound	Cut off top, bottom, and skin. Chop or slice as desired.
Plums	4 to 5 servings per pound	Wash; keep whole, or cut in half and remove pit.
Raspberries	4 servings per pound	Rinse lightly just before serving.
Strawberries	2 to 3 servings per pound	Rinse and remove stems just before serving. Leave whole, slice, or chop.

*The preparation instructions are general; refer to your recipe for more detailed directions.

FRESH VEGETABLE PREPARATION GUIDE

VEGETABLE	APPROXIMATE SERVINGS	PREPARATION*
Artichoke	2 servings per pound (2 artichokes)	Wash; cut off stem and ½ inch off top. Remove loose bottom leaves. Cut off thorny tips with scissors. Rub cut surfaces with lemon.
Asparagus	3 to 4 servings per pound	Snap off tough ends. Remove scales, if desired.
Beans, green	4 servings per pound	Wash; trim ends, and remove strings.
Beets	3 to 4 servings per pound	Leave root and 1 inch of stem; scrub with vegetable brush.
Broccoli	3 to 4 servings per pound	Remove outer leaves and tough ends of lower stalks. Wash. Cut into spears or chop.
Brussels sprouts	4 servings per pound	Wash; remove discolored leaves. Cut off stem ends; cut an x in the bottom of each sprout.
Cabbage	4 servings per pound	Remove outer leaves; wash. Shred, chop, or cut into wedges.
Carrots	4 servings per pound	Scrape; remove ends, and rinse. Leave tiny carrots whole; slice, chop, or cut as necessary.

VEGETABLE	APPROXIMATE SERVINGS	PREPARATION*
Cauliflower	4 servings per head	Remove outer leaves and stalk; wash. Leave whole, or break into florets.
Celery	4 servings per bunch	Separate stalks; trim off leaves and base. Rinse. Slice diagonally, or chop.
Corn	4 servings per 4 large ears	Remove husks and silks. Leave corn on cob, or cut off kernels.
Cucumbers	2 servings per cucumber	Peel, if desired; slice or chop.
Eggplant	2 to 3 servings per pound	Wash and peel, if desired. Cut into cubes, or cut crosswise into slices.
Greens	3 to 4 servings per pound	Remove stems; wash thoroughly. Tear into bite-sized pieces.
Mushrooms	4 servings per pound	Just before using, wipe with damp paper towels, or wash gently and pat dry. Cut off tips of stems. Slice, if desired.

*The preparation instructions are general; refer to your recipe for more detailed directions.

VEGETABLE	APPROXIMATE SERVINGS	PREPARATION*
Okra	4 servings per pound	Wash and pat dry. Trim ends.
Onions	4 servings per pound	Peel; cut large onions into quarters or slices, or leave small onions whole.
Peas, green	2 servings per pound unshelled; 4 servings per pound shelled	Shell and wash.
Peas, snow	4 servings per pound	Wash; trim ends, and remove tough strings.
Peppers, bell	1 serving per pepper	Cut off top, and remove seeds and membranes. Leave whole to stuff, slice into thin strips, or chop.
Potatoes, baking	2 to 3 servings per pound	Scrub potatoes; peel, if desired.
Potatoes, new, red	3 to 4 servings per pound	Scrub potatoes; peel, if desired. Leave whole, or slice or cut into chunks.
Potatoes, sweet	2 to 3 servings per pound	Scrub potatoes. Leave whole to bake, or peel, if desired, and slice or cut into chunks.

VEGETABLE	APPROXIMATE SERVINGS	PREPARATION*
Squash, spaghetti	2 servings per pound	Rinse; cut in half lengthwise, and discard seeds.
Squash, summer	3 to 4 servings per pound	Wash; trim ends. Slice or chop.
Squash, winter (acorn, butternut, hubbard)	2 servings per pound	Rinse; cut in half, and remove seeds.
Tomatoes	4 servings per pound	Wash; peel, if desired. Slice or chop.
Turnips	3 servings per pound	Wash; peel, and slice or cube.

*The preparation instructions are general; refer to your recipe for more detailed directions.

MY CAN'T-MISS SHOPPING LIST

In addition to staples, condiments, and seasonings, I always keep my pantry stocked with the following healthy convenience products and basic quick-fix items. I keep a copy posted on my refrigerator. That way, I don't forget to pick something up on my next shopping trip.

EGGS AND DAIRY

____ Eggs/egg substitute
____ Cheeses *(reduced-fat)*
____ Grated Parmesan cheese
____ Margarine or light butter
____ Milk *(fat-free, low-fat)*
____ Buttermilk *(low-fat)*
____ Sour cream *(low-fat)*
____ ⅓-less-fat cream cheese
____ Tub-style light cream cheese
____ Yogurt *(fat-free, low-fat)*

BREAD

____ Flour tortillas
____ French bread
____ Pita bread rounds
____ Pizza crust, Italian cheese flavored
____ White or whole wheat bread

BAKING PRODUCTS

____ Biscuit mix *(low-fat)*
____ Breadcrumbs, dry
____ Hot roll mix
____ Rapid-rise yeast

GRAINS

____ Couscous
____ Rice; quick-cooking, long-grain, and brown
____ Pasta, variety of shapes

CONDIMENTS

____ Fruit spreads
____ Mayonnaise *(reduced-fat)*
____ Mustards; plain, flavored
____ Salad dressings and vinaigrettes *(fat-free, reduced-fat)*
____ Soy sauce/teriyaki sauce *(low-sodium)*
____ Vinegars
____ Worcestershire sauce

CANNED, PACKAGED, AND BOTTLED ITEMS

_____ Beans

_____ Broths, chicken and beef
(*fat-free, less-sodium*)

_____ Caramel-flavored syrup
(*fat-free*)

_____ Fruit, dried

_____ Fruit, packed in juice

_____ Fudge topping (*fat-free*)

_____ Garlic, minced

_____ Ginger

_____ Green chilies

_____ Lemon juice

_____ Maple syrup
(*reduced-calorie*)

_____ Milk; nonfat dry milk
powder, fat-free
evaporated

_____ Pasta sauce

_____ Pimiento, diced

_____ Salsa

_____ Soups (*reduced-sodium,
reduced-fat*)

_____ Tomatoes, canned

_____ Tomato sauce and paste

_____ Tuna, packed in water

"Make a copy of this page
and use it as the basis for
your grocery shopping list."

REFRIGERATOR

_____ Breadstick dough

_____ French bread dough

_____ Pizza crust dough

FREEZER

_____ Assorted fruit

_____ Assorted vegetables

_____ Bread dough

_____ Cooked chicken, diced
or strips

_____ Green bell pepper, chopped

_____ Juice concentrates

_____ Phyllo pastry

_____ Potatoes; mashed, hash
brown

_____ Vegetable blends
(chopped onion and
green bell pepper)

_____ Whipped topping
(*reduced-calorie*)

10 Smart Cooking Secrets

1. **Nibble** while you work. Buy baby carrots, whole mushrooms, and broccoli florets to munch on while you cook.

2. **Stick** to it. Serve hard breadsticks rather than buttery dinner rolls. *3.* **Flavor** up. Stir-fry veggies in a flavored oil and get more flavor from a small amount. *4.* **Pass the bread**, please. Brush your bread with a little heart-healthy olive oil, rather than butter or margarine. *5.* Swap **sauces**. Opt for low-cal red sauces, such as marinara or red clam sauce, rather than high-fat white sauces. *6.* One **crust** does the trick. Make fruit pies with a single crust to save loads of fat.

7. Cook with a **cube.** Season vegetables with a beef, chicken, or vegetable bouillon cube instead of fat. *8.* **Go** for the **green**. Add chopped broccoli, spinach, or green beans to your rice or pasta in the last few minutes of cooking time.

9. **Spice** it up. Make pudding with fat-free milk, then boost the flavor with spices such as nutmeg, cinnamon, cloves, or ginger. *10.* Season with **herbs**. Herbs add flavor without fat.

Chapter 9

Cook Quick, Cook Healthy

5 Ways to Cook Smart

How you cook is just as important as what you cook!

You know I believe in quick and easy cooking solutions! I also think you should get the most possible flavor and nutrients from foods. That's why *how* you cook is just as important as *what* you cook. Too often, folks buy healthy foods such as broccoli and bell peppers, but destroy the nutrients by improperly storing or cooking them.

That's why I want to tell you about the five fastest and healthiest ways to cook:

1. Steaming
2. Sautéing or stir-frying
3. Grilling
4. Roasting
5. Microwaving

These cooking methods are my favorites because they're the best ways to retain a food's color, flavor, shape, texture, and nutrients.

I know you don't like uncertainty in the kitchen, so I'm going to give you a step-by-step guide for each of these cooking methods, an easy-to-follow recipe, and some of my secrets that'll help take the guesswork out of cooking. Okay, now let's get cooking!

Steamy Stuff

Steaming (as well as microwaving) is one of the most gentle ways to cook foods, particularly fruit and vegetables. It's also one of the most nutritious methods because it preserves the vitamins and minerals in foods. Seafood lovers like myself also like to cook delicate foods, such as shellfish, with this method.

HOW-TO: You can steam foods by placing them in a steamer basket over simmering water in a covered pan.

HEALTH TIP: The recipe for Broccoli with Garlic-Lemon Pepper Sauce below is one of my favorites. I steam the broccoli just until it's crisp-tender, or slightly firm to the bite. When they're cooked just until crisp-tender, vegetables such as broccoli retain more flavor, B vitamins, and vitamin C than if they were boiled.

Broccoli with Garlic-Lemon Pepper Sauce

Makes 4 servings

1 pound fresh broccoli
3 tablespoons light butter
2 garlic cloves, minced
3 tablespoons lemon juice
1½ tablespoons white wine Worcestershire sauce
⅓ cup water
1 tablespoon Dijon mustard
¼ teaspoon salt
⅛ teaspoon crushed red pepper flakes

1 Remove and discard broccoli leaves and tough ends of stalks, cut broccoli into spears. Steam broccoli, covered, 7 minutes or until crisp-tender. Transfer to a serving bowl, and keep warm.

2 Melt butter in a large nonstick skillet over medium-high heat; add garlic. Sauté garlic 1 minute or until golden. Add lemon juice and remaining 5 ingredients; bring to a boil. Pour over broccoli; toss gently. Serve immediately.

Per Serving: Calories 86 Fat 5.2g (saturated 3.1g) Protein 4.7g Carbohydrate 8.9g Fiber 3.1g Cholesterol 15mg Sodium 372mg
Exchanges: 2 Vegetable, 1 Fat

Sizzling Sautés

Sauté is a fancy-schmancy word that means practically the same thing as stir-fry. I know what you're thinking: "You can't fry foods and lose weight!" Well, my friends, yes you can! Sautéing is one of my favorite cooking methods because foods are cooked at such a high heat that very little oil is needed. And foods that are sautéed have a wonderful texture and flavor!

HOW-TO: To sauté, use a small amount of fat. Heat the fat until it's very hot but not burning or smoking, then add the food.

Sauté is a French word, and it means "to jump." When you sauté, push the food quickly back and forth across the pan to prevent it from burning. It's important to cut the pieces of food the same size and to stir constantly so the food will cook evenly.

HEALTH TIP: Sautéing is a great low-fat cooking method because you only cook in a small amount of fat. Sautéing also preserves the nutrients in vegetables because you only have to cook the vegetables a short time to get them crisp-tender.

"Once you start cooking the low-fat way, you'll start enjoying a trimmer profile!"

Beef-and-Broccoli Stir-Fry

Makes 6 servings (serving size: 1 cup beef mixture and 1 cup rice)

1	pound boneless sirloin steak
1	cup beef broth
¼	cup low-sodium soy sauce
1	tablespoon cornstarch
2	teaspoons dark sesame oil, divided
1	tablespoon bottled minced ginger
3	garlic cloves, minced
4	cups broccoli florets
2½	cups sliced onion (about 1 large)
1	cup thinly sliced carrot
6	cups hot cooked quick-cooking brown rice

1 Trim fat from steak. Cut steak diagonally across grain into very thin slices.

2 Combine broth, soy sauce, and cornstarch in a small bowl; stir with a whisk until blended.

3 Heat 1 teaspoon oil in a large nonstick skillet or wok over high heat. Add ginger and garlic; sauté 2 minutes. Add steak; sauté 5 minutes. Remove mixture from pan; keep warm. Add remaining 1 teaspoon oil; add broccoli, onion, and carrot. Sauté 7 minutes or until vegetables are crisp-tender. Return steak mixture to pan, and stir in cornstarch mixture; sauté 2 minutes or until thick and bubbly. Serve over rice.

Per Serving: Calories 402 Fat 8.3g (saturated 2.5g) Protein 25.6g
Carbohydrate 55.6g Fiber 6.3g Cholesterol 51mg Sodium 609mg
Exchanges: 3 Starch, 2 Vegetable, 2 Very Lean Meat, 1 Fat

Great Grilling

There's nothing that I love more than firing up the grill! Grilling is one of my all-time favorite cooking methods because of the wonderful flavor it gives to food. And with my new gas grill, it's so-o-o easy! There are two methods for grilling foods: direct or indirect. With the **direct** method, you cook food over the direct heat of the flame or directly over the burners. For **indirect** cooking, you place the food on an area of the grill where the burners are turned off. When the grill lid is down, the heat rises, reflects off the lid, and circulates around the food.

HOW-TO: If you want to be a grill master, then you have to know that the heat must be evenly distributed. Often I've gone to backyard cookouts and noticed that one side of the grill was hotter than the other. Uneven cooking wastes good food because the meat on one side of the grill gets overcooked, and the meat on the other side is undercooked!

I also recommend turning food only once, using long-handled tongs rather than a meat fork. Forks pierce meat, causing it to release it's flavor and juices. When you're grilling meat covered, open the grill lid only when basting, turning, or removing food so you don't lose heat. And if you're grilling delicate fish or small pieces of food, I recommend using a grill basket.

HEALTH TIP: Grilling is a cooking method of choice for health-conscious cooks because it gives foods, particularly meat, a great flavor without a lot of added fat. Most folks associate grilling with hamburgers or other meat dishes, but grilling is a good option for all kinds of poultry, fish, vegetables, fruit, and breads. I think it's especially tasty to grill vegetables and bread, even some sliced fruit, alongside my main course. That prevents me from dirtying saucepans or baking sheets, and I can stay outside and tend the star attraction!

Herb-Crusted Pork with Pineapple Sauce

Makes 6 servings (3 ounces pork and 2 tablespoons sauce)

1   teaspoon dried thyme
1   teaspoon dried oregano
½   teaspoon salt
½   teaspoon ground coriander
½   teaspoon freshly ground black pepper
2   (¾-pound) pork tenderloins, trimmed
Cooking spray
1½   cups pineapple juice
2   tablespoons spicy brown mustard
4   teaspoons cornstarch

1 Preheat the grill. Combine first 5 ingredients in a small bowl. Rub mixture over pork. Insert a meat thermometer into thickest part of tenderloin, if desired.

2 Place tenderloins on grill rack coated with cooking spray; grill, covered, 20 minutes or until meat thermometer registers 160°.

3 Combine pineapple juice, mustard, and cornstarch in a small saucepan, stirring well with a whisk. Bring to a boil over medium heat. Cook, stirring constantly, 2 minutes or until thick.

4 Let pork stand 10 minutes before cutting into thin slices; serve pork with pineapple sauce.

Per Serving: Calories 193 Fat 4.3g (saturated 1.4g) Protein 24.6g
Carbohydrate 11.9g Fiber 1.1g Cholesterol 67mg Sodium 322mg
Exchanges: 1 Fruit, 3 Lean Meat

A Toast to Roasting

Roasting is a super-simple cooking technique that produces tender, juicy meat and poultry entrées, and draws out the natural sweetness in vegetables. Even better, roasting uses just one pan, so there's little cleanup!

HOW-TO: By definition, foods that are roasted are cooked uncovered in an oven. Unlike broiling, where the heat source is overhead, roasted foods are surrounded by heat. And foods are usually roasted at a very high temperature. Roasted foods do need some space, so spread out the pieces of food in a roasting or shallow baking pan so that they have plenty of room.

HEALTH TIP: Roasting intensifies the flavor of fruit and vegetables, especially root vegetables such as beets and sweet potatoes. They require little seasoning or additional fat. Since you don't add any liquid when roasting, it's a terrific way to preserve vitamins and minerals in foods. Roasting foods caramelizes the natural sugar in them, adding sweetness and depth of flavor, especially to high-sugar vegetables like beets.

Gingered Orange Beets

Makes 4 (½-cup) servings

6 medium beets, peeled and sliced into ¼-inch-thick slices
  (about 2 pounds)
2 teaspoons olive oil
½ teaspoon salt
¼ teaspoon pepper
1½ teaspoons bottled minced ginger
¼ cup orange marmalade
1 tablespoon orange juice

1 Preheat oven to 450°. Combine first 4 ingredients in a large bowl. Combine ginger, marmalade, and orange juice in a small bowl, stirring well. Set aside.

2 Place beets in a single layer in a shallow roasting pan or jelly-roll pan. Bake at 450° for 12 minutes.

3 Remove beets from oven, and brush with ginger-orange mixture. Return to oven, and bake 10 to 12 minutes or until tender.

Per Serving: Calories 147 Fat 2.6g (saturated 0.4g) Protein 2.9g
Carbohydrate 30.5g Fiber 4.9g Cholesterol 0mg Sodium 437mg
Exchanges: 1 Starch, 3 Vegetable, ½ Fat

Microwave Magic

I don't know how I ever got along without my microwave oven! The microwave has come a long way since its debut, and I think it's a wonderful tool for busy cooks.

Here are just a few of my favorite microwave shortcuts:

• **EXTRACT JUICE:** Microwave a whole lemon, lime, or orange at HIGH 20 seconds to extract more juice from fruit.

• **MAKE BREADCRUMBS:** Stack 6 slices of bread, and cut bread into cubes. Place cubes in a microwave-safe dish. Microwave at HIGH 7 minutes or until cubes are dry, stirring after 3½ minutes.

• **CRISP SNACKS:** Place stale pretzels or crackers in a paper bag. Microwave, uncovered, at HIGH 30 seconds to 2 minutes, depending on the amount. Stir and let stand 5 minutes before serving.

• **TOAST NUTS:** Place ½ cup nuts in a 9-inch microwave-safe pie plate coated with cooking spray. Microwave at HIGH 4 to 5 minutes or until lightly browned, stirring every 2 minutes.

HOW-TO: Microwave ovens vary significantly by manufacturer and model, and most of the newer models are more powerful (indicated by the higher wattage). If you don't know the wattage of your microwave, do this simple test: Pour 1 cup tap water into a 2-cup glass measure, and watch how long it takes to come to a boil at HIGH power. Then check your time and wattage in the chart below.

TIME (in minutes)	OVEN WATTAGE
less than 2	850-1000 watts
2 to 3	650-850 watts
3 to 4	400-650 watts

You may have to add or deduct time from a recipe, depending on how powerful your microwave is.

HEALTH TIP: Like steaming, cooking vegetables in the microwave is a good way to preserve nutrients and flavor, and it's often the quickest way to cook them. I usually cook vegetables at HIGH in a baking dish covered with wax paper until they're crisp-tender. If you use plastic wrap to cover the dish, be sure to turn back one corner to allow steam to escape.

Couscous-Stuffed Peppers

Makes 3 servings

1 (5.8-ounce) package roasted garlic- and olive oil-flavored couscous
3 small yellow, red, or green bell peppers
1 cup chopped fresh spinach
⅓ cup grated Parmesan cheese
2 tablespoons slivered almonds, toasted
2 tablespoons sliced green onions

1 Prepare couscous according to package directions, omitting fat.

2 Cut each bell pepper in half lengthwise; discard seeds and membranes.

3 Combine couscous, spinach, and cheese; spoon evenly into pepper halves. Place in a microwave-safe 2½-quart baking dish. Cover with heavy-duty plastic wrap, and vent. Microwave at HIGH 8 minutes or until peppers are tender. Sprinkle with almonds and green onions.

Per Serving: Calories 338 Fat 7.0g (saturated 2.0g) Protein 13.3g
Carbohydrate 51.4g Fiber 5.6g Cholesterol 7mg Sodium 660mg
Exchanges: 3 Starch, 1 Vegetable, 1 Medium-Fat Meat

10 Ways to Lighten Up

1. Make **smarter** salads. Load up the greens with plenty of veggies, but keep the meat, cheese, and high-fat dressing to a minimum. *2.* **Beans,** please. Cut fat and add fiber to hamburgers by replacing some of the meat with rinsed, drained, and mashed black beans. *3.* **Say cheese.** Switch to reduced-fat cheeses. *4.* **Juice** up. Drink 100 percent juice instead of juice blends with added sugar. *5.* Hold the **mayo.** Save fat by spreading mustard instead of mayonnaise on your sandwich. *6.* Get **milk.** Add calcium and cut fat by using fat-free or low-fat milk instead of half-and-half to lighten coffee. *7.* Bake a better **spud.** Bake sweet potatoes instead of plain russets and get three times more fiber plus extra vitamin A. *8.* Broil, don't brown. Broil meats used in stews, soups, and roasts rather than browning them in oil. *9.* Smart **eggs.** Use 2 egg whites or ¼ cup egg substitute instead of a whole egg. *10.* Get **saucy.** Instead of heavy sauces or gravies, try fruit juices, salsas, pureed vegetables, broth, and wine for flavor.

Chapter 10

Make It Healthy

Makeover Magic

I didn't believe rich dips, cheese-topped casseroles, and ooey-gooey desserts could be good for you and still taste great.

I used to be one of those critics who cringed when someone brought "healthy" food to a party. Like a lot of folks, I didn't believe that any food that was good for you could taste great!

But now I know the truth. When I developed my weight-loss plan, I put a lot of thought into how I could make my recipes healthier without sacrificing flavor. I researched the best ways to trim the fat in everything from appetizers to side dishes. I also talked to dietitians and fellow professional cooks about substituting ingredients to keep the nutrition numbers in the healthy range. But most importantly, I went into the kitchen and started cooking. I wanted to experiment with lower-fat substitutes and find out for myself what products and methods work best.

As I experimented with ingredient substitutions, I wanted to make sure I kept the great taste intact. You know I believe in getting gratification from the foods you eat to lose weight. If food doesn't taste good, it doesn't matter how good it is for you, you'll give it up and go back to the other stuff.

Revamping Recipes

When it comes to good taste and good health, can you really have the best of both worlds? Yes, You Can! I'm gonna let you in on some of my test kitchen secrets. That's right! I want to share with you the tricks and techniques I used to transform fatty dishes into smart food choices.

I've discovered loads of ways to shave fat, calories, and cholesterol from some of my favorite recipes. In fact, I recently did a recipe makeover for a close friend who is a registered nurse. She brought me her family's favorite chicken casserole in cream sauce, which is loaded with artery-clogging fat. I made some quick substitutions and challenged her with a blind taste test. You know what? She couldn't tell the difference between the before and after casseroles!

> I've discovered loads of ways to shave fat, calories, and cholesterol from some of my favorite recipes.

Take a look at my recipe makeover on the next page to see what a difference a few simple changes can make. I cut the fat and calorie content of the original recipe and kept an eye on both sodium and cholesterol without losing the rich taste and creamy texture of this delicious dish.

The recipe chapters of this book are packed with recipes I've made both light and luscious. And you'll get plenty of how-to's in the following pages so that you can lighten up some of your own family favorites, too.

Recipe Improvement Project

The top card is the high-fat casserole from my friend. The recipe on the bottom is the new-and-improved version with a lot less fat!

Before Chicken Casserole in Cream Sauce

1   (10.75-ounce) can **cream of chicken soup,** undiluted
1   (8-ounce) carton **sour cream**
1   tablespoon poppy seeds
3   cups chopped cooked **chicken**
1½   cups crushed round **buttery crackers** (about 40)
½   cup **butter or margarine,** melted

Combine first 4 ingredients; spoon into a **lightly greased** 7 x 11-inch baking dish. Combine crushed crackers and butter, and sprinkle over chicken mixture. Bake at 350° for 30 minutes. Makes 4 servings.

After Ooh-It's-So-Creamy Chicken Casserole

Makes 4 (1-cup) servings

1   (10.75-ounce) can **reduced-fat, reduced-sodium cream of chicken soup,** undiluted
1   (8-ounce) carton **low-fat sour cream**
1   tablespoon poppy seeds
2   cups chopped cooked **chicken breast**
Cooking spray
15   **reduced-fat round buttery crackers,** crushed
1½   tablespoons **reduced-calorie margarine,** melted

Preheat oven to 350°. Combine first 4 ingredients. Pour mixture into a 2-quart baking dish **coated with cooking spray.** Combine crushed crackers and margarine; sprinkle over chicken mixture. Bake, uncovered, at 350° for 30 minutes.

Per Serving: Calories 270 Fat 10.5g (saturated 3.9g) Protein 26.9g Carbohydrate 14.1g Fiber 0.2g Cholesterol 83mg Sodium 520mg
Exchanges: 1 Starch, 3 Lean Meat

How I Lightened It

See what a difference a few simple changes can make in the nutrient values of a recipe:

BEFORE & AFTER	
Serving Size	
1 cup	1 cup
Calories	
690	270
Fat	
46.0g	10.5g
Cholesterol	
166mg	83mg
Sodium	
1,067mg	520mg

- Use reduced-fat, reduced-sodium cream of chicken soup.
- Substitute low-fat sour cream for regular sour cream.
- Use all white meat (breast) instead of a mix of white and dark meat and reduce the amount.
- Switch to reduced-fat buttery crackers and reduce the number.
- Substitute reduced-calorie margarine for butter and reduce the amount.
- Coat the baking dish with cooking spray instead of margarine or shortening.

TOP 15 FAT-TRIMMING TIPS

These simple ideas are sure-fire ways to save calories before a dish ever gets to the table!

1. Shop Around There are plenty of reduced-fat products that taste great! Find the ones you like, check the calories, and substitute these products for their higher-fat alternatives.

2. Make It Sizzle When you stir-fry meats or vegetables, keep the oil in the skillet or wok very hot. Foods soak up cold oil much more quickly than hot oil.

3. Chill Out Chill soups right after you make them. Before you heat them up to serve, remove the fat layer that forms on top.

4. Ground Rules If a recipe calls for ground beef, use lean ground round. Brown the meat in a nonstick skillet, and drain it in a paper towel-lined colander. Wipe the skillet with paper towels to get rid of even more fat before returning the meat to the pan.

5. Beef Tips Choose whole cuts of beef with the least amount of marbling (flecks of fat within the lean part of the meat). And trim all visible fat before cooking.

6. A Little Skin It's fine to cook chicken or turkey with the skin on, but remove the skin before you eat it to get rid of some fat.

7. Sauce Savvy Use fat-free half-and-half, low-fat sour cream, or evaporated fat-free milk as a creamy replacement for regular half-and-half and whipping cream in sauces.

8. Spray Away Use cooking spray instead of oil to coat skillets and baking dishes. It also makes cleanup a breeze.

9. Get Juicy If you love vegetables bathed in butter or margarine, get that flavor by using one part fat with one part lemon juice. Gradually decrease the amount of fat until you're only using a scant amount.

10. Cheese, Please Switch from higher-fat cheeses to sharp-flavored cheeses like reduced-fat sharp Cheddar cheese or feta and decrease the amount.

11. Chicken Stock Keep chopped, cooked chicken breasts in the freezer and bags of frozen chicken or a rotisserie chicken on hand so you'll always have an easy-to-fix main dish.

12. Drain It If you pan-fry foods, drain them on a paper towel to absorb excess grease.

13. Go Nuts Toasting nuts before adding them to a recipe enhances their flavor without adding fat. Try chopping them a little finer than normal so that you get nutty flavor in every bite.

14. Dressing Down To reduce the fat in a regular salad dressing, dilute it with a little lemon juice or vinegar. It will be thinner, so a little bit of dressing will go further.

15. 'Tater Talk If you're making mashed potatoes, try using Yukon Golds. They have a naturally rich, buttery flavor, so you don't have to add much fat to make them taste great.

SEND IN THE SUBSTITUTES

You can reduce fat by making some simple substitutions.

INGREDIENT	SUBSTITUTION
FATS AND OILS	
Butter and/or margarine	Reduced-calorie margarine or margarine made with safflower, soybean, corn, or canola oil
Mayonnaise	Low-fat or light mayonnaise
Oil	Safflower, soybean, corn, canola, olive, or peanut oil in reduced amount
Salad dressing	Reduced-fat or fat-free dressings and vinaigrettes
DAIRY PRODUCTS	
Sour cream	Low-fat sour cream; low-fat or nonfat yogurt
Half-and-half	Fat-free half-and-half
American, Cheddar, Colby, Edam, Swiss cheese	Cheese with 5 grams of fat or less per ounce like reduced-fat and part-skim cheeses
Cottage cheese	1% low-fat cottage cheese
Cream cheese	Light cream cheese; ⅓-less-fat cream cheese
Ricotta cheese	Part-skim ricotta cheese
Milk, whole or 2%	Fat-free milk; low-fat (1%) milk
Ice cream	Fat-free or low-fat frozen yogurt; fat-free or low-fat ice cream; sherbet; sorbet
MEATS, POULTRY, AND EGGS	
Bacon	Canadian bacon; turkey bacon; lean ham
Beef, veal, lamb, pork	Chicken, turkey, or lean cuts of meat trimmed of all visible fat
Ground beef	Ground round; ground turkey breast
Luncheon meat	Skinned, sliced turkey or chicken breast; lean ham; lean roast beef
Poultry	Skinned poultry
Tuna, packed in oil	Tuna, packed in water
Turkey, self-basting	Turkey basted with fat-free broth
Egg, whole	2 egg whites or ¼ cup egg substitute
MISCELLANEOUS	
Fudge sauce	Fat-free fudge sauce or chocolate syrup
Nuts	One-third to one-half less, toasted
Cream soups, canned	Reduced-fat, reduced-sodium condensed cream soups

Follow the Rainbow

*Pick the foods with the brightest colors and
you'll be assured you're getting the nutrients
you need for good health!*

Nutritionally speaking, the more colorful the food, the more vitamins, minerals, and other nutrients it contains. "Color my diet" is my new motto when I buy groceries or prepare meals.

The next time you sit down at the table, take a look at your plate. Pick the foods with the brightest colors, and you'll be assured you're getting the nutrients you need for good health! Fruit and vegetables, whether fresh, frozen, canned, or dried, are a great way to add variety to your meals year-round. By filling up on these flavorful foods, you'll boost the nutrients in your diet, reduce your fat intake, and possibly prevent weight gain.

In addition, all fruit and vegetables are loaded with nutrients and other protective properties. Turn to the next page for my "Top 10 Fruits and Veggies" that I always have on hand. Loading up on these foods is a safe bet toward ensuring lifelong good health.

TOP 10 FRUITS AND VEGGIES

As a person who loves food, I'm excited that there are things I can eat that will help me ward off some diseases. After learning more about what makes up a healthy diet, I'm convinced that fruit and vegetables should be a mainstay at every meal. The best part is that all these foods are easy to prepare and satisfy the "OOH IT'S SO GOOD!!" factor!

1. Broccoli   Loaded with the antioxidants beta-carotene and vitamin C, broccoli protects against cancer. It's also a great choice for women of child-bearing age because of its high folic acid content, which helps to prevent neural tube birth defects such as spina bifida.

2. Tomatoes   In any form—fresh, canned, or as juice—tomato products are superfoods because they contain vitamins A and C and the nutrient lycopene, all of which may help fight certain types of cancer. And lycopene is more active in canned tomato products than fresh, so keep your pantry stocked!

3. Sweet Potatoes   These are one of nature's most nutrient-dense foods. These root vegetables are loaded with fiber, vitamin C, and beta carotene, an antioxidant prized for its possible ability to protect against heart disease and certain types of cancer.

4. Citrus Fruit   Lemons, limes, and oranges are versatile fruits well known for their vitamin C content. Preserve this antioxidant by storing vitamin C-containing fruit in the refrigerator's crisper drawer.

5. Berries Summer brings a bounty of wonderful berries—from delicate blueberries and raspberries to sweet strawberries and tart blackberries. These fruits are terrific fiber sources that have tons of vitamins and minerals in a small package.

6. Spinach This dark leafy green offers an arsenal of nutrients. It is loaded with folic acid, beta carotene, and vitamin C. It also contains some of the highest levels of lutein of any vegetable. Lutein is a phytochemical that protects the eyes from harmful ultraviolent rays.

7. Bell Peppers Whether they're green, red, or yellow, bell peppers are a great source of vitamin C. One bell pepper has more vitamin C than an orange.

8. Squash The deeper the orange or yellow of a squash, the more vitamin A it has. And the more vitamin A you eat, the more you can reduce your risk of cancer and heart disease.

9. Beans Dried beans such as pinto, kidney, navy, black, and garbanzo are inexpensive sources of protein, iron, folic acid, and fiber. And although the canned versions can be higher in sodium than dried, they're still full of all the good stuff.

10. Carrots You've heard that eating carrots helps you see better, and it's true! They have beta carotene, which not only improves your night vision, but also protects against macular degeneration, a leading cause of blindness in adults.

6 Speedy Supper Tips

The ten 30-minute meals in this chapter feature these time-saving menu ideas: *1.* **Make a list** so you can quickly pick up everything you need at the grocery store. I've included a grocery list with each of my menus! *2.* Choose **one-dish meals** so you only have to mess up one pan. *3.* Use frozen, canned, or precut **vegetables** so you don't have to spend time chopping. *4.* **Buy bread** at the bakery instead of baking your own. Or check out the freezer and refrigerator sections for quick and easy bread doughs. *5.* Put the **rice** or **pasta** on to cook first so it can be cooking while you prepare the rest of the meal. *6.* Serve **fresh fruit** or low-fat **ice cream** for dessert.

Chapter 11

Magic Meals

Greek Snapper

Makes 4 servings

Cooking spray
- ½ cup chopped onion (about 1 small)
- ½ cup chopped green bell pepper (about 1 small)
- 1 teaspoon bottled minced garlic
- 1 (14½-ounce) can no-salt-added stewed tomatoes, undrained
- 1 tablespoon lemon juice
- 1 teaspoon Greek seasoning
- ½ teaspoon dried oregano
- 4 (6-ounce) red snapper fillets
- ¼ cup (1 ounce) crumbled feta cheese

1 Coat a large nonstick skillet with cooking spray; place over medium-high heat until hot. Add chopped onion, green pepper, and garlic; sauté until tender. Add tomatoes and next 3 ingredients; bring to a boil.

2 Reduce heat, and add fish, spooning tomato mixture over fish. Cover and simmer 15 minutes or until fish flakes easily when tested with a fork. Transfer fish to serving plates, and spoon tomato mixture evenly over fish. Sprinkle evenly with feta cheese.

Per Serving: Calories 200 Fat 2.9g (saturated 1.4g) Protein 34.0g
Carbohydrate 8.7g Fiber 1.9g Cholesterol 131mg Sodium 359mg
Exchanges: 2 Vegetable, 4 Very Lean Meat

Cucumber-Green Onion Salad

Makes 4 (1-cup) servings

2 large cucumbers, sliced
1 green onion, sliced
¼ cup light ranch dressing
¼ teaspoon cracked black pepper

1 Combine all ingredients in a medium bowl, tossing well. Cover and chill.

Per Serving: Calories 55 Fat 3.6g (saturated 0.3g)
Protein 1.0g Carbohydrate 5.0g Fiber 1.1g
Cholesterol 4mg Sodium 154mg
Exchanges: 1 Vegetable, ½ Fat

GROCERY LIST

1 small onion
1 small green bell pepper
2 cucumbers
Green onions
Pita bread
1 (14½-ounce) can no-salt-added stewed tomatoes
4 (6-ounce) red snapper fillets
Feta cheese
Light ranch dressing

SEASONINGS AND STAPLES

Bottled minced garlic
Cracked black pepper
Dried oregano
Greek seasoning
Lemon juice

Super Shrimp Supper
······················· SERVES 4 ·······················

Skillet Barbecued Shrimp
Corn on the cob
Shredded Apple Slaw

Skillet Barbecued Shrimp

Makes 4 servings
(serving size: about 3 ounces cooked shrimp and ¾ cup rice)

1 **family-size bag quick-cooking boil-in-bag rice (3 cups hot
    cooked rice)**
1 **pound peeled and deveined large shrimp**
2 **teaspoons no-salt-added Creole seasoning**
Cooking spray
½ **cup chili sauce**
½ **teaspoon hot sauce**

1 Prepare rice according to package directions, omitting any salt
and fat.

2 Toss shrimp with Creole seasoning. Coat a large nonstick skillet
with cooking spray; place over medium-high heat until hot.
Add shrimp; cook 3 to 5 minutes or until shrimp are done, stirring
often. Add chili sauce and hot sauce; reduce heat, and cook 2 minutes. Serve over rice.

Per Serving: Calories 293 Fat 2.4g (saturated 0.4g) Protein 26.4g
Carbohydrate 39.6g Fiber 0.8g Cholesterol 172mg Sodium 629mg
Exchanges: 2½ Starch, 3 Very Lean Meat

Shredded Apple Slaw

Makes 4 (¾-cup) servings

¼ cup light mayonnaise
1 tablespoon cider vinegar
1 to 1½ teaspoons sugar
¼ teaspoon salt
1 (8-ounce) Granny Smith apple
3 cups finely shredded cabbage

1 Combine first 4 ingredients in a small bowl, and stir until smooth with a whisk.

2 Shred apple. Combine shredded apple and cabbage in a large bowl; add mayonnaise mixture, and toss gently to coat.

Per Serving: Calories 84 Fat 4.3g (saturated 1.0g)
Protein 0.9g Carbohydrate 12.1g Fiber 2.5g
Cholesterol 5mg Sodium 267mg
Exchanges: 1 Vegetable, ½ Fruit, 1 Fat

Tip: Cook corn in microwave.

GROCERY LIST

1 Granny Smith apple
1 package cabbage, shredded
Family bag quick-cooking boil-in-bag rice
1 pound peeled and deveined large shrimp
Fresh or frozen corn on the cob

SEASONINGS AND STAPLES

Cider vinegar
Chili sauce
Cooking spray
Hot sauce
Light mayonnaise
No-salt-added Creole seasoning
Salt
Sugar

Quick Italian Fare

Linguine with Vegetables
Caesar Salad
Crusty rolls
Lemon sorbet

Linguine with Vegetables

Makes 4 (1¾-cup) servings

8   ounces uncooked linguine or fettuccine
¾   cup vegetable broth
1   (16-ounce) package fresh broccoli, cauliflower, carrot medley
½   (10-ounce) container light Alfredo sauce
½   cup (2 ounces) preshredded fresh Parmesan cheese
Freshly ground black pepper

1 Cook pasta according to package directions, omitting any salt and oil.

2 Combine broth and vegetables in a medium saucepan over low heat. Cover and simmer 5 minutes or until vegetables are crisp-tender. Add Alfredo sauce, stirring well.

3 Drain pasta, and place in a serving bowl. Add vegetable mixture, and toss. Top with cheese, and sprinkle with pepper.

Per Serving: Calories 341 Fat 6.9g (saturated 3.7g) Protein 16.7g
Carbohydrate 53.5g Fiber 4.4g Cholesterol 19mg Sodium 550mg
Exchanges: 3 Starch, 2 Vegetable, 1 Medium-Fat Meat

Caesar Salad

Makes 10 (1-cup) servings

2	tablespoons water
1½	tablespoons white wine vinegar
1	tablespoon olive oil
1½	teaspoons Dijon mustard
½	teaspoon Worcestershire sauce
¼	teaspoon garlic-pepper seasoning
1	garlic clove, minced
5	cups torn romaine lettuce
½	cup fat-free Caesar croutons
1	tablespoon preshredded fresh Parmesan cheese

Freshly ground black pepper

1 Combine first 7 ingredients in a small bowl; stir well with a whisk.

2 Combine lettuce and dressing in a large bowl; toss well. Add croutons and cheese; toss well. Sprinkle with pepper.

Per Serving: Calories 49 Fat 3.2g (saturated 0.6g)
Protein 1.3g Carbohydrate 3.2g Fiber 0.7g
Cholesterol 1mg Sodium 119mg
Exchanges: 1 Vegetable, ½ Fat

Tip: Pair the leftover salad with grilled chicken strips for another quick-and-easy meal.

GROCERY LIST

1 (16-ounce) package fresh broccoli, cauliflower, carrot medley
1 (10-ounce) package torn romaine lettuce
Crusty rolls
1 (8-ounce) package linguine
Vegetable broth
Fat-free Caesar croutons
1 (10-ounce) container light Alfredo sauce
Preshredded fresh Parmesan cheese
Lemon sorbet

SEASONINGS AND STAPLES
Dijon mustard
Garlic cloves
Garlic-pepper seasoning
Olive oil
Pepper
White wine vinegar
Worcestershire sauce

Company Curry Dinner

Curried Vegetable Gratin
Gingered Fruit
Crisp breadsticks

Curried Vegetable Gratin

Makes 4 servings

 1 (16-ounce) package frozen carrots, cauliflower, and snow pea pods
 2 tablespoons all-purpose flour
1⅓ cups fat-free milk, divided
 1 tablespoon reduced-calorie margarine
 ½ cup (2 ounces) shredded reduced-fat Swiss cheese
 ½ teaspoon curry powder
 ¼ teaspoon salt
Cooking spray
 2 tablespoons dry breadcrumbs

1 Steam frozen vegetables, covered, 8 minutes or until crisp-tender; drain. Set aside, and keep warm.

2 Combine flour and ⅓ cup milk in a saucepan, stirring until smooth. Add remaining 1 cup milk and the margarine; stir well. Cook over medium heat, stirring constantly, until milk mixture is thick and bubbly. Remove from heat; add Swiss cheese, curry powder, and salt, stirring until cheese melts.

3 Preheat broiler. Spoon vegetables evenly into 4 (1½-cup) broiler-proof baking dishes coated with cooking spray. Spoon cheese mixture over vegetables. Sprinkle with breadcrumbs. Broil 4 to 5 minutes or until lightly browned.

Per Serving: Calories 153 Fat 4.8g (saturated 1.8g)
Protein 10.9g Carbohydrate 17.3g Fiber 2.8g
Cholesterol 10mg Sodium 299mg
Exchanges: ½ Starch, 2 Vegetable, 1 Lean Meat

Tip: If you don't have individual baking dishes, cook this cheesy vegetable casserole in a shallow broiler-proof 1-quart baking dish.

Gingered Fruit

Makes 4 (1-cup) servings

½ cup sugar
½ cup hot water, divided
2 tablespoons lime juice
1 tablespoon grated peeled fresh ginger
2 cups pineapple cubes
2 bananas, halved lengthwise, and cut into
   2-inch pieces

1 Combine sugar and 1 tablespoon water in a large skillet; place over medium heat. Cook 5 minutes or until sugar mixture is golden, stirring frequently. Add remaining water, the lime juice, and ginger; bring to a boil. Reduce heat, and simmer, uncovered, until sugar dissolves, stirring occasionally.

2 Remove sugar mixture from heat. Add pineapple and banana; toss well.

Per Serving: Calories 261 Fat 1.2g (saturated 0.2g)
Protein 1.5g Carbohydrate 66.7g Fiber 4.0g
Cholesterol 0mg Sodium 3mg
Exchanges: 1 Starch, 3 Fruit

GROCERY LIST

2 bananas
Fresh ginger
Fresh pineapple
  chunks or canned
  pineapple cubes
  in juice
Crisp breadsticks
1 (16-ounce)
  package frozen
  carrots, cauli-
  flower, and snow
  pea pods
Dry breadcrumbs
Shredded reduced-
  fat Swiss cheese

SEASONINGS AND
STAPLES
All-purpose flour
Cooking spray
Curry powder
Fat-free milk
Lime juice
Reduced-calorie
  margarine
Salt
Sugar

Gourmet Pizza Night

Beef Pizza Portobellos
Herb-and-Garlic Breadsticks
Honeydew melon cubes
Light beer

Beef Pizza Portobellos

Makes 4 servings

    4 portobello mushroom caps (about 1 pound)
Cooking spray
    2 teaspoons extra-virgin olive oil
    ¾ pound ground round
    1 tablespoon dried basil
    ⅛ teaspoon fennel seeds
    1 (14-ounce) jar pizza sauce
    ⅔ cup (2⅔ ounces) shredded part-skim mozzarella cheese

1 Preheat oven to 400°.

2 Using a spoon, remove gills from undersides of mushrooms. Place mushrooms, underside up, on a baking sheet coated with cooking spray. Coat mushrooms with cooking spray. Drizzle ½ teaspoon olive oil over each mushroom. Bake, uncovered, at 400° for 8 minutes or until tender. Remove from oven. Set aside, and keep warm.

3 Cook ground round, basil, and fennel in a nonstick skillet over medium heat until beef is browned, stirring to crumble. Drain well.

4 Spoon pizza sauce evenly over mushrooms; top evenly with beef mixture and cheese. Broil 2 minutes or until cheese melts.

Per Serving: Calories 297 Fat 13.5g (saturated 5.5g)
Protein 27.2g Carbohydrate 16.5g Fiber 3.4g
Cholesterol 41mg Sodium 704mg
Exchanges: 3 Vegetable, 3 Medium-Fat Meat

Tip: Cook the ground round while the mushrooms bake.

Herb-and-Garlic Breadsticks

Makes 8 servings (serving size: 2 breadsticks)

1   (8-ounce) loaf sourdough bread
2   tablespoons olive oil
1½ teaspoons dried Italian seasoning
¼   teaspoon garlic powder

1 Preheat broiler. Slice bread in half lengthwise. Slice each half into 8 long sticks.

2 Combine olive oil, Italian seasoning, and garlic powder. Brush bread sticks evenly with oil mixture. Place on a baking sheet.

3 Broil 1 to 2 minutes or until lightly browned. Serve warm.

Per Serving: Calories 110 Fat 4.4g (saturated 0.7g)
Protein 2.5g Carbohydrate 15g Fiber 1g
Cholesterol 0mg Sodium 173mg
Exchanges: 1 Starch, 1 Fat

GROCERY LIST

4 portobello
   mushroom caps
Honeydew melon
   cubes
1 (8-ounce) loaf
   sourdough bread
¾ pound ground
   round
1 (14-ounce) jar
   pizza sauce
Shredded part-skim
   mozzarella
   cheese
Light beer

SEASONINGS AND
STAPLES
Cooking spray
Dried basil
Dried Italian
   seasoning
Fennel seeds
Garlic powder
Olive oil

Taste of the Tropics

Rum-Marinated Pork Chops
Baked sweet potato (½ per serving)
Steamed broccoli
Cinnamon Ice Cream

Rum-Marinated Pork Chops

Makes 4 servings

1½ cups coarsely chopped onion (about 1 large)
 ¼ cup dark rum (or ¼ cup apple juice)
 2 tablespoons lemon juice
 ½ teaspoon garlic powder
 ½ teaspoon dried crushed red pepper
 ½ teaspoon dried thyme
 ½ teaspoon ground cinnamon
 ⅛ teaspoon ground nutmeg
 4 (5-ounce) lean center-cut pork loin chops (½ inch thick), trimmed
Cooking spray

1 Combine first 8 ingredients in a large heavy-duty zip-top bag. Add pork, and seal bag; turn to coat. Marinate in refrigerator at least 8 hours, turning occasionally. Remove chops from marinade, discarding marinade.

2 Preheat the grill. Place pork chops on grill rack coated with cooking spray; grill, covered, 10 minutes or until done, turning once.

Per Serving: Calories 206 Fat 8.9g (saturated 3.1g) Protein 27.1g
Carbohydrate 3.1g Fiber 0.5g Cholesterol 82mg Sodium 66mg
Exchanges: 1 Vegetable, 3 Lean Meat

Tip: Leave the chops marinating in the refrigerator while you're at work. When you get home, you can have dinner on the table in about 10 minutes!

Cinnamon Ice Cream

Makes 4 (½-cup) servings

2   cups vanilla fat-free ice cream or frozen yogurt, softened
1   teaspoon ground cinnamon

1 Combine ice cream and cinnamon in a medium bowl; stir until well blended.

2 Cover and freeze until ready to serve.

Per Serving: Calories 101 Fat 0.0g (saturated 0.0g)
Protein 3.0g Carbohydrate 23.5g Fiber 0.3g
Cholesterol 0mg Sodium 45mg
Exchanges: 1½ Starch

GROCERY LIST

1 large onion
1 (16-ounce)
  package frozen
  broccoli
2 sweet potatoes
4 (5-ounce) lean
  center-cut pork
  loin chops
  (½ inch thick)
Dark rum (Note:
  substitute apple
  juice, if desired)
Vanilla fat-free ice
  cream or frozen
  yogurt

SEASONINGS AND
STAPLES

Cooking spray
Dried crushed red
  pepper
Dried thyme
Garlic powder
Ground cinnamon
Ground nutmeg
Lemon juice

Cajun Fire Chicken

Makes 4 servings

Cooking spray
4   **(4-ounce) skinless, boneless chicken breast halves**
1   **green bell pepper, coarsely chopped**
1   **(14½-ounce) can stewed tomatoes, undrained and chopped**
2   **teaspoons hot sauce**
⅓   **cup chopped fresh cilantro, divided**
½   **teaspoon dried thyme**
2   **teaspoons olive oil**

1 Coat a large nonstick skillet with cooking spray; place over medium-high heat until hot. Add chicken, bell pepper, tomatoes, 2 teaspoons hot sauce, ¼ cup cilantro, and the dried thyme. Bring to a boil; cover, reduce heat, and simmer 10 minutes.

2 Uncover and simmer 10 minutes. Stir remaining cilantro and olive oil into chicken mixture.

Per Serving: Calories 192 Fat 3.8g (saturated 0.7g) Protein 27.6g
Carbohydrate 11.8g Fiber 2.1g Cholesterol 66mg Sodium 323mg
Exchanges: 2 Vegetable, 3 Very Lean Meat

Tip: Put the rice on first and let it cook while you make the chicken and the salad.

Creole Rice

Makes 4 (¾-cup) servings

2¼   cups water
1   cup uncooked converted rice
½   teaspoon Creole seasoning

1 Bring water to a boil in a medium saucepan; stir in rice and Creole seasoning. Cover; reduce heat, and simmer 20 minutes.

2 Remove from heat; let stand, covered, 5 minutes or until water is absorbed. Fluff with a fork.

Per Serving: Calories 185 Fat 0.4g (saturated 0.1g)
Protein 3.8g Carbohydrate 40.1g Fiber 0.6g
Cholesterol 0mg Sodium 80mg
Exchanges: 2½ Starch

GROCERY LIST

1 bag mixed salad greens
1 green bell pepper
Fresh cilantro
4 (4-ounce) skinless, boneless chicken breast halves
Converted rice
1 (14½-ounce) can stewed tomatoes

SEASONINGS AND STAPLES

Creole seasoning
Dried thyme
Hot sauce
Low-fat vinaigrette
Olive oil

Special Occasion Dinner

SERVES 4

Balsamic Turkey
New Potatoes in Seasoned Butter
Fresh pear slices
White wine

Balsamic Turkey

Makes 4 servings

1   **pound turkey breast cutlets**
½   **teaspoon salt**
¼   **teaspoon garlic powder**
¼   **teaspoon black pepper**
Cooking spray
2   **teaspoons olive oil**
1   **large red bell pepper, sliced into rings**
⅓   **cup balsamic vinegar**

1 Rub both sides of turkey with salt, garlic powder, and black pepper. Coat a large nonstick skillet with cooking spray. Add oil, and place over medium-high heat until hot. Add turkey, and cook 2 minutes on each side or until lightly browned. Transfer turkey to a serving platter; keep warm.

2 Add red bell pepper to pan, and sauté 3 minutes or until crisp-tender. Top turkey with red pepper. Add vinegar to pan; cook 2 minutes or until slightly reduced. Spoon sauce over cutlets.

Per Serving: Calories 172 Fat 3.1g (saturated 0.6g)   Protein 30.0g
Carbohydrate 4.5g Fiber 0.3g Cholesterol 82mg Sodium 350mg
Exchanges: 4 Very Lean Meat

New Potatoes in Seasoned Butter

Makes 4 (⅔-cup) servings

1   **pound new potatoes, quartered**
1   **tablespoon light butter**
1½ **teaspoons lime juice**
¾   **teaspoon paprika**
½   **teaspoon salt**
3   **tablespoons chopped fresh parsley**

1 Steam potatoes, covered, 6 minutes or until tender. Transfer to a large serving bowl, and keep warm.

2 Combine butter and next 3 ingredients. Add to potatoes, and toss gently. Sprinkle potatoes with parsley, and toss again.

Per Serving: Calories 105 Fat 1.7g (saturated 1.0g)
Protein 2.8g Carbohydrate 21.0g Fiber 2.0g
Cholesterol 5mg Sodium 319mg
Exchanges: 1½ Starch

GROCERY LIST

1 large red bell
  pepper
4 pears
1 pound new
  potatoes
Fresh parsley
1 pound turkey
  breast cutlets
1 bottle white wine

SEASONINGS AND STAPLES
Balsamic vinegar
Cooking spray
Garlic powder
Light butter
Lime juice
Olive oil
Paprika
Pepper
Salt

Sandwich Supper for 2

SERVES 2

Fresh Slaw Reubens
Baked low-fat potato chips
Tart Spiced Apples

Fresh Slaw Reubens

Makes 2 servings

2 cups country-style shredded coleslaw mix
2 tablespoons white wine vinegar
3 tablespoons fat-free Thousand Island dressing
4 (1.1-ounce) slices rye bread
2 ounces thinly sliced low-fat deli corned beef
2 (1-ounce) slices reduced-fat Swiss cheese
2 teaspoons yogurt-based spread (such as Brummel and Brown)

1 Combine coleslaw mix and vinegar in a medium bowl; toss well. (Discard slaw dressing envelope if there is one in the package.)

2 Spread dressing evenly on one side of bread slices. Top two bread slices evenly with corned beef and cheese slices. Spoon slaw evenly over cheese. Top with remaining bread slices, dressing side down. Spread both sides of sandwiches evenly with yogurt-based spread.

3 Place sandwiches in a large skillet over medium-high heat. Cook 1 to 2 minutes on each side or until golden.

Per Serving: Calories 349 Fat 10.8g (saturated 5.3g) Protein 19.5g
Carbohydrate 43.2g Fiber 6.0g Cholesterol 35mg Sodium 919mg
Exchanges: 3 Starch, 2 Medium-Fat Meat

Tart Spiced Apples

Makes 2 (1-cup) servings

1   (20-ounce) can sliced apples
2   teaspoons lemon juice
2   tablespoons brown sugar
1   tablespoon reduced-calorie margarine
½   teaspoon apple pie spice

1 Drain apples, reserving juice. Add water to juice to equal ½ cup; set aside. Combine apple slices and lemon juice; toss lightly.

2 Combine apple slices, apple juice mixture, brown sugar, margarine, and apple pie spice in a saucepan. Bring to a boil. Reduce heat, and simmer, uncovered, 15 minutes, stirring occasionally. Serve warm.

Per Serving: Calories 135 Fat 3.7g (saturated 0.5g) Protein 0.1g Carbohydrate 26.3g Fiber 2.1g Cholesterol 0mg Sodium 81mg
Exchanges: 2 Starch, ½ Fat

Tip: Prepare the apples and let them cook while you make the sandwiches.

GROCERY LIST

Country-style shredded coleslaw mix
1 (20-ounce) can sliced apples
Fat-free Thousand Island dressing
Baked low-fat potato chips
Rye bread
Reduced-fat Swiss cheese slices
Low-fat deli corned beef

SEASONINGS AND STAPLES

Apple pie spice
Brown sugar
Lemon juice
Reduced-calorie margarine
White wine vinegar
Yogurt-based spread

Spicy Tomato-Corn Chowder

Makes 4 (1-cup) servings

Cooking spray
2 teaspoons vegetable oil
1 (10-ounce) package frozen whole-kernel corn, thawed
1½ teaspoons dried basil
1 (14¼-ounce) can fat-free, less-sodium chicken broth
1 (10¾-ounce) can condensed reduced-fat, reduced-sodium tomato
    soup, undiluted
½ teaspoon hot sauce
¼ teaspoon salt
¼ teaspoon pepper

1 Coat a large saucepan with cooking spray; add oil, and place over medium-high heat until hot. Add corn and basil; sauté 2 minutes. Add broth and next 4 ingredients. Bring to a boil; cover, reduce heat, and simmer 20 minutes.

Per Serving: Calories 140 Fat 4.0g (saturated 0.7g) Protein 3.4g
Carbohydrate 24.8g Fiber 2.4g Cholesterol 0mg Sodium 385mg
Exchanges: 1½ Starch, 1 Fat

Cheddar Drop Biscuits

Makes 12 biscuits

2   cups low-fat biscuit mix
½   cup (2 ounces) shredded reduced-fat
       Cheddar cheese
¾   cup fat-free milk
Cooking spray
2   tablespoons reduced-calorie margarine, melted
¼   teaspoon garlic powder
½   teaspoon dried parsley flakes, crushed

1 Preheat oven to 450°.

2 Combine biscuit mix and cheese in a bowl; make a well in center of mixture. Add milk, stirring just until dry ingredients are moistened.

3 Drop dough by rounded tablespoonfuls, 2 inches apart, onto a baking sheet coated with cooking spray. Bake at 450° for 8 to 10 minutes or until golden.

4 Combine margarine, garlic powder, and parsley flakes; brush over warm biscuits.

Per Biscuit: Calories 106 Fat 3.5g (saturated 1.0g)
Protein 3.4g Carbohydrate 15.0g Fiber 0.3g
Cholesterol 3mg Sodium 291mg
Exchanges: 1 Starch, ½ Fat

Tip: Place remaining biscuits in a zip-top plastic bag and store in refrigerator up to 2 days.

GROCERY LIST

1 (14¼-ounce) can fat-free, less-sodium chicken broth
1 (10¾-ounce) can condensed reduced-fat, reduced-sodium tomato soup
Low-fat biscuit mix
Shredded reduced-fat Cheddar cheese
1 (10-ounce) package frozen whole-kernel corn
Gingersnaps
Vanilla reduced-fat ice cream

SEASONINGS AND STAPLES

Cooking spray
Dried basil
Dried parsley flakes
Fat-free milk
Garlic powder
Hot sauce
Pepper
Reduced-calorie margarine
Salt
Vegetable oil

On the Move

with Mr. Food

YOU NOW KNOW A LOT ABOUT LOSING WEIGHT the right way. We've talked about smart eating habits, staying motivated, and low-fat cooking techniques. Now it's time to get moving!

Every weight-loss expert I spoke with told me exercise is the key to successful weight loss and long-term weight control. When I wanted to lose weight, I knew I had to carve out time for more physical activity. But how? Between my travel schedule, work, and family responsibilities, I didn't have time to hit the gym. And I sure didn't want to buy a lot of expensive equipment!

That's when I started thinking about all the different ways I could move more each day. But I realized I didn't *have* to move much, thanks to elevators, remote controls, and my golf cart!

That's when I decided to make some changes. I found tons of ways to take more steps, and I walked off 35 pounds. Now I want to show you how easy squeezing fitness into your hectic schedule can be. Trust me, you can do it!

7 Reasons to Get Moving Today!

1. **Stronger muscles** Keep your muscles strong so that you can lift groceries and grandkids with ease! And muscle tissue burns more calories than fat tissue does. **2.** **Stronger bones** Weight-bearing exercises such as walking, running, and strength training help to strengthen your bones and reduce the risk of fractures. **3.** **Better sleep** If you work out emotional stress with regular physical activity, you'll sleep better. **4.** **Easy moves** When your joints are stiff, your range of motion drops. Stay flexible by stretching regularly. **5.** **Fabulous figure** A trimmer figure is an added benefit of regular exercise and good eating habits. **6.** **Healthy body** If you have a medical condition such as diabetes, regular exercise is a must to control blood sugar. Physical activity is also a terrific way to reduce the risk of heart disease. **7.** **Clear mind** Folks who exercise regularly say that it helps them erase worries by releasing tension.

Chapter 12

Time to Move

Ready, Set, Go!

*Begin with a realistic plan to fit exercise
into your schedule.*

How many times have you promised yourself that today you will start exercising and make it a life-long habit? We often promise ourselves a fresh start, but typically those new beginnings don't last long.

I've finally been able to follow through with my exercise resolutions and make permanent lifestyle changes for the better. I want to tell you how to do that for yourself.

Begin with a realistic plan to fit exercise into your schedule. Think about any obstacles that you'll need to work around, such as carpool duties, business meetings, and household chores. You may want to put this plan on paper, and keep it in a location where you can review it often.

Next, think of at least three ways in which you can add more physical activity each day. For example, you can decide to (1) take the stairs instead of the elevator at work, (2) park your car in the far corner of the parking lot, far from the entrance, and (3) walk the dog farther every morning. Then, I want you to list your goals, and your reasons for making them. (See the chart on the next page.) Writing down your goals will help you keep them in mind. Maybe you want to lose weight so you can keep up with your children or grandchildren. Or perhaps you want to get in shape so that your back and knees won't hurt anymore. Make sure the goals you list are realistic. If you've never run before, don't decide you'll run a marathon in two months!

Make sure the goals you list are realistic.

Then, write down ways to make those exercise resolutions a reality. Will you plan to sneak in exercise by walking laps around your office? Or will you lace up your tennis shoes and hit the pavement after work?

Also, write down your current weight, Body Mass Index, and waist-to-hip ratio. (See the assessments on pages 174-176.) In a couple of months, you'll want to take these assessments again and see how far you've come!

Finally, mark your goals on a calendar so that you have deadlines to check your progress. Make today the day you start to make regular exercise a part of your daily schedule.

ACTIVITY GOAL	REASONS TO EXERCISE	WHEN I PLAN TO EXERCISE
1._____ _____	_____ _____	_____ _____
2._____ _____	_____ _____	_____ _____
3._____ _____	_____ _____	_____ _____

Assess Yourself

Losing weight is not just about looking good—it's also about getting healthier. As a starting point, you might want to assess your current health risk by determining your Body Mass Index and your waist-to-hip ratio. These assessments can help you see if your weight might contribute to health problems. Be sure to let your doctor or other health care provider know that you're starting an exercise program.

Size up Your Body Weight

The **Body Mass Index (BMI)** is a measure of your weight relative to your height. It's considered a more accurate measurement of your body fat than the former "ideal" weight charts.

To use the BMI table on the facing page:
1. Find your height in inches on the left side of the table.
2. On the row corresponding to your height, find your current weight.
3. Look at the numbers at the very top of the column to find your BMI.
4. Use the BMI and Health Risk table on the bottom of the page to determine your health risk.

Your Current BMI_____   **Your Health Risk**_____

BODY MASS INDEX (BMI)

BMI	19	21	23	25	27	30	32	34	36	38
Height					Weight (pounds)					
58"	91	100	110	119	129	143	152	162	172	181
59"	94	104	114	124	134	149	159	169	179	188
60"	97	107	117	127	138	153	163	173	183	194
61"	101	111	122	132	143	159	169	180	191	201
62"	103	114	125	136	147	163	174	185	196	206
63"	107	119	130	141	152	169	181	192	203	214
64"	111	123	135	146	158	176	187	199	211	223
65"	114	126	138	150	162	180	192	204	216	228
66"	118	131	143	156	168	187	199	212	224	236
67"	121	134	147	159	172	191	204	217	229	242
68"	125	139	152	165	178	198	211	224	238	251
69"	128	142	155	169	182	203	216	230	243	257
70"	133	147	161	175	189	210	224	237	251	265
71"	136	150	164	179	193	214	229	243	257	271
72"	140	155	170	185	199	221	236	251	266	281
73"	143	158	174	189	204	226	241	257	272	287
74"	148	164	179	195	210	234	249	265	281	296

BMI AND HEALTH RISK

Below 18.5   = Underweight

18.5 to 24.9 = Healthy Weight

25.0 to 29.9 = Overweight

30+   = Obesity

For example, if you are 5 feet 7 inches (67") and weigh 147 pounds, your BMI is 23. This means that you are in the healthy weight range and have a reduced risk of developing a weight-related disease, such as heart disease or Type 2 diabetes. If you are in the overweight weight range, you are at moderate risk, and if you are in the obese range, you are at high risk.

Determine Your Body Shape

Are you shaped like an apple or a pear? The **waist-to-hip ratio** will help you answer that question. This measurement is a good indicator of the amount of abdominal fat you have. If you are shaped like an apple, you carry more weight around your waist and might be at greater risk of heart disease. If you are shaped like a pear, you carry more weight around your hips and your risk for heart disease isn't as high. Either way, exercise will help decrease the risk of heart disease.

To measure yourself:

1. Using a tape measure, measure your waist (at the navel).
2. Measure your hips at the widest point of your buttocks and hips.
3. Divide your waist measurement by your hip measurement.

Waist measurement _____ ÷

Hip measurement _____ =

Waist-to-hip ratio _____

Your body shape:

❑ **Apple**　　　❑ **Pear**

WAIST-TO-HIP RATIO AND HEALTH RISK

1.0 or more　= Apple　= greater risk of heart disease

Less than 1.0 = Pear　= lower risk of heart disease

Less than .80 = normal for women

Less than .95 = normal for men

TOP 20 REASONS TO KEEP MOVING

Health experts say that regular exercise is the key to weight maintenance and has a bounty of health benefits.

1. Burns calories
2. Promotes weight loss
3. Increases heart rate
4. Increases good cholesterol (HDL)
5. Improves cardiovascular fitness
6. Improves muscle strength
7. Strengthens bones
8. Increases flexibility
9. Increases energy
10. Strengthens lungs
11. Improves sleep
12. Lowers blood pressure
13. Improves circulation
14. Improves posture
15. Strengthens heart muscles
16. Relieves stress
17. Helps prevent binge eating
18. Boosts self-esteem
19. Improves endurance
20. Increases alertness

Feel Younger and Stronger

Don't think of exercise as punishment—think of it as an opportunity to spread your wings.

Physical activity is the key to long-term weight control and freedom from "old age disease." Don't think of exercise as punishment—think of it as an opportunity to spread your wings. In addition to aerobic activities such as walking and swimming, I learned that there are a couple of other easy things that you can do to feel younger and stronger: stretching and strength training.

Stretching: The Truth

Stretching shouldn't just be something you do when you get out of bed in the morning. It needs to be part of your fitness routine. If you don't do any other form of activity all day except some stretching exercises, you will have done something important for your well-being.

Stretching can help you relax and reduce stress. Not only does it feel good, it also helps keep you flexible—no matter what your age—by improving your range of motion. And let me tell you, the more flexible you are, the younger you'll feel! Stretching tight muscles makes them less vulnerable to pulls and tears, so it prevents injuries. And even though you don't burn a lot of calories stretching, it helps you burn more calories during other types of activities. You should always do some light stretches before and after you exercise.

That's a Stretch!

- Before you stretch, warm up your muscles with some light movement like marching in place or swinging your arms.
- Stretch slowly and evenly without bouncing, and hold the stretch for 10 to 30 seconds.
- Stretch only to the point of tension, not pain. Don't force a stretch.
- After stretching one side of the body, do the same stretches on the other side.

Weight Up

As we age, our metabolism slows down and sometimes this results in a few extra pounds, even when our diets are about the same. One of the reasons that our metabolism slows down is because we tend to lose muscle as we age. But there's no reason that you have to continue on the muscle-losing path! Strength training can help you build back that muscle mass and turn you into a calorie-burning machine.

Lifting weights will make you stronger. Groceries will seem lighter to carry, stairs easier to climb, and grandchildren easier to lift. For all you women, don't worry that you're gonna look like Mr. Universe! It's not likely because women just don't have the hormones to form big, bulky muscles like some men. You'll simply look firm, fit, and fabulous.

There are quite a few ways that you can start a strength-training program, and you can do it at home or at a gym. Read up on weight training in fitness magazines, or talk to a fitness trainer at the local YMCA or sports club. All it takes to get stronger and leaner is about 20 minutes, three times a week. You'll be amazed at the difference you start seeing and feeling immediately in your body.

8 Ways to Fit in Fitness Today!

1. **Park** it. Don't drive up to the supermarket door. Instead, carry your grocery bags to your car, and then unload them bag by bag when you get home. *2.* **Speak** up. Take advantage of a cordless phone so that you can get up and move around during phone calls. *3.* **Fill** up. Fill up your water bottle regularly with frequent trips to the tap or water cooler. Every extra step counts!

4. **Do lunch.** If you're pressed for time in the afternoons or evenings because of your job, try exercising during lunch. Check out health clubs near your workplace, or buddy up with a coworker for a brisk walk after lunch. *5.* **Take the stairs.** If your home, office, or apartment complex has a staircase, go up and down it as often as possible. *6.* **Pencil** it in. Schedule your exercise time by writing it on your calendar so you'll be less tempted to skip it for another commitment. *7.* **Travel** light. If you'll be traveling, plot a walking course around your hotel or around the lobby.

8. **Wait and walk.** While you're waiting for a meeting or doctor's appointment to start, walk a few laps around the office.

Chapter 13

Feet First

Walk On!

Walking is easy, enjoyable, economical, and a great way to burn off calories!

If you're like me, you need a super-simple exercise plan that can be done anywhere and doesn't come with a hefty price tag. My friends, all you have to do is put one foot in front of the other and walk! Walking is easy, enjoyable, economical (it's free!), and a great way to burn off calories. It's amazing that something so simple can make such a difference in your health!

Walking has helped me keep the weight off for several years now, and while I'm no marathon runner, I've covered a lot of ground! In addition to my regular walking program, I look for ways during the day to be as "inefficient" as possible! Instead of saving steps, I try to see how many more steps I can take. For example, I always park my car in the far corner of the parking lot so that I have to walk a long way to get to my office entrance.

Get Moving

Now it's time for you to hit the ground running—er, walking—with my super-simple nine-week walking plan. (See "Walk Your Way to Fitness" on page 187.) This step-by-step program starts you out at a beginner's level, then shows you how to advance to pro status!

I've also included some stretching exercises to help strengthen your muscles and increase your flexibility. But first I want to get you on your feet with some commonsense tips for starting a walking program.

Rules of the Road

• **Get the green light.** If you have a medical condition or history of illness that might be affected by exercise, see your doctor before you begin any type of exercise program.

• **Be safe.** Find a safe place to walk. Consider school tracks, bicycle paths, or even the mall. Or check to see if your community has a walking club.

• **Pair up.** If you decide to walk with a partner or group, pair up with someone who has a similar pace.

• **Dress up.** Wear comfortable, seasonal clothing. Cotton clothing is best for the summer because it keeps your body cool by absorbing sweat and allowing it to evaporate. In colder months, layer clothing so that you can peel off layers as you warm up.

• **Stretch it.** Do some stretches before you step out and at the end of your walk. (See page 179 and "Stretching Exercises" on page 188.) When you stretch, you're less likely to pull muscles or feel sore. Plus, it feels good!

• **Follow the rule of three.** Divide your walk into three sections to make sure that you warm up and cool down properly. Begin at a slow pace with a five-minute warm-up. Then increase your speed and maintain it until almost the end of your walk. Cool down with a five-minute slow walk. (See "Walk Your Way to Fitness" on page 187 for a sample walking program.)

- **Make it a habit.** You'll see the greatest effects if you walk at least three times a week. That's a minimum, however. My wife and I like to hit the pavement after we've cleared away the dinner dishes. Walking gets us out of the house (and off the couch!), and because we go together, we're more likely to stick with our program.

"Since I started my walking program, I've gotten back the energy and stamina I had in my younger days."

A Perfect Fit

If you plan to walk, make sure you wear well-fitting shoes. Ill-fitting shoes can cause blisters. If you plan to buy new shoes, it's a good idea to shop smart. Here are a few tips to get a good fit:

- Shop late in the day, when your feet are at their largest size.
- Choose shoes with a thick, flexible sole that will cushion your feet and absorb shock.
- Check the toe to ensure that there's plenty of room. You need at least a half-inch between the end of your longest toe and the inner toe of the shoe.

Straighten Up

When you have poor posture, you're more prone to injury and you burn fewer calories. Here are four simple tips to fix your form:

1. Keep your chin up and pull your shoulders back. If you catch yourself drooping a little, imagine that there's a pull cord centered at the top of your head and someone is pulling up on it.

2. Stand tall and walk so that the heel of your foot touches the ground first, and roll your weight forward. Focus your eyes on the street or track about 10 to 20 feet ahead. Don't look down at your feet.

3. Hold in your abdominal muscles to help keep your back straight and strengthen those abs.

4. Swing your arms back and forth, not side to side.

Get with the Program

I love meeting folks like the Longs who have made exercise a habit!

I asked Ellen and Bones Long to be models for my walking program and stretching exercises because they are two of the most physically active folks I've ever met! At 70, Bones could outpace any teenager, and 55-year-old Ellen is a walking billboard for the benefits of fitness. The couple heads to the YMCA at least four times a week for some light toning exercises. On weekends, you can usually find them circling the track at their local high school. Ellen says she clocks over 4½ miles on those walks! I love meeting folks like the Longs who have made exercise a habit!

Ellen and Bones Long, of Birmingham, AL, exercise together about five times each week.

WALK YOUR WAY TO FITNESS

If you're a beginner, start with week 1. If you're already fairly active, you might want to start at the week 5 or 6 level.

	Warm-Up Time (Slow Walk)	Fast Walk Time (Brisk Walk)	Cool-Down Time (Slow Walk)	Total Time
Week 1	5 min.	5 min.	5 min.	15 min.
Week 2	5 min.	8 min.	5 min.	18 min.
Week 3	5 min.	11 min.	5 min.	21 min.
Week 4	5 min.	14 min.	5 min.	24 min.
Week 5	5 min.	17 min.	5 min.	27 min.
Week 6	5 min.	20 min.	5 min.	30 min.
Week 7	5 min.	23 min.	5 min.	33 min.
Week 8	5 min.	26 min.	5 min.	36 min.
Week 9 & beyond	5 min.	30 min.	5 min.	40 min.

From the Weight-Control Information Network, a program of the National Institute of Diabetes and Digestive and Kidney Disease

Before and after you walk, complete each of these stretching exercises three to five times, holding each stretch 10 to 30 seconds without bouncing.

Chest, Shoulders, and Upper Back Stand or sit, making sure your back is straight. First, pull your shoulders back, squeezing your shoulder blades together. Try to get your elbows as close as possible behind your back. Then straighten your arms, reach behind your back at waist level, and press your arms back.

Buttocks and Lower Back Lie on your back and gently pull both legs to your chest, clasping your hands between your thighs and calves. Curl your torso up toward your knees to increase the stretch.

Front of Thighs Lie on your right side. Your hips should be lined up so that one hip is directly above the other hip. Bend your left knee, reach back with your left hand, and hold onto your left heel. Pull slightly. Reverse the position and repeat with the other leg.

Back of Thighs Lie on your back, one leg bent, foot flat on the floor. Keep the other leg straight, and lift it straight up, bending just at the hip. Wrap your hands behind the thigh for support, but don't pull hard. Repeat with the other leg.

Abdomen, Chest, and Back Lie on your stomach and prop yourself up with your elbows. Slowly lift your torso up, making sure to keep your forearms and pelvis on the ground.

This exercise plan was reviewed by Nancy McCracken, M.S., P.T., senior physical therapist at HealthSouth Lakeshore Rehabilitation Hospital in Birmingham, Alabama.

5 Fantastic Ways to Keep Exercise Interesting

1. Play ball. Sign up for a community sports team or a work-related team. You'll have so much fun making new friends that you'll never notice you're exercising! **2. Strike!** Try out new activities, such as bowling or dancing. And make it a family activity so that everyone gets involved. **3. Pair up.** Find a workout partner who will keep you honest about getting fit. Don't buddy up with someone who'll tempt you to skip a workout. **4. Reward yourself.** Stay motivated by rewarding yourself when you reach fitness goals. For example, buy a new pair of tennis shoes, or treat yourself to a sports headphone set. **5. Do what you love.** Start off on the right foot by choosing activities that you enjoy doing. You're far more likely to keep on movin'!

Chapter 14

Beating Burnout

Bust Boredom

You've got to vary your activity habits in order to sustain your interest.

If you've been faithful to your walking program and stayed with it weekly, congratulations! But if you feel like you've been traveling down the same road (literally) far too long, then I have some suggestions.

Folks who maintain their weight loss know you've got to vary your activity habits in order to sustain your interest over the long haul. You know I walked off my extra weight, and I still hit the pavement regularly. Lately, I've even been known to park the golf cart and walk the greens!

But sometimes I want to try new things that'll test my muscles and spark my interest. As I've searched for fun activities, I've developed some hobbies as well. Now my wife and I take regular spins on the dance floor. In fact, we've recently learned the tango!

20 EXERCISE BOREDOM BUSTERS

Dancing is just one way we've worked extra activities into our exercise habits. I've found plenty of other fun ways to sneak in exercise! You've got to keep moving to keep the weight off, and these tips are sure-fire ways to burn fat and bust boredom.

1. Change your scenery. If you're bored to tears by the thought of a treadmill, then hit the pavement or walk to the mall.

2. Reset the clock. Change the time you work out. Lots of afternoon exercisers I know switched to the morning hours and loved it.

3. Gear up. Track your progress with exercise equipment such as a pedometer, which clocks the number of steps you take. I know a couple who competes to see who can log the most number of steps in a day!

4. Swing out. Take advantage of new dance crazes like swing dancing by registering for classes.

5. Walk for a cause. Charity fund-raising events such as walks, bike races, and runs are terrific ways to get in shape. Besides the health benefits, you'll feel good about what you're doing.

6. Do double time. Use an exercise machine, stretch, or do your muscle-toners while you're watching television. I do my daily crunches and push-ups while I'm catching up on the morning's television news headlines.

7. Act like a kid. During the summer months, I love to take my six grandchildren to the beach for an afternoon of kite-flying. If you take children on an outing and actually play with them, I promise you'll get a workout!

8. Make a date. Make exercise a social occasion by pairing up with a friend or spouse. You're more likely to keep the date if you make a commitment to someone else.

9. Clean up. Housework burns lots of calories, so get busy washing windows, vacuuming, and dusting. Turn on some tunes while you're working to keep you moving.

10. Hide the remote. Try getting up to change the television channel! (If you change it as much as I do, you'll be in great shape!)

11. Be old-fashioned. Pass up modern conveniences such as elevators in favor of a few more steps.

12. Join an exercise class. Try several classes until you find the one that's right for you, and don't be distracted by the perfect bodies in the room. Those people are there for the same reason you are: to get in shape and stay there. And many of them started where you are now.

13. Watch more TV. That's right! Check out the variety of fitness videos or exercise classes that cable television offers. At home, you don't have to compare yourself to others. Find an instructor you like, and work out at your own pace. Some folks like to tape their favorite shows and use the tape to exercise at their convenience.

14. Try a treadmill. According to a study published in the Journal of the American Medical Association, women who walk on treadmills in their homes lose an average of 8 more pounds than women who walk on the street or at a gym. In the study, women from ages 25 to 45 were told to walk briskly for 30 minutes every day for 18 months. One-third of the women were given treadmills, others were left to their own devices. The treadmill group also exercised more frequently.

15. Work smart. If you're stuck at your desk from 9 to 5, here are some great tips for adding a little physical activity to your day:
- Stretch your legs while you're on the phone.
- Hop up frequently to file papers.
- Take your fingers off the keyboard and point them upward, rotating them both ways at the wrist.
- Walk to a colleague's office instead of picking up the phone or sending an e-mail.
- Set your clock or program your computer to remind you to take brief walking and/or stretching breaks periodically.

16. Find a hobby. Did you always want to try horseback riding? Or perhaps in-line skating? Pick a sport and learn some new skills!

17. Take flights. Flights of stairs, that is. Go up and down the stairs as often as you can when you're at home or in an office building. You can burn 18 calories per minute of climbing.

18. Practice aerobic shopping. Take a lap around the mall or grocery store before you begin to shop. If you have to wait in line, practice good posture and stretch your back muscles.

19. Dig in the dirt. Gardening is a nice way to get in a little exercise. Plus, you can enjoy the results of beautiful flowers or tasty vegetables afterward. Although gardening may not be as vigorous as aerobics or running, it can be key to achieving a long, healthy life.

Take a few minutes to stretch, warm up, and loosen your muscles before beginning work in your garden, just as you would before any other workout. And be sure to wear plenty of sunscreen, a hat, and protective clothing as needed.

Here are some gardening activities that will give you a great workout:
- raking leaves
- carrying brush
- stacking wood
- digging
- laying stones or sod
- mowing grass
- planting trees or shrubs
- trimming trees with power tools
- weeding

20. Get your hair wet. If you have a medical problem that forces you to limit some activities, water workouts may be your answer to losing weight. They are low impact, and let you work out at your own intensity. Swimming and water aerobics are especially beneficial if you have trouble with your knees.

FUN WAYS TO BURN CALORIES

Enjoying these favorite activities can help you lose pounds, build energy, and get fit.

Note: These figures are approximate and are based on a body weight of 150 pounds. If you weigh more, you'll burn even more calories. If you weigh less, you'll burn fewer calories.

Exercise for 30 Minutes:	Burn this many calories:
Archery	120 calories
Badminton	122 calories
Bicycling (moderate pace)	221 calories
Bowling	102 calories
Canoeing	203 calories
Dancing (ballroom or square)	153 calories
Dancing (slow, fox-trot, or waltz)	102 calories
Gardening	258 calories
Golf (carrying clubs)	184 calories
Golf (using cart)	120 calories
Hiking	230 calories
Horseback riding	234 calories
Snorkeling	180 calories
Softball	180 calories
Swimming laps	360 calories
Swimming for fun	144 calories
Tennis (singles)	320 calories
Volleyball (vigorous)	293 calories
Walking (3.5 mph)	162 calories
Waterskiing (beginner)	170 calories

What's for Dinner

Menu Plans & Recipes

NOW THAT YOU KNOW ABOUT HEALTHY WEIGHT LOSS, motivation, attitudes, and exercise, let's eat! In this section, we're gonna put all you've learned about healthy cooking and eating into action. So many folks tell me, "If I could just have a menu to follow, I could do better!" Well, I've made it ooh-so-easy for you with six whole weeks of menus to get you started. Each day's menu includes at least one recipe from the recipe chapters in this book. (And even though I'm eating in a whole new way, I still believe in quick-and-easy recipes, so that's what you'll get.)

But don't stop with these menus! Beginning with Chapter 16, there are over 240 recipes, from Beverages to Soups & Sandwiches, so you can create your own menus.

Every recipe has the nutrient numbers listed so you can see how many calories and how much fat you're getting in one serving. But you don't really have to worry about that, because I've made sure that all of my recipes fit into the current nutrition guidelines. And I've shared some extra tidbits of information so you'll be "in the know." Happy meals!

6 Shortcuts for Meal Planning

1. **Pick three.** Always plan your meals with three food groups in mind. Pick a protein source, coming from meat, poultry, fish, or other foods such as beans or cheese. Then choose a grain source, such as pasta or rice. Round out the meal with plenty of vegetables and/or fruit. *2.* **Plan ahead.** Decide what you'll eat before you're hungry. That way, you're more likely to plan on healthy menu items. *3.* **Get fresh.** Plan menus around seasonal produce. Fresh fruits and veggies taste great and usually require very little preparation. *4.* **Make a list.** From the menus you've planned, make a shopping list and buy only what's on the list. *5.* **Snack smart.** Plan your snacks ahead of time so that you'll have low-fat snacks on hand when you get hungry. *6.* **Shop once.** Stop by the market only once a week. You'll save time, money, and the temptation to buy high-fat, high-sugar foods!

CHAPTER 15

Easy Menus for You

How to Plan a Meal

Before you know it, preparing healthy, delicious meals will become second nature.

By now you've learned how to read food labels. And you know to eat lots of fruits and vegetables and drink plenty of water. But are you still a little confused about how to put it all together to make a healthy meal? Keep reading, my friends, because this chapter is guaranteed to help you plan and cook healthy meals, and before you know it, preparing healthy, delicious meals will become second nature.

Think back to the Food Guide Pyramid I showed you in Chapter 6. This diagram holds the basic keys to healthy menu planning. By using the Food Guide Pyramid as a model, it's easy to create well-balanced meals. The Food Guide Pyramid is based on the concept that you should eat the most servings from the largest area of the pyramid, and you should eat fewer servings from the other food groups in the smaller areas of the pyramid. Notice that the largest area of the pyramid is the base, which is bread and other starchy foods. You'll see on my menu planners (pages 204-215) that each day is packed full of breads and grains, fruits and vegetables. Each day also has at least two low-fat milk servings and two lean protein servings. Sweets and fats are also included, but only in healthy moderation. (Remember, it's not about deprivation, it's about moderation!) If you pattern your food choices after the Food Guide Pyramid, you're sure to eat a healthy diet that will have you losing pounds just like I have!

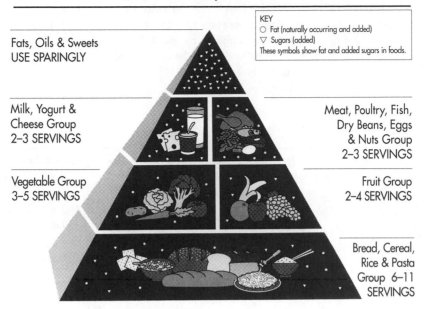

FOOD GUIDE PYRAMID
A Guide to Daily Food Choices

KEY
○ Fat (naturally occurring and added)
▽ Sugars (added)
These symbols show fat and added sugars in foods.

Fats, Oils & Sweets
USE SPARINGLY

Milk, Yogurt &
Cheese Group
2–3 SERVINGS

Meat, Poultry, Fish,
Dry Beans, Eggs
& Nuts Group
2–3 SERVINGS

Vegetable Group
3–5 SERVINGS

Fruit Group
2–4 SERVINGS

Bread, Cereal,
Rice & Pasta
Group 6–11
SERVINGS

Source: U.S. Department of Agriculture/U.S. Department of Health and Human Services

Explanation of Menu Plans

Planning an entire day of healthy meals may seem overwhelming, but I've included six weeks of menus to get you started. Beginning on page 204, you'll find a day-by-day meal plan. Each day gives you ideas for breakfast, lunch, and dinner. There's also a snack each day that you can eat anytime. The menus feature recipes from this book, and the page numbers are provided so you can find the recipes quickly. The other items in the menus will help round out the meals and are nutritious items you may already have in your pantry.

If you start with my menu plan, you'll quickly get the hang of how easy it is to put together your own healthy, delicious meals. Before you know it, you'll be creating your own meal plans using the other recipes in this book.

	MONDAY	TUESDAY	WEDNESDAY	THURSDAY
BREAKFAST	**Granola Muffins** (p. 246), 2 muffins Apple juice, 1 cup Fat-free milk, 1 cup	Cheese Muffin (Broil ½ ounce Cheddar cheese on cut sides of English muffin) Banana, 1 Orange juice, 1 cup	Scrambled egg, 1 Whole wheat bread, 2 slices Grapefruit, 1 Fat-free milk, 1 cup	Oatmeal, 1 cup Brown sugar, 1 tablespoon Raisins, 2 tablespoons Fat-free milk, 1 cup
LUNCH	**Grilled New Yorker** (p. 465), 1 serving Apple, 1 small	**Fresh Tomato, Basil, and Cheese Pizza** (p. 341), 1 serving Carrot sticks, 1 cup Fat-free milk, 1 cup	**New England Clam Chowder** (p. 453), 1 serving Saltine crackers, 6 Apple, 1 small	**Confetti Cheese Omelet** (p. 325), 1 serving Whole wheat bread, 1 slice Fat-free yogurt, 8 ounces
DINNER	**Tortellini and Salmon Dinner** (p. 308), 1 serving Salad greens, 2 cups Reduced-fat balsamic vinegar dressing, 2 tablespoons	**Maple-Glazed Ham** (p. 382), 1 serving **Sweet Potatoes in Orange Syrup** (p. 439), 1 serving Steamed broccoli, 1 cup Whole wheat roll, 1	**All-American Grilled Steak** (p. 361), 1 serving Boiled new potatoes, 1 cup **Spinach-Artichoke Bake** (p. 435), 1 serving	**Quick Curried Chicken** (p. 387), **Quick Mini Muffins** (p. 244), 2 muffins Canned pineapple, 1 cup Fat-free milk, 1 cup
SNACK	**Peanut Butter Bread** (p. 253), 1 slice Fat-free milk, 1 cup	Graham crackers, 2 sheets Fat-free yogurt, 8 ounces	**Caramel Swirl Icebox Cake** (p. 273), 1 serving	Reduced-fat popcorn, 3 cups popped
	TOTAL CALORIES: 1584	TOTAL CALORIES: 1543	TOTAL CALORIES: 1614	TOTAL CALORIES: 1577

FRIDAY	SATURDAY	SUNDAY	
Bran cereal, 1 cup Banana, 1 Fat-free milk, 1 cup	English muffin, 1 Jelly, 2 tablespoons Orange juice, 1 cup	Oatmeal, 1 cup Brown sugar, 1 tablespoon Banana, 1 Fat-free milk, 1 cup	BREAKFAST

Fruited Chicken Salad
  (p. 424), 1 serving
Pretzels, 2 ounces
Fat-free yogurt,
  8 ounces
	Veggie-Bean Tostadas
	  (p.330), 1 serving
	Grapes, 1 cup
	Fat-free milk, 1 cup
		Vegetable Fried Rice
		  (p. 335), 1 serving
		Carrot sticks, 1 cup
		Fat-free yogurt,
		  8 ounces
			LUNCH

Herbed Potato
  Frittata (p. 324),
  1 serving
Salad greens, 2 cups
Reduced-fat Italian
  dressing,
  2 tablespoons
Whole wheat roll, 1
	Broiled boneless pork
	  chop, 3 ounces
	Macaroni and Cheese
	  (p. 444), 2 servings
	Steamed green beans,
	  1 cup
	Whole wheat roll, 1
	Peach, 1
		Southwestern Chicken
		  Casserole (p. 384),
		  1 serving
		Low-fat deli coleslaw,
		  ½ cup
		Grapes, 1 cup
		Fat-free milk, 1 cup
			DINNER

Strawberry
  Milkshake (p. 220),
  1 serving
	Saltine crackers, 6
	Cheddar cheese,
	  1 ounce
		French Toast-Peach
		  Cobbler (p. 282),
		  1 serving
			SNACK

TOTAL CALORIES: 1578	TOTAL CALORIES: 1592	TOTAL CALORIES: 1570	

7-DAY MENU PLANNER
WEEK 1

	MONDAY	TUESDAY	WEDNESDAY	THURSDAY
BREAKFAST	Waffles, 2 Maple syrup, 2 tablespoons Blueberries, ¾ cup Fat-free milk, 1 cup	Bagel, 1 small Light cream cheese, 2 tablespoons Orange juice, 1 cup	Cinnamon Toast (1 slice whole wheat bread, 1 teaspoon butter, 1 teaspoon cinnamon-sugar), 2 slices Banana, 1 Fat-free milk, 1 cup	Cheese Toast (1 slice toast, 1 ounce cheese) Orange juice, 1 cup Fat-free yogurt, 8 ounces
LUNCH	**Quick Chicken Gumbo** (p. 457), 1 serving French bread, 2 ounces Pear, 1 Fat-free milk, 1 cup	**Garden Vegetable Wraps** (p. 460), 1 serving Reduced-fat baked chips, 1 ounce Fat-free yogurt, 8 ounces	**Barbecued Pork Sandwiches** (p. 467), 1 serving Baked beans, 1 cup Carrot sticks, 1 cup	**Tortellini with Pesto Sauce** (p. 348), 1 serving Salad greens, 2 cups Reduced-fat Italian dressing, 2 tablespoons
DINNER	**Lamb Shish Kabob** (p. 369), 1 serving Couscous, 1 cup Salad greens, 2 cups Reduced-fat balsamic vinegar dressing, 2 tablespoons	**Shrimp with Feta** (p. 320), 1 serving Angel hair pasta, 1 cup Sautéed spinach, ½ cup French bread, 1 ounce	**Chicken-Almond Stir-Fry** (p. 389), 1 serving Steamed snow peas, 1 cup Fat-free milk, 1 cup	**Barbecue Meatloaf** (p. 356), 1 serving Mashed potatoes, 1 cup Sautéed squash and zucchini, 1 cup Strawberries, 1¼ cups
SNACK	**Café Mocha Granita** (p. 262), 1 serving	**Blueberry-Yogurt Muffins** (p. 245), 1 muffin Fat-free milk, 1 cup	**Cookies and Cream Ice Cream** (p. 264), 1 serving	**Caramel Hot Cocoa** (p. 224), 1 serving
	TOTAL CALORIES: 1622	TOTAL CALORIES: 1521	TOTAL CALORIES: 1563	TOTAL CALORIES: 1523

FRIDAY	SATURDAY	SUNDAY	
Bagel, 1 small Reduced-fat peanut butter, 2 tablespoons Orange juice, 1 cup	**Buttermilk Biscuits** (p. 248), 2 biscuits Jelly, 2 tablespoons Grapefruit juice, 1 cup Fat-free milk, 1 cup	Waffles, 2 Maple syrup, 2 tablespoons Fat-free milk, 1 cup Blueberries, ¾ cup	BREAKFAST
Dump-and-Stir Chili (p. 458), 1 serving Oyster crackers, 22 **Cantaloupe Salad** (p. 407), 1 serving	**French Dip Sandwiches** (p. 463), 1 serving Reduced-fat baked chips, 1 ounce Nectarine, 1 small Fat-free milk, 1 cup	**Minestrone** (p. 450), 1 serving Grilled Cheese Sandwich (2 slices whole wheat bread, 2 ounces Cheddar cheese, 1 teaspoon butter) Banana, 1	LUNCH
Southwestern Vegetable Bake (p. 337), 1 serving Pineapple chunks, 1 cup Fat-free milk, 1 cup	**Cranberry-Ginger Grilled Turkey** (p. 403), 1 serving Wild rice, 1 cup Steamed green beans, 1 cup	**Indonesian Pork Tenderloin** (p. 378), 1 serving Yellow saffron rice, 1 cup Steamed broccoli, 1 cup	DINNER
Graham crackers, 2 sheets **Tangy Fruit Cup** (p. 267), 1 serving	**Whole Wheat Quick Bread** (p. 252), 1 slice Swiss cheese, 1 ounce	Apple, 1 small Fat-free milk, 1 cup	SNACK
TOTAL CALORIES: 1515	TOTAL CALORIES: 1612	TOTAL CALORIES: 1555	

7-DAY MENU PLANNER
WEEK 2

	MONDAY	TUESDAY	WEDNESDAY	THURSDAY
BREAKFAST	Whole wheat toast, 2 slices Scrambled egg, 1 Butter, 2 teaspoons Tomato juice, 1 cup	Grits, 1 cup Turkey bacon, 2 slices Dried plums, 3	Whole wheat toast, 2 slices Reduced-fat peanut butter, 2 tablespoons Grapefruit juice, 1 cup	**Granola Muffins** (p. 246), 1 muffin Turkey bacon, 2 slices Blueberries, ¾ cup Fat-free milk, 1 cup
LUNCH	**Sloppy Joes** (p. 350), 1 serving Reduced-fat baked chips, 1 ounce Celery sticks, 1 cup Fat-free yogurt, 8 ounces	**Fettuccine Alfredo** (p. 342), 1 serving Raspberries, 1 cup Fat-free milk, 1 cup	**Vegetable-Beef Soup** (p. 455), 1 serving Grilled cheese sandwich (2 slices whole wheat bread, 2 ounces Cheddar cheese, 1 teaspoon butter)	**Caesar-Tortellini Salad** (p. 420), 1 serving French bread roll, 1 Fat-free yogurt, 8 ounces
DINNER	**Marmalade Pork Chops** (p. 374), 1 serving Rice, 1 cup Steamed broccoli, 1 cup	**Oven-Fried Chicken** (p. 393), 1 serving Mashed potatoes, 1 cup **Succotash Slaw** (p. 415), 1 serving	**Grilled Portobello Pizzas** (p. 339), 1 serving Strawberries, 1¼ cups Fat-free milk, 1 cup	**Halibut with Teriyaki Sauce** (p. 303), 1 serving Couscous, 1 cup Steamed asparagus, 12 spears
SNACK	**Thumbprint Cookies** (p. 278), 1 cookie Fat-free milk, 1 cup	Pretzels, 1 ounce Pear, 1	Animal crackers, 8 Fat-free milk, 1 cup	**Strawberry-Merlot Ice** (p. 263), 1 cup
	TOTAL CALORIES: 1646	TOTAL CALORIES: 1567	TOTAL CALORIES: 1636	TOTAL CALORIES: 1592

FRIDAY	SATURDAY	SUNDAY	
Shredded wheat cereal, 1 cup Banana, 1 Fat-free milk, 1 cup	English muffin, 1 Jelly, 2 tablespoons Poached egg, 1 Grapefruit juice, 1 cup	**Buttermilk Pancakes** (p. 242), 2 servings Maple syrup, 2 tablespoons Orange juice, 1 cup Fat-free milk, 1 cup	BREAKFAST
Barbecued Beans 'n' Rice (p. 327), 1 serving Salad greens, 2 cups Reduced-fat ranch dressing, 2 tablespoons	**Cajun Catfish Sandwiches** (p. 461), 1 serving Low-fat deli coleslaw, ½ cup Watermelon wedge, 1	**Cheese and Onion Quesadillas** (p. 326), 1 serving Fruit cocktail, 1 cup Fat-free milk, 1 cup	LUNCH
Southwestern-Style Spaghetti (p. 401), 1 serving **Crisp-and-Spicy Cheese Twists** (p. 255), 1 serving Peach, 1	**Ham and Hash Brown Casserole** (p. 381), 1 serving Green peas, ½ cup Fat-free milk	**Gingered Beef Stir-Fry** (p. 359), 1 serving Rice, 1 cup Pineapple chunks, 1 cup	DINNER
Mocha Pudding Cake (p. 275), 1 serving Fat-free milk, 1 cup	Saltines, 6 Reduced-fat peanut butter, 1 tablespoon	**Popovers** (p. 243), 1 serving	SNACK
TOTAL CALORIES: 1598	TOTAL CALORIES: 1566	TOTAL CALORIES: 1625	

7-DAY MENU PLANNER
WEEK 3

	MONDAY	TUESDAY	WEDNESDAY	THURSDAY

BREAKFAST	Bran cereal, 1 cup
	Raisins,
	   2 tablespoons
	Orange juice, 1 cup
	Fat-free milk, 1 cup
		Shredded wheat cereal,
		   1 cup
		Banana, 1
		Apple juice, 1 cup
		Fat-free milk, 1 cup
			Cinnamon Toast
			   (1 slice whole wheat
			   bread, 1 teaspoon
			   cinnamon-sugar,
			   1 teaspoon butter),
			   2 slices
			Blueberries, ¾ cup
			Fat-free milk, 1 cup
				Breakfast Bagel
				   Stack-Ups
				   (p. 459), 1 serving
				Orange juice, 1 cup

LUNCH	**Crab Cakes** (p. 316),
	   1 serving
	Salad greens, 2 cups
	Reduced-fat balsamic
	   vinegar dressing,
	   2 tablespoons
		Mexicali Macaroni
		   and Cheese
		   (p. 343), 1 serving
		Orange, 1 medium
		Fat-free milk, 1 cup
			Oriental Chicken
			   Wraps (p. 469),
			   1 serving
			Fat-free yogurt,
			   8 ounces
			Grapes, 1 cup
				Gazpacho (p. 448),
				   2 servings
				Saltines, 6
				Fat-free yogurt,
				   8 ounces
				Grapes, 1 cup

DINNER	**Grilled Tomato-Basil**
	   Chicken (p. 395),
	   1 serving
	Feta Mashed
	   Potatoes
	   (p. 438), 2 servings
	Steamed asparagus,
	   12 spears
	Banana, 1
		Veal Marsala
		   (p. 365), 1 serving
		Spaghetti, 1 cup
		Mediterranean
		   Tossed Salad
		   (p. 414), 1 serving
		French bread, 1 ounce
			Sunflower Orange
			   Roughy (p. 306),
			   1 serving
			Rice, 1 cup
			Green Beans with
			   Onions and Garlic
			   (p. 431), 1 serving
				Garlic-Studded Pork
				   Loin Roast
				   (p. 379), 1 serving
				Microwave Risotto
				   (p. 441), 1 serving
				Steamed sugar snap
				   peas, 1 cup

SNACK	Whole wheat toast,
	   1 slice
	Reduced-fat peanut
	   butter, 2 tablespoons
	Fat-free milk, 1 cup
		Tutti-Frutti Smoothie
		   (p. 219), 1 serving
			Whole wheat bread,
			   2 slices
			Lean deli roast beef,
			   2 ounces
			Lettuce and tomato
				Chilled Mexican
				   Coffee (p. 223),
				   1 serving

	TOTAL CALORIES: 1621	TOTAL CALORIES: 1539	TOTAL CALORIES: 1544	TOTAL CALORIES: 1567

FRIDAY	SATURDAY	SUNDAY	
Whole wheat toast, 2 slices Hard-boiled egg, 1 Orange juice, 1 cup	**Sticky Caramel-Pecan Rolls** (p. 258), 1 serving Fat-free milk, 1 cup	Oatmeal, 1 cup Dried cranberries, 2 tablespoons Brown sugar, 1 tablespoon Orange juice, 1 cup	**BREAKFAST**
Turkey Pepperoni-Stuffed Pitas (p. 470), 1 serving Reduced-fat baked chips, 1 ounce Apple, 1 small	**Red Beans and Rice** (p. 400), 1 serving **Corn Bread Salad** (p. 412), 1 serving Melon wedge, 1	**Roast Beef and Blue Cheese Salad** (p. 421), 1 serving Whole wheat roll, 1 Fat-free yogurt, 8 ounces	**LUNCH**
Vegetable Lasagna (p. 346), 1 serving Salad greens, 2 cups Reduced-fat Italian dressing, 2 tablespoons Breadstick, 1 Fat-free milk, 1 cup	**Creamy Poblano Chicken** (p. 388), 1 serving Rice, 1 cup Steamed broccoli, 1 cup	**Balsamic Glazed Scallops** (p. 317), 1 serving Sautéed squash and zucchini, 1 cup Pear, 1	**DINNER**
Mom's Banana Bread (p. 250), 1 slice Fat-free milk, 1 cup	Low-fat ice cream, ½ cup	**Easy Peanut Butter Cookies** (p. 296), 2 cookies Fat-free milk, 1 cup	**SNACK**
TOTAL CALORIES: 1577	TOTAL CALORIES: 1601	TOTAL CALORIES: 1516	

7-DAY MENU PLANNER

WEEK 4

	MONDAY	TUESDAY	WEDNESDAY	THURSDAY

BREAKFAST	English muffin, 1
	Jelly, 2 tablespoons
	Orange juice, 1 cup
		Oatmeal, 1 cup
		Brown sugar,
		  1 tablespoon
		Raisins, 2 tablespoons
		Fat-free milk, 1 cup
			Waffles, 2
			Maple syrup,
			  2 tablespoons
			Blueberries, ¾ cup
			Fat-free milk, 1 cup
				Bagel, 1 small
				Reduced-fat peanut
				  butter,
				  2 tablespoons
				Banana, 1
				Fat-free milk, 1 cup

LUNCH	**Spinach Fettuccine**
	with Bacon-
	Cheese Sauce
	  (p. 380), 1 serving
	Strawberries,
	  1¼ cups
	Fat-free milk, 1 cup
		Taco Salad (p. 422),
		  1 serving
		Orange, 1 medium
		Fat-free yogurt,
		  8 ounces
			Deli-roasted chicken
			  breast, 3 ounces
			Whole wheat bread,
			  2 slices
			Lettuce, 2 leaves
			Reduced-fat baked
			  chips, 1 ounce
				Stuffed Poblanos
				  (p. 329), 1 serving
				Grapes, 1 cup
				Fat-free milk, 1 cup

DINNER	**Old-Fashioned**
	Turkey Hash
	  (p. 402), 1 serving
	Salad greens, 2 cups
	Reduced-fat balsamic
	  vinegar dressing,
	  2 tablespoons
		Grilled Mustard-Beer
		Shrimp (p. 322),
		  1 serving
		Steamed new
		  potatoes, 3 small
		Steamed asparagus,
		  12 spears
		Fat-free milk, 1 cup
			Extra-Easy Lasagna
			  (p. 355), 1 serving
			Salad greens, 2 cups
			Reduced-fat Italian
			  dressing,
			  2 tablespoons
			Apple, 1 small
				Asian Tuna Steaks
				  (p. 313), 1 serving
				Oriental noodles,
				  1 cup
				Grilled Eggplant
				  (p. 432), 1 serving
				Raspberries, 1 cup

SNACK	**Peanut Butter-**
	Banana Pudding
	  (p. 293), 1 serving
	Fat-free milk, 1 cup
		Tutti-Frutti Smoothie
		  (p. 219), 1 serving
			Caramel Corn Crunch
			  (p. 234), 1 serving
			Fat-free milk, 1 cup
				Low-fat ice cream,
				  ½ cup

	TOTAL: CALORIES 1563	TOTAL CALORIES: 1549	TOTAL CALORIES: 1635	TOTAL CALORIES: 1540

FRIDAY	SATURDAY	SUNDAY	
Bran flakes, 1 cup Strawberries, 1¼ cups Apple juice, 1 cup Fat-free milk, 1 cup	Bagel, 1 small Light cream cheese, 2 tablespoons Fat-free yogurt, 8 ounces Orange juice, 1 cup	English muffin, 1 Cheddar cheese, 1 ounce Grapefruit juice, 1 cup Fat-free yogurt, 8 ounces	**BREAKFAST**
Mostaccioli with Red Pepper Sauce (p. 345), 1 serving **Mandarin Salad** (p. 411), 1 serving Peach, 1	**French Onion Soup** (p. 449), 1 serving French bread, 1 ounce Raspberries, 1 cup	**Cheesy Bean and Rice Casserole** (p. 328), 1 serving Apple, 1 small Fat-free milk, 1 cup	**LUNCH**
Chicken Pot Pie (p. 386), 1 serving **Cranberry Waldorf Salad** (p. 410), 1 serving Fat-free milk, 1 cup	**Peppery Mushroom Burgers** (p. 351), 1 serving **Cheese Fries** (p. 437), 2 servings Steamed squash, 1 cup	**Chicken Parmesan Tenders** (p. 390), 1 serving Mashed potatoes, 1 cup Green peas, ½ cup	**DINNER**
Cheese toast (1 slice bread and 1 ounce cheese) Orange juice, 1 cup	Applesauce, ½ cup Graham crackers, 2 sheets	Pretzels, 1 ounce Carrot sticks, 1 cup	**SNACK**
TOTAL CALORIES: 1589	TOTAL CALORIES: 1564	TOTAL CALORIES: 1646	

7-DAY MENU PLANNER
WEEK 5

	MONDAY	TUESDAY	WEDNESDAY	THURSDAY
BREAKFAST	Whole wheat toast, 1 slice Poached egg, 1 Turkey bacon, 2 slices Orange juice, 1 cup	Bran cereal, 1 cup Banana, 1 Fat-free milk, 1 cup	**Orange Gingerbread Muffins** (p. 247), 2 muffins Apple juice, 1 cup Fat-free milk, 1 cup	Grits, 1 cup Turkey bacon, 2 slices Orange juice, 1 cup
LUNCH	**Apple-Chicken Salad Sandwiches** (p. 468), 1 serving Reduced-fat baked chips, 1 ounce Fat-free milk, 1 cup	**Curried Vegetable Couscous** (p. 336), 1 serving Pita chips, 1 ounce Orange, 1 medium	**Spinach Pockets** (p. 338), 1 serving Strawberries, 1¼ cups	Whole wheat bread, 2 slices Reduced-fat peanut butter, 2 tablespoons Jelly, 2 tablespoons Apple, 1 small Fat-free milk, 1 cup
DINNER	**Grilled Herbed Grouper** (p. 301), 1 serving **Garlic-Herb Cheese Grits** (p.440), 1 serving Steamed asparagus, 12 spears	**Quick Beef Stroganoff** (p. 354), 1 serving Egg noodles, 1 cup **Carrots and Zucchini in Browned Pecan Butter** (p. 430), 1 serving	**Moroccan Chicken** (p. 398), 1 serving Couscous, 1 cup Steamed broccoli, 1 cup	**Clam Fettuccine with Mushrooms** (p. 315), 1 serving Sautéed spinach, 1 cup Whole wheat roll, 1
SNACK	**Crunchy Oat-Apricot Bars** (p. 280), 1 serving Fat-free milk, 1 cup	Reduced-fat baked chips, 1 ounce Fat-free yogurt, 8 ounces	**Caramel Apple Dumplings** (p. 285), 1 serving Fat-free milk, 1 cup	Reduced-fat popcorn, 3 cups popped Fat-free yogurt, 8 ounces
	TOTAL CALORIES: 1602	TOTAL CALORIES: 1590	TOTAL CALORIES: 1596	TOTAL CALORIES: 1576

FRIDAY	SATURDAY	SUNDAY	
Whole wheat toast, 2 slices Jelly, 2 tablespoons Scrambled egg, 1 Grapefruit, 1	Bran cereal, 1 cup Blueberries, ¾ cup Orange juice, 1 cup Fat-free milk, 1 cup	**Buttermilk Pancakes** (p. 242), 2 servings Maple syrup, 2 tablespoons Strawberries, 1¼ cups Apple juice, 1 cup	BREAKFAST
Quick Chicken Gumbo (p. 457), 1 serving Salad greens, 2 cups Reduced-fat Italian dressing, 2 tablespoons	**Shrimp Rémoulade Loaf** (p. 462), 1 serving Reduced-fat baked chips, 1 ounce Fat-free yogurt, 8 ounces	**Barbecued Chicken Pizza** (p. 385), 1 serving Salad greens, 2 cups Reduced-fat ranch dressing, 2 tablespoons	LUNCH
Sausage-Beef Enchiladas (p. 352), 1 serving Grapes, 1 cup Fat-free milk, 1 cup	**Turkey Cutlets in Orange Sauce** (p. 404), 1 serving Wild rice, 1 cup Steamed green beans, 1 cup	**Spinach-Stuffed Shells** (p. 347), 1 serving French bread, 1 ounce Fat-free milk, 1 cup	DINNER
Bagel, 1 small Light cream cheese, 2 tablespoons	**Ooey Gooey Peanut Butter-Chocolate Brownies** (p. 279), 1 brownie Fat-free milk, 1 cup	Reduced-fat chocolate sandwich cookies, 2 Fat-free milk, 1 cup	SNACK
TOTAL CALORIES: 1667	TOTAL CALORIES: 1550	TOTAL: CALORIES 1635	

7-DAY MENU PLANNER

WEEK 6

Nutrition Notes

The recipes in the *Mr. Food Yes You Can Weight Loss Plan* can help you lose weight as well as meet the healthy eating recommendations of the U.S. Dietary Guidelines. Use the nutrient analysis following each recipe to see how the recipe fits into your healthy eating plan.

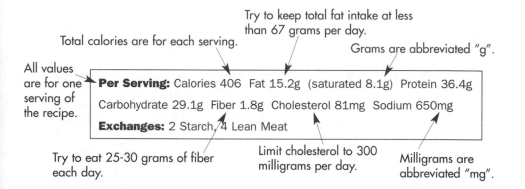

Try to keep total fat intake at less than 67 grams per day.

Total calories are for each serving.

Grams are abbreviated "g".

All values are for one serving of the recipe.

Per Serving: Calories 406 Fat 15.2g (saturated 8.1g) Protein 36.4g
Carbohydrate 29.1g Fiber 1.8g Cholesterol 81mg Sodium 650mg
Exchanges: 2 Starch, 4 Lean Meat

Try to eat 25-30 grams of fiber each day.

Limit cholesterol to 300 milligrams per day.

Milligrams are abbreviated "mg".

FAT

Your daily fat intake should be 30 percent or less of your total calories for the day. This doesn't mean that every single food you eat has to be under 30 percent.

Recipes with over 30 percent calories from fat can still be healthy. For example, salmon is higher in fat than other fish, but it is omega-3 fat, a healthier kind of fat.

Here's how the 30 percent recommendation translates to actual fat grams per day:
If you should eat 2000 calories per day, you can have up to 67 grams of fat.
2000 calories x 30% = 600 calories
Fat has 9 calories per gram, so
600 calories ÷ 9 = 67 grams fat

SODIUM

The current dietary recommendations advise us to limit our sodium to 2,400 milligrams a day. As you enjoy the ease of using convenience products, be aware that many of them are high in sodium, even when they are low in fat and calories. If you're watching your sodium intake carefully, read food labels and note the sodium value in the nutrient analysis following each recipe.

DIABETIC EXCHANGES

Exchange values are provided for those who use them for meal planning. They are based on the *Exchange Lists for Meal Planning* developed by the American Diabetes Association and The American Dietetic Association.

Chapter 16

Beverages
& Snacks

Old-Fashioned Lemonade

Makes 6 (1-cup) servings

1¼ cups fresh lemon juice (about 8 lemons)
¾ cup sugar
4¼ cups cold water
6 lemon slices

1 Combine lemon juice and sugar in a large pitcher, and stir until sugar dissolves. Stir in water and lemon slices; chill. Pour lemonade with lemon slices over ice.

Per Serving: Calories 109 Fat 0.0g (saturated 0.0g) Protein 0.2g
Carbohydrate 29.4g Fiber 0.0g Cholesterol 0mg Sodium 1mg
Exchanges: 1 Starch, 1 Fruit

"Quench your thirst with a glass of chilled lemonade instead of popping the top on a can of carbonated soda."

Tutti-Frutti Smoothie

Makes 3 (1-cup) servings

1   cup sliced ripe banana (about 1 medium)
1   cup orange juice
¾   cup sliced peeled peaches
¾   cup sliced strawberries
1   tablespoon honey

1 Combine all ingredients in a blender; process until smooth. Serve immediately.

Per Serving: Calories 134 Fat 0.5g (saturated 0.1g) Protein 1.6g
Carbohydrate 33.8g Fiber 3.3g Cholesterol 0mg Sodium 2mg
Exchanges: 2 Fruit

"This ooh-so-easy smoothie is a simple start toward the recommended five fruits and vegetables a day. I like to have it as an energy booster after exercising."

Strawberry Milkshake

Makes 4 (¾-cup) servings

3   cups vanilla low-fat ice cream or frozen yogurt
1   cup quartered fresh or frozen strawberries
½   cup low-fat (1%) milk

1 Combine all ingredients in a blender; process until smooth. Serve immediately.

Per Serving: Calories 197   Fat 3.4g   (saturated 1.7g)   Protein 5.7g
Carbohydrate 35.0g   Fiber 2.7g   Cholesterol 9mg   Sodium 84mg
Exchanges: 2 Starch, ½ Fat

"If you don't like to drink plain milk, or you're avoiding dairy products to fight fat, think again. Research suggests that eating low-fat calcium-containing foods may actually help you burn fat!"

Pineapple-Rum Slush

Makes 6 (1-cup) servings

3   cups pineapple juice
1   cup fresh lemon juice (about 5 large lemons)
¾   cup golden or dark rum (see tip below)
¾   cup water
½   cup sugar

1 Combine all ingredients in a large plastic pitcher; cover and freeze at least 4 hours or until slushy.

Per Serving: Calories 228 Fat 0.1g (saturated 0.0g) Protein 0.6g
Carbohydrate 37.4g Fiber 0.3g Cholesterol 0mg Sodium 2mg
Exchanges: ½ Starch, 2 Fruit

Tip: For a nonalcoholic version of this drink, substitute orange juice for the rum.

Hot Mulled Cider

Makes 6 (1-cup) servings

6   cups apple cider
3   tablespoons brown sugar
12 whole cloves
6   lemon slices (about 1 large lemon)
8   (3-inch) sticks cinnamon
½   cup light rum (see tip below)

1 Combine cider and sugar in a medium saucepan. Place 2 cloves in rind of each lemon slice. Add prepared lemon slices, cinnamon sticks, and rum to cider.

2 Bring to a boil; cover, reduce heat, and simmer 5 minutes. Remove cinnamon sticks and lemon slices; set aside for garnish if desired. Serve immediately.

Per Serving: Calories 155 Fat 0.3g (saturated 0.1g) Protein 0.2g
Carbohydrate 33.4g Fiber 0.3g Cholesterol 0mg Sodium 9.3mg
Exchanges: 1 Starch, 1 Fruit

Tip: If you want to make this without rum, just add an extra ½ cup of cider.

Chilled Mexican Coffee

Makes 5 servings
(serving size: 1 cup coffee mixture and ¼ cup ice cream)

4½ cups brewed coffee, chilled
 ½ cup chocolate syrup
 ½ teaspoon ground cinnamon
1¼ cups coffee or chocolate low-fat ice cream

1 Combine first 3 ingredients. Pour into individual mugs. Top each serving with ¼ cup ice cream. Serve immediately.

Per Serving: Calories 172 Fat 1.6g (saturated 1.0g) Protein 3.4g
Carbohydrate 36.0g Fiber 0.9g Cholesterol 13mg Sodium 67mg
Exchanges: 2 Starch

"Using chocolate syrup is a great way to curb a chocolate craving. One tablespoon has less than half a gram of fat!"

Caramel Hot Cocoa

Makes 2 servings (serving size: about 1 cup)

1 tablespoon sugar
1 tablespoon unsweetened cocoa
1¾ cups fat-free milk
2 tablespoons caramel ice cream topping

1 Combine sugar and cocoa in a small saucepan; stir in milk and topping. Cook, stirring constantly, over medium heat until mixture is thoroughly heated and caramel topping dissolves. Serve immediately.

Per Serving: Calories 175 Fat 0.9g (saturated 0.6g) Protein 10.1g
Carbohydrate 33.7g Fiber 0.9g Cholesterol 4mg Sodium 172mg
Exchanges: 1½ Starch, ½ Skim Milk

"A steamin' cup of cocoa is a soothing way to fill up on calcium-rich milk."

Russian Tea

Makes 1 serving

¾ cup boiling water
1 regular-size English Breakfast tea bag (see tip below)
¼ cup orange juice
1 teaspoon sugar
¼ teaspoon ground cinnamon
⅛ teaspoon ground cloves

1 Combine boiling water and tea bag in a large mug; cover and steep 5 minutes. Discard tea bag. Stir orange juice, sugar, cinnamon, and cloves into mug.

Per Serving: Calories 46 Fat 0.1g (saturated 0.0g) Protein 0.5g
Carbohydrate 11.2g Fiber 0.5g Cholesterol 0mg Sodium 1mg
Exchanges: 1½ Starch

Tip: If you're cutting back on caffeine, substitute decaf tea. And for an extra-zesty punch, try an orange-flavored tea.

Quick and Zesty Refried Bean Dip

Makes 1¾ cups (serving size: 1 tablespoon)

¼ cup chopped red onion
2 tablespoons bottled salsa
1 tablespoon fresh lime juice
1 teaspoon hot sauce
1 (16-ounce) can fat-free refried beans
¼ cup chopped fresh cilantro
¼ cup (1 ounce) shredded sharp Cheddar cheese

1 Combine first 5 ingredients in a small saucepan; cook over medium-low heat 5 minutes or until thoroughly heated.

2 Add chopped cilantro and cheese, stirring mixture until cheese melts. Serve warm with low-fat tortilla chips (chips not included in analysis).

Per Tablespoon: Calories 18 Fat 0.3g (saturated 0.2g) Protein 1.1g
Carbohydrate 2.6g Fiber 0.8g Cholesterol 1mg Sodium 73mg
Exchange: Free (up to 3 tablespoons)

"Want to know my secret to staying slim during the party season? I always take a healthy dip like this to get-togethers when I'm asked to bring a dish. No one ever guesses that it's good for you!"

Creamy Marshmallow Dip

Makes 1 cup (serving size: 1 tablespoon)

½   cup tub-style light cream cheese
½   cup strawberry low-fat yogurt
¼   cup marshmallow creme

1 Combine all ingredients in a medium bowl; beat at low speed of a mixer until well blended. Cover and chill 2 hours. Serve with fresh fruit (fruit not included in analysis).

Per Tablespoon: Calories 21.8 Fat 0.7g (saturated 0.4g) Protein 1.0g
Carbohydrate 72.8g Fiber 0.0g Cholesterol 3mg Sodium 31mg
Exchange: Free (up to 3 tablespoons)

"If you're not a fruit fan, you will be when you dip into this marshmallow dream. I like it best with apples, pineapple, and strawberries."

Peanut Butter Dip

Makes 1¼ cups (serving size: 1 tablespoon)

⅔   cup 1% low-fat cottage cheese
¼   cup reduced-fat creamy peanut butter
1   tablespoon honey
1   teaspoon vanilla extract
Ground cinnamon (optional)

1 Place all ingredients except cinnamon in a food processor; process until smooth. Cover and chill. Sprinkle with cinnamon, if desired. Serve with fresh fruit or graham crackers. (Fruit and crackers not included in analysis.)

Per Tablespoon: Calories 4 Fat 0.2g (saturated 0.0g) Protein 0.3g
Carbohydrate 0.4g Fiber 0.0g Cholesterol 0mg Sodium 8mg
Exchange: Free

"This is a super snack that'll fill you up quickly, thanks to high-protein cottage cheese and peanut butter."

Toffee Dip with Apples

Makes 16 appetizer servings
(serving size: 2 tablespoons dip and 3 apple wedges)

¾ cup packed brown sugar
½ cup sifted powdered sugar
1 teaspoon vanilla extract
1 (8-ounce) block ⅓-less-fat cream cheese, softened
¾ cup toffee bits (about 4 ounces)
1 cup pineapple juice
3 Red Delicious apples, each cored and cut into 8 wedges
3 Granny Smith apples, each cored and cut into 8 wedges

1 Combine first 4 ingredients in a bowl; beat at medium speed of a mixer until smooth. Stir in toffee bits. Cover and chill.

2 Combine pineapple juice and apple wedges; toss well. Drain apples, and serve dip with apple wedges.

Per Serving: Calories 173 Fat 6.0g (saturated 3.7g) Protein 1.5g
Carbohydrate 29.0g Fiber 1.9g Cholesterol 16mg Sodium 121mg
Exchanges: 1 Fruit, ½ Fat

"This dip is my secret weapon to get my grandkids to eat fruit. (They think it's some kind of treat— and it is!)"

Southwestern Dip

Makes 24 (¼-cup) servings

1 (16-ounce) can fat-free refried beans
1 medium avocado, chopped
½ teaspoon lemon juice
⅛ teaspoon salt
⅛ teaspoon pepper
1 (16-ounce) carton reduced-fat sour cream
1 (1¼-ounce) envelope 40%-less-sodium taco seasoning mix
⅓ cup sliced green onions
2 large tomatoes, chopped
1 (2¼-ounce) can sliced ripe olives
1 cup (4 ounces) shredded reduced-fat Cheddar cheese

1 Spread beans into a 10-inch deep-dish pie plate. Combine avocado and next 3 ingredients; spread over beans.

2 Combine sour cream and seasoning mix; spread evenly over avocado mixture.

3 Combine green onions, tomato, and olives; arrange mixture around the outside edge of pie plate. Sprinkle cheese in the center of dip mixture.

Per Serving: Calories 82 Fat 4.7g (saturated 2.3g) Protein 3.5g
Carbohydrate 6.6g Fiber 1.7g Cholesterol 12mg Sodium 273mg
Exchanges: ½ Starch, ½ High-Fat Meat

Tip: Make your own tortilla chips to serve with this dip by cutting flour tortillas into wedges and baking them at 400° for 4 to 5 minutes or until they're crisp and lightly browned.

Hot Artichoke Spread

Makes 48 appetizers
(serving size: 1 Melba round and about 1 tablespoon dip)

 1 cup 1% low-fat cottage cheese
½ cup grated Parmesan cheese
 3 tablespoons reduced-fat mayonnaise
 2 garlic cloves, minced
¼ teaspoon hot sauce
 1 (14-ounce) can artichoke hearts, drained and finely chopped
Cooking spray
48 Melba rounds

1 Preheat oven to 350°.

2 Combine first 5 ingredients in a food processor; process until smooth. Transfer mixture to a bowl; stir in artichokes.

3 Spoon mixture into a 1-quart baking dish coated with cooking spray. Bake at 350° for 20 minutes or until thoroughly heated. Serve with Melba rounds.

Per Appetizer: Calories 25 Fat 0.8g (saturated 0.3g) Protein 1.5g
Carbohydrate 2.9g Fiber 0.3g Cholesterol 1mg Sodium 87mg
Exchange: Free (up to 2 appetizers)

"Everybody loves to serve this easy dip at parties. A mix of low-fat cottage cheese and Parmesan cheese is my trick to trim the fat but keep the traditional version's creamy texture."

Fresh Tomato Salsa

Makes 2 cups (serving size: 1 tablespoon)

3 cups diced seeded tomato (about 3 large)
½ cup diced red onion
3 tablespoons chopped fresh cilantro
3 tablespoons fresh lime juice
½ teaspoon salt
2 garlic cloves, minced
1 jalapeño pepper, seeded and diced

1 Combine all ingredients in a medium bowl. Let stand for 30 minutes at room temperature before serving. Or cover and chill until ready to serve.

Per Tablespoon: Calories 4 Fat 0.0g (saturated 0.0g) Protein 0.2g
Carbohydrate 0.9g Fiber 0.2g Cholesterol 0mg Sodium 38mg
Exchange: Free

"This fresh tangy dip is TERRIFIC with low-fat tortilla chips. And, at only 4 calories per serving, it's a great way to add flavor to a piece of grilled chicken or fish."

Lemon-Garlic Pita Chips

Makes 4 servings (serving size: 6 chips)

3 (6-inch) pita bread rounds, split in half horizontally
2 teaspoons olive oil
1½ teaspoons lemon pepper
¼ teaspoon garlic powder

1 Preheat oven to 400°.

2 Cut each pita half into 4 wedges; place on a baking sheet. Drizzle oil evenly over wedges. Combine lemon pepper and garlic powder; sprinkle evenly over wedges. Bake at 400° for 5 minutes or until crisp.

Per Serving: Calories 108 Fat 3.3g (saturated 0.6g) Protein 2.9g
Carbohydrate 16.7g Fiber 0.8g Cholesterol 1mg Sodium 308mg
Exchanges: 1 Starch, ½ Fat

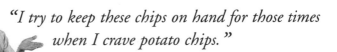

"I try to keep these chips on hand for those times when I crave potato chips."

Caramel Corn Crunch

Makes 14 (1-cup) servings

 1 (3-ounce) package reduced-fat microwave popcorn
⅔ cup packed brown sugar
¼ cup plus 2 tablespoons reduced-calorie margarine
¼ cup plus 2 tablespoons reduced-calorie maple-flavored syrup
 1 teaspoon vanilla extract
¼ teaspoon baking soda
Cooking spray

1 Preheat oven to 250°.

2 Cook popcorn according to package directions. Place popped popcorn in a large bowl; set aside.

3 Combine sugar, margarine, and syrup in a 2-quart saucepan; place over medium heat. Bring to a boil, stirring constantly. Cook 5 minutes, without stirring, or until candy thermometer registers 250°. Remove from heat, and stir in vanilla and baking soda.

4 Pour syrup mixture over popcorn; stir until evenly coated. Spread onto 2 jelly-roll pans coated with cooking spray. Bake at 250° for 20 to 25 minutes or until crisp. Cool in pans on wire racks; break into small pieces. Store in an airtight container.

Per Serving: Calories 89 Fat 3.2g (saturated 0.4g) Protein 0.8g
Carbohydrate 15.8g Fiber 0.0g Cholesterol 0mg Sodium 123mg
Exchanges: 1 Starch, ½ Fat

Garlic-Cheese Toasts

Makes 24 appetizers

½   cup (4 ounces) light cream cheese, softened
1½   tablespoons chopped fresh chives (see tip below)
1   tablespoon grated Parmesan cheese
1   teaspoon bottled minced garlic
24   (½-inch-thick) slices French baguette, toasted

1 Combine first 4 ingredients in a small bowl, stirring until smooth. Spread 1 teaspoon cream cheese mixture over one side of each toasted baguette slice.

Per Appetizer: Calories 51   Fat 1.2g   (saturated 0.7g)   Protein 1.8g
Carbohydrate 7.7g   Fiber 0.4g   Cholesterol 2mg   Sodium 113mg
Exchange: ½ Starch

Tip: If you don't have fresh chives, use 1½ tablespoons of any fresh herb, or a couple of teaspoons of your favorite dried herb.

Skewered Tortellini Appetizers

Makes 12 servings (serving size: 1 skewer)

36   fresh uncooked cheese tortellini (about 4 ounces)
¼   cup reduced-calorie Italian dressing
1   tablespoon chopped fresh parsley
36   (¾-inch) squares red bell pepper (about 2 large)

1 Cook pasta according to package directions, omitting any salt and oil. Drain.

2 Combine pasta and remaining ingredients in a bowl; toss. Thread 3 tortellini and 3 bell pepper squares alternately onto each of 12 (6-inch) skewers.

Per Skewer: Calories 46 Fat 1.1g (saturated 0.3g) Protein 2.1g
Carbohydrate 6.7g Fiber 0.5g Cholesterol 6mg Sodium 118mg
Exchange: ½ Starch

Tip: If you want to make these appetizers ahead of time, put the prepared skewers in a shallow baking dish and let them soak in the Italian dressing for a couple of hours.

Deviled Eggs

Makes 12 servings (serving size: 1 egg half)

     6   hard-cooked large eggs, peeled (see tip below)
  2½   tablespoons reduced-fat mayonnaise
     1   tablespoon sweet pickle relish, drained
     1   tablespoon grated onion
     1   teaspoon prepared mustard
     ⅛   teaspoon salt
Dash of ground white pepper
Paprika

1 Slice eggs in half lengthwise. Scoop out yolks, and place 4 yolks in a small bowl. (Reserve remaining yolks for another use.) Set whites aside.

2 Mash yolks with a fork. Add mayonnaise, pickle relish, onion, mustard, salt, and pepper; stir well.

3 Spoon mixture evenly into egg whites. Sprinkle with paprika.

Per Serving: Calories 39 Fat 2.6g (saturated 0.5g) Protein 2.7g
Carbohydrate 1.1g Fiber 0.0g Cholesterol 74mg Sodium 90mg
Exchange: ½ Medium-Fat Meat

Tip: For perfect-every-time hard-cooked eggs, place eggs in a single layer in a saucepan. Add enough cold water to measure at least 1 inch above eggs. Cover and quickly bring to a boil. Remove from heat. Let stand, covered, in hot water 15 minutes for large eggs. Pour off water. Immediately run cold water over eggs or place them in ice water until completely cooled.

Sausage-Cheese Balls

Makes 24 balls (serving size: 1 ball)

½ pound turkey breakfast sausage
1 cup (4 ounces) shredded reduced-fat sharp Cheddar cheese
3 tablespoons chopped fresh parsley
¼ teaspoon ground red pepper
1¼ cups low-fat biscuit mix
Cooking spray

1 Preheat oven to 350°.

2 Combine first 4 ingredients in a medium bowl, stirring well. Stir in biscuit mix.

3 Shape meat mixture into 1-inch balls; place balls on a baking sheet coated with cooking spray. Lightly coat sausage balls with cooking spray.

4 Bake at 350° for 20 to 25 minutes or until lightly browned. Serve warm.

Per Ball: Calories 61 Fat 3.3g (saturated 0.6g) Protein 3.3g
Carbohydrate 4.5g Fiber 0.2g Cholesterol 11mg Sodium 180mg
Exchanges: ½ Starch, ½ Fat

"The secret ingredients in these savory little low-fat snacks are low-fat biscuit mix and turkey sausage."

Potato Skins with Cheese and Bacon

Makes 8 servings (serving size: 1 shell)

 4 medium baking potatoes (about 2 pounds)
Cooking spray
 4 turkey bacon slices
 ¾ cup (3 ounces) shredded reduced-fat sharp Cheddar cheese
 ¼ cup reduced-fat sour cream
 1 tablespoon minced fresh chives

1 Preheat oven to 425°. Bake potatoes at 425° for 1 hour or until done. Cool slightly. Cut each potato in half lengthwise, and scoop out potato pulp, leaving a ¼-inch-thick shell. Reserve pulp for another use.

2 Place shells on a baking sheet. Spray inside of shells with cooking spray. Bake at 425° for 8 minutes or until crisp; set aside.

3 Cook bacon in microwave according to package directions; cool slightly. Chop cooked bacon.

4 Sprinkle cheese evenly in potato shells. Bake at 425° for 5 minutes or until cheese melts. Sprinkle evenly with bacon. Dollop each shell with sour cream; sprinkle with chives.

Per Serving: Calories 110 Fat 4.3g (saturated 2.2g) Protein 6.4g
Carbohydrate 12.0g Fiber 1.1g Cholesterol 15mg Sodium 177mg
Exchanges: 1 Starch, ½ Fat

Party Shrimp

Makes 12 appetizer servings (serving size: about 3 shrimp)

3 tablespoons finely chopped green onions
3 tablespoons minced red onion
1 tablespoon olive oil
2 tablespoons lemon juice
¼ teaspoon salt
⅛ teaspoon ground red pepper
1 pound large shrimp, cooked and peeled (see note below)

1 Combine first 6 ingredients; add shrimp, tossing well. Cover and chill at least 3 hours.

Per Serving: Calories 37 Fat 1.4g (saturated 0.2g) Protein 5.1g
Carbohydrate 0.6g Fiber 0.1g Cholesterol 47mg Sodium 103mg
Exchange: 1 Very Lean Meat

"Don't stress out over the shrimp—you can buy peeled, steamed shrimp in the seafood department of most grocery stores."

Chapter 17

Breads

Buttermilk Pancakes

Makes 9 pancakes

1 cup all-purpose flour
2 tablespoons sugar
1 teaspoon baking powder
½ teaspoon baking soda
1 cup low-fat buttermilk
1 tablespoon vegetable oil
1 large egg, lightly beaten
Reduced-calorie pancake syrup (optional)

1 Combine flour, sugar, baking powder, and baking soda in a large bowl. Combine buttermilk, oil, and egg; add to flour mixture, stirring until smooth.

2 Spoon about ¼ cup batter onto a hot nonstick griddle or nonstick skillet. Turn pancakes when tops are covered with bubbles and edges look cooked. Serve with reduced-calorie pancake syrup, if desired.

Per Pancake: Calories 92 Fat 2.6g (saturated 0.8g) Protein 3.0g
Carbohydrate 14.0g Fiber 0.3g Cholesterol 25mg Sodium 102mg
Exchange: 1 Starch

"Breakfast is a must when you're trying to lose weight, so why not start your day with a stack of warm pancakes topped with fresh fruit or drizzled with reduced-calorie syrup?"

Popovers

Makes 8 popovers

1 cup all-purpose flour
1 cup low-fat (1%) milk
¾ cup egg substitute
1 tablespoon sugar
1 tablespoon vegetable oil
¼ teaspoon salt
Cooking spray

1 Combine flour and next 5 ingredients in a food processor; process until smooth, stopping once to scrape down sides.

2 Pour batter into popover pans coated with cooking spray, filling one-half full. Place in a cold oven. Turn oven to 450°, and bake 15 minutes. Reduce heat to 350°, and bake 35 to 40 additional minutes or until popovers are crusty and brown.

Per Popover: Calories 109 Fat 2.5g (saturated 0.6g) Protein 5.3g
Carbohydrate 15.9g Fiber 0.4g Cholesterol 1mg Sodium 123mg
Exchanges: 1 Starch, ½ Fat

For Sweet Orange Popovers, add 1 tablespoon orange juice and 2 teaspoons grated orange rind to flour mixture, and proceed with recipe as directed.

For Savory Dill Popovers, add ½ teaspoon dried dill and ⅛ teaspoon onion powder to flour mixture, and proceed with recipe as directed.

Tip: You don't have to have a popover pan to make these. Your muffin pan will work just fine.

Quick Mini Muffins

Makes 16 muffins

½ cup all-purpose flour
½ cup uncooked quick-cooking farina (such as Cream of Wheat)
1½ teaspoons baking powder
½ teaspoon salt
1 cup low-fat buttermilk
1½ teaspoons vegetable oil
1 large egg white, lightly beaten
Cooking spray

1 Preheat oven to 450°.

2 Stir together all ingredients except cooking spray until blended. Spoon batter into miniature muffin cups coated with cooking spray (filling to top).

3 Bake at 450° for 12 minutes or until lightly browned. Remove muffins from pans immediately; place on a wire rack.

Per Muffin: Calories 46 Fat 0.7g (saturated 0.2g) Protein 1.8g
Carbohydrate 8.0g Fiber 0.3g Cholesterol 1mg Sodium 160mg
Exchange: ½ Starch

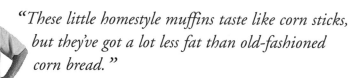

"These little homestyle muffins taste like corn sticks, but they've got a lot less fat than old-fashioned corn bread."

Blueberry-Yogurt Muffins

Makes 12 muffins

  2   cups all-purpose flour
⅓   cup sugar
  1   teaspoon baking powder
  1   teaspoon baking soda
¼   teaspoon salt
¼   cup orange juice
  2   tablespoons vegetable oil
  1   teaspoon vanilla extract
  1   (8-ounce) carton vanilla low-fat yogurt
  1   large egg, lightly beaten
  1   cup fresh or frozen blueberries, thawed
Cooking spray
  1   tablespoon sugar

1 Preheat oven to 400°.

2 Combine flour, ⅓ cup sugar, baking powder, baking soda, and salt in a large bowl; make a well in center of mixture. Combine orange juice and next 4 ingredients; add to dry ingredients, stirring just until moist. Gently fold in blueberries.

3 Spoon batter into 12 muffin cups coated with cooking spray; sprinkle 1 tablespoon sugar evenly over muffins. Bake muffins at 400° for 18 minutes or until a wooden toothpick inserted in center comes out clean. Remove muffins from pans immediately; place on a wire rack.

Per Muffin: Calories 150 Fat 3.4g (saturated 0.7g) Protein 3.5g
Carbohydrate 26.4g Fiber 1.1g Cholesterol 19mg Sodium 161mg
Exchanges: 1 Starch, ½ Fruit, 1 Fat

Granola Muffins

Makes 14 muffins

1½ cups low-fat biscuit mix
1½ cups low-fat granola cereal with raisins
½   cup packed brown sugar
1   teaspoon ground cinnamon
1   large egg, lightly beaten
¾   cup fat-free milk
1   tablespoon vegetable oil
Cooking spray

1 Preheat oven to 375°.

2 Combine first 4 ingredients in a bowl; make a well in center of mixture. Combine egg, milk, and oil; add to cereal mixture, stirring just until moist. (Batter will be thin.)

3 Spoon batter into muffin cups coated with cooking spray, filling two-thirds full. Bake at 375° for 20 minutes or until golden. Remove muffins from pans immediately.

Per Muffin: Calories 134 Fat 2.7g (saturated 0.6g) Protein 2.8g
Carbohydrate 25.3g Fiber 0.8g Cholesterol 18mg Sodium 187mg
Exchanges: 1 Starch, ½ Fruit, ½ Fat

"I like to keep these hearty muffins in the freezer for a quick but filling breakfast when I'm on the go."

Orange Gingerbread Muffins

Makes 12 muffins

2 cups low-fat biscuit mix
¼ cup cinnamon sugar, divided
½ teaspoon ground ginger
⅔ cup fat-free milk
¼ cup molasses
1 large egg, lightly beaten
1 tablespoon grated orange rind
Butter-flavored cooking spray

1 Preheat oven to 400°.

2 Combine biscuit mix, 3½ tablespoons cinnamon sugar, and ginger in a bowl; make a well in center of mixture. Combine milk and next 3 ingredients, stirring well. Add milk mixture to dry ingredients, stirring just until moist.

3 Spoon batter into muffin cups coated with cooking spray, filling one-half full; sprinkle remaining 1½ teaspoons cinnamon sugar over batter. Bake at 400° for 12 minutes. Remove muffins from pans immediately.

Per Muffin: Calories 122 Fat 2.0g (saturated 0.4g) Protein 2.5g
Carbohydrate 24.0g Fiber 0.3g Cholesterol 19mg Sodium 247mg
Exchanges: 1½ Starch

"Sh-h-h! Don't tell anyone these scrumptious muffins start with low-fat biscuit mix!"

Buttermilk Biscuits

Makes 16 biscuits

2	cups all-purpose flour
2½	teaspoons baking powder
¼	teaspoon baking soda
¼	teaspoon salt
2	teaspoons sugar
3	tablespoons chilled reduced-calorie stick margarine, cut into small pieces
¾	cup low-fat buttermilk

Butter-flavored cooking spray
Reduced-calorie jelly (optional)

1 Preheat oven to 425°.

2 Combine flour and next 4 ingredients in a medium bowl; cut in margarine with a pastry blender until mixture resembles coarse meal. Add buttermilk; stir just until moist.

3 Turn dough out onto a heavily floured surface; knead lightly 10 to 12 times. Roll dough to ½-inch thickness; cut with a 2-inch biscuit cutter.

4 Place on an ungreased baking sheet. Bake at 425° for 10 to 12 minutes or until golden. Lightly spray biscuits with cooking spray. Serve with reduced-calorie jelly, if desired.

Per Biscuit: Calories 75 Fat 1.6g (saturated 0.1g) Protein 2.0g
Carbohydrate 13.2g Fiber 0.4g Cholesterol 0mg Sodium 167mg
Exchange: 1 Starch

Corn Bread

Makes 9 servings (serving size: 1 square)

¾   cup all-purpose flour
1¼ cups yellow cornmeal
 2 teaspoons baking powder
½   teaspoon baking soda
¼   teaspoon salt
 1 tablespoon sugar
 1 cup low-fat buttermilk
 1 (8.5-ounce) can cream-style corn
 1 large egg, lightly beaten
Cooking spray

1 Preheat oven to 425°.

2 Lightly spoon flour into a dry measuring cup; level with a knife. Combine flour, cornmeal, and next 4 ingredients in a medium bowl; stir well.

3 Stir together buttermilk, corn, and egg in a small bowl. Add to cornmeal mixture, stirring just until moist. Pour batter into an 8-inch square baking pan coated with cooking spray.

4 Bake at 425° for 20 to 22 minutes or until golden. Cool 5 minutes in pan on a wire rack. Remove from pan and cut into squares. Serve warm.

Per Serving: Calories 145 Fat 1.6g (saturated 0.4g) Protein 4.6g
Carbohydrate 28.6g Fiber 2.6g Cholesterol 25mg Sodium 367mg
Exchanges: 2 Starch

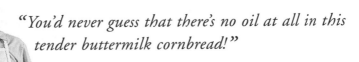

"You'd never guess that there's no oil at all in this tender buttermilk cornbread!"

Mom's Banana Bread

Makes 1 loaf or 18 (½-inch) slices (serving size: 1 slice)

1	cup sugar
¼	cup light butter, softened
1⅔	cups mashed ripe banana (about 3 bananas)
¼	cup fat-free milk
¼	cup reduced-fat sour cream
2	large egg whites
2	cups all-purpose flour
1	teaspoon baking soda
½	teaspoon salt

Cooking spray

1 Preheat oven to 350°.

2 Beat sugar and butter at medium speed of a mixer until well blended. Add mashed banana, milk, sour cream, and egg whites; beat well.

3 Combine flour, baking soda, and salt. Add flour mixture to sugar mixture, beating until blended.

4 Spoon batter into a 5 x 9-inch loaf pan coated with cooking spray. Bake at 350° for 1 hour and 10 minutes or until a wooden toothpick inserted in center comes out clean. Cool in pan 10 minutes on a wire rack; remove from pan. Cool completely on wire rack.

Per Slice: Calories 132 Fat 2.0g (saturated 1.2g) Protein 2.5g
Carbohydrate 27.0g Fiber 0.9g Cholesterol 6mg Sodium 161mg
Exchanges: 1 Starch, 1 Fruit

"Don't tell Mom, but I lightened up her banana bread recipe. And I added another banana, so it's sweeter than ever!"

Beer Bread

Makes 1 loaf or 16 (½-inch) slices (serving size: 1 slice)

3 cups self-rising flour
¼ cup sugar
1 (12-ounce) bottle light or dark beer (see tip below)
Cooking spray

1 Preheat oven to 375°.

2 Stir together first three ingredients; spoon dough into a 4½ x 8½-inch loaf pan coated with cooking spray.

3 Bake at 375° for 55 to 60 minutes or until lightly browned. Cool in pan 5 minutes on a wire rack . Remove from pan, and cool completely on wire rack.

Per Slice: Calories 96 Fat 0.2g (saturated 0.0g) Protein 2.3g
Carbohydrate 20.6g Fiber 0.6g Cholesterol 0mg Sodium 298mg
Exchange: 1 Starch

Tip: Alcohol and extra calories from the beer evaporate as the bread bakes, leaving only the hearty flavor behind.

Whole Wheat Quick Bread

Makes 1 loaf or 18 (½-inch) slices (serving size: 1 slice)

2	cups whole wheat flour
1½	cups all-purpose flour
1¼	teaspoons salt
¼	cup unsalted sunflower seed kernels
1	teaspoon baking soda
1½	cups low-fat buttermilk
1	large egg, lightly beaten
3	tablespoons honey
2	tablespoons margarine, melted

Cooking spray

| 3 | tablespoons regular oats |

1 Preheat oven to 375°.

2 Combine flours, salt, and sunflower kernels in a large bowl. Combine baking soda and buttermilk; stir and let stand 5 minutes. Add egg, honey, and margarine to buttermilk mixture; stir well. Add buttermilk mixture to dry ingredients, stirring well.

3 Spoon batter into a 5 x 9-inch loaf pan coated with cooking spray. Coat top of dough lightly with cooking spray, and sprinkle with oats.

4 Bake at 375° for 55 minutes or until a wooden toothpick inserted in center comes out clean. Cool in pan 10 minutes on a wire rack. Remove from pan, and cool on wire rack.

Per Slice: Calories 132 Fat 3.1g (saturated 0.6g) Protein 4.5g
Carbohydrate 22.7g Fiber 2.2g Cholesterol 13mg Sodium 274mg
Exchanges: 1½ Starch, ½ Fat

Peanut Butter Bread

Makes 1 loaf or 18 (½-inch) slices (serving size: 1 slice)

2   cups all-purpose flour
½   cup sugar
2   teaspoons baking powder
1   teaspoon salt
¾   cup reduced-fat peanut butter
1   large egg, lightly beaten
1   cup low-fat (1%) milk
Cooking spray

1 Preheat oven to 350°.

2 Stir together first 4 ingredients in a medium bowl. Cut in peanut butter with a fork or pastry blender until crumbly. Combine egg and milk in a small bowl; stir into dry ingredients just until blended.

3 Spoon batter into a 5 x 9-inch loaf pan coated with cooking spray. Bake at 350° for 1 hour or until a wooden toothpick inserted in center comes out clean. Remove from pan immediately, and cool on a wire rack.

Per Slice: Calories 136 Fat 4.1g (saturated 0.8g) Protein 5.1g
Carbohydrate 20.4g Fiber 1.0g Cholesterol 12mg Sodium 254mg
Exhanges: 1 Starch, 1 Fat

"I go nuts over this bread! My favorite way to eat it is toasted for breakfast. With a tad of low-sugar jelly, I've got a breakfast PB&J!"

Stuffed Tex-Mex Loaf

Makes 10 servings (serving size: 1 slice)

1   cup bottled salsa
1   (16-ounce) loaf French bread, cut in half lengthwise
1   cup (4 ounces) shredded reduced-fat Mexican cheese blend
1   (4.5-ounce) can chopped green chilies, drained
1   (2¼-ounce) can sliced ripe olives, drained

1 Preheat oven to 400°.

2 Spread salsa over bottom half of bread. Top with cheese, chilies, olives, and top half of bread.

3 Wrap in foil; bake at 400° for 20 minutes or until cheese melts and bread is toasted. Let stand 5 minutes. Cut into slices, using a serrated knife.

Per Serving: Calories 168 Fat 4.0g (saturated 1.6g) Protein 7.6g
Carbohydrate 26.0g Fiber 2.0g Cholesterol 4mg Sodium 526mg
Exchanges: 1½ Starch, 1 Fat

"If you're crazy about spicy food like I am, use hot salsa. The hotter the better, in my opinion! And the good news is that salsa is VERY low in calories and is a super way to sneak extra veggies into your day!"

Crisp-and-Spicy Cheese Twists

Makes 16 twists

¼ cup grated Parmesan cheese
1 teaspoon paprika
⅛ teaspoon ground red pepper
1 (10-ounce) can refrigerated pizza crust dough
Butter-flavored cooking spray

1 Preheat oven to 425°.

2 Combine cheese, paprika, and pepper.

3 Unroll dough; roll dough into an 8 x 12-inch rectangle. Lightly coat surface of dough with cooking spray, and sprinkle with 2 tablespoons cheese mixture. Fold dough in half to form a 6 x 8-inch rectangle. Re-roll dough into an 8 x 12-inch rectangle. Lightly coat surface of dough with cooking spray, and sprinkle dough with remaining cheese mixture. Using fingertips, press cheese mixture into dough.

4 Cut dough into 16 (8-inch-long) strips. Gently pick up both ends of each strip, and twist dough. Place twists ½ inch apart on a large baking sheet coated with cooking spray. Bake at 425° for 8 minutes or until lightly browned. Remove from pan; cool on wire racks.

Per Twist: Calories 68 Fat 1.1g (saturated 0.5g) Protein 2.7g
Carbohydrate 11.9g Fiber 0.6g Cholesterol 1mg Sodium 189mg
Exchange: 1 Starch

Quick Focaccia

Makes 8 servings

  1 (10-ounce) can refrigerated pizza crust dough
Cooking spray
  1 tablespoon olive oil
1⅓ cups sliced mushrooms
 ¼ cup (1 ounce) crumbled goat cheese
  1 teaspoon dried thyme
 ½ teaspoon freshly ground black pepper
 ¼ teaspoon salt

1 Preheat oven to 375°.

2 Unroll dough on a baking sheet coated with cooking spray; pat dough into an 8 x 10-inch rectangle. Brush dough with olive oil; sprinkle mushrooms and remaining 4 ingredients evenly over dough.

3 Bake at 375° for 17 minutes or until crust is lightly browned.

Per Serving: Calories 127 Fat 4.0g (saturated 1.0g) Protein 4.0g
Carbohydrate 18.0g Fiber 0.6g Cholesterol 3mg Sodium 330mg
Exchanges: 1 Starch, 1 Fat

"Focaccia is just a fancy name for Italian flatbread. My easy version has less olive oil and salt than a traditional focaccia. It gets its flavor punch from hearty mushrooms and a sprinkling of sharp goat cheese."

Parsley-Garlic Rolls

Makes 12 rolls

2 tablespoons chopped fresh parsley
2 tablespoons reduced-calorie margarine, melted
2 garlic cloves, pressed
1 (16-ounce) loaf frozen bread dough, thawed
Cooking spray

1 Combine first 3 ingredients.

2 Roll bread dough to a 12-inch square; spread parsley mixture over dough, leaving a ½-inch border on top and bottom edges. Roll dough tightly, jelly-roll fashion, from bottom edge. Press top edge of dough into roll to seal edge. Cut roll into 1-inch slices. Place slices, cut sides down, in muffin cups coated with cooking spray.

3 Cover and let rise in a warm place (85°), free from drafts, 1 hour or until doubled in size.

4 Preheat oven to 400°.

5 Bake at 400° for 9 to 11 minutes or until golden. Remove from pans, and serve warm.

Per Roll: Calories 101 Fat 2.6g (saturated 0.0g) Protein 3.0g
Carbohydrate 17.1g Fiber 0.6g Cholesterol 0mg Sodium 206mg
Exchanges: 1 Starch, ½ Fat

"There's no need to give up bread when you're trying to lose weight, especially when you can have these tasty low-fat rolls on the table in minutes."

Sticky Caramel-Pecan Rolls

Makes 8 rolls

¼ cup fat-free caramel sundae syrup
Cooking spray
1 (8-ounce) can refrigerated reduced-fat crescent dinner rolls
¼ cup packed brown sugar
2 tablespoons finely chopped pecans
½ teaspoon ground cinnamon

1 Preheat oven to 375°.

2 Spoon 1½ teaspoons syrup into each of 8 muffin cups coated with cooking spray; set aside.

3 Unroll dough; separate into 4 rectangles. Combine brown sugar, pecans, and cinnamon. Sprinkle sugar mixture evenly over each rectangle; press gently into dough. Beginning at 1 long edge, roll up jelly-roll fashion. Pinch ends of dough to seal.

4 Cut each roll into 6 slices. Place 3 slices, cut side down, in each muffin cup. Bake at 375° for 14 minutes. Run a knife around edges of cups; invert onto a platter.

Per Roll: Calories 172 Fat 5.8g (saturated 0.1g) Protein 2.2g
Carbohydrate 26.9g Fiber 0.2g Cholesterol 0mg Sodium 260mg
Exchanges: 1½ Starch, 1 Fat

"These decadently delightful sticky buns are made with reduced-fat crescent roll dough. So not only are they easy, they have half the fat of old-fashioned cinnamon rolls!"

Caraway-Swiss Casserole Bread

Makes 14 servings

1   (16-ounce) package hot roll mix
1⅓ cups warm water (100° to 110°)
1   cup (4 ounces) shredded reduced-fat Swiss cheese
¼   cup finely chopped onion
2   tablespoons margarine, melted
1   tablespoon caraway seeds
1   teaspoon cracked pepper
Cooking spray

1 Combine yeast packet from roll mix and warm water in a large bowl. Let stand 5 minutes. Add three-fourths of flour packet from roll mix, cheese, and next 4 ingredients. Beat with a mixer at low speed until blended. Stir in remaining flour from roll mix.

2 Scrape dough from sides of bowl. Cover and let rise in a warm place (85°), free from drafts, 30 minutes or until doubled in size. Stir dough 25 strokes.

3 Preheat oven to 350°.

4 Coat a 2-quart round casserole dish with cooking spray. Spoon dough into dish. Bake at 350° for 45 to 50 minutes or until loaf is browned and sounds hollow when tapped. Remove from dish immediately, and cool on a wire rack.

Per Serving: Calories 160 Fat 4.4g (saturated 1.1g) Protein 6.1g
Carbohydrate 23.1g Fiber 0.7g Cholesterol 5mg Sodium 246mg
Exchanges: 1½ Starch, 1 Fat

Romano-Oregano Bread

Makes 12 servings (serving size: 1 slice)

 3 cups bread flour (see tip below)
 1 cup water
 ¾ cup (3 ounces) grated fresh Romano cheese
 3 tablespoons sugar
 1 tablespoon dried oregano
1½ tablespoons olive oil
 1 teaspoon salt
 1 package dry yeast (about 2¼ teaspoons)

1 Follow manufacturer's instructions for placing all ingredients into bread pan; select bake cycle, and start bread machine.

Per Serving: Calories 181 Fat 4.2g (saturated 1.5g) Protein 6.6g
Carbohydrate 28.7g Fiber 0.2g Cholesterol 7mg Sodium 281mg
Exchanges: 2 Starch, 1 Fat

Tip: It's best to use bread flour in this bread machine recipe because bread flour has more gluten (protein) than all-purpose flour. It's the gluten that helps the bread dough have the elastic structure it needs to rise.

Chapter 18

Desserts

Café Mocha Granita

Makes 4 (1-cup) servings

2   cups water
2   tablespoons sugar
2   tablespoons instant espresso granules or instant coffee
1   cup low-fat (1%) milk
¼   cup chocolate syrup
¼   cup Kahlúa or other coffee-flavored liqueur

1 Combine water and sugar in a medium saucepan; bring to a boil. Cook, stirring until sugar dissolves. Remove from heat, and stir in espresso granules. Stir in milk, chocolate syrup, and liqueur. Pour mixture into a 9-inch square baking pan. Cover and freeze 4 hours or until firm.

2 Remove mixture from freezer; let stand 10 minutes. Scrape mixture with the tines of a fork until fluffy. Spoon into goblets or dessert dishes.

Per Serving: Calories 153 Fat 0.9g (saturated 0.4g) Protein 2.9g
Carbohydrate 25.6g Fiber 0.1g Cholesterol 2mg Sodium 44mg
Exchanges: 2 Starch

"Granita is the Italian word for an 'ice'—a frozen dessert treat. The great thing about granitas and ices is that they're practically fat-free and much better choices than ice cream."

Strawberry-Merlot Ice

Makes 12 (½-cup) servings

1 (16-ounce) package frozen whole strawberries
2 cups dry red wine (see tip below)
1 cup thawed white grape juice concentrate

1 Combine all ingredients in a blender; process until smooth, stopping once to scrape down sides.

2 Pour mixture into a 9 x 13-inch baking dish; cover and freeze at least 8 hours or until firm.

3 Remove mixture from freezer, and scrape mixture with the tines of a fork until fluffy. Serve immediately or spoon into a freezer-safe container; cover and freeze up to 1 month.

Per Serving: Calories 98 Fat 0.3g (saturated 0.0g) Protein 0.1g
Carbohydrate 18.2g Fiber 0.5g Cholesterol 0mg Sodium 10mg
Exchange: 1 Fruit

Tip: For a nonalcoholic version, use 2 cups of red grape juice instead of the red wine.

Cookies and Cream
Ice Cream

Makes 16 (½-cup) servings

1   quart fat-free half-and-half
1   (14-ounce) can fat-free sweetened condensed milk
¾   cup coarsely crushed reduced-fat chocolate sandwich cookies
      (about 9 cookies)

1 Combine half-and-half and milk; stir well. Stir in crushed cookies.

2 Pour mixture into a 9 x 13-inch baking pan and freeze about 2 hours or until firm.

3 Cut frozen mixture into chunks. Place in a food processor, and process until smooth. Serve immediately.

Per Serving: Calories 159 Fat 0.7g (saturated 0.0g) Protein 3.2g
Carbohydrate 31.1g Fiber 0.3g Cholesterol 2mg Sodium 116mg
Exchanges: 2½ Starch

*"This soft-serve ice cream is so sweet and creamy—
you'll never believe it's practically fat-free! The
secret is the fat-free half-and-half and sweetened
condensed milk!"*

Ice Cream Sandwich Dessert

Makes 12 servings (serving size: 1 square)

1½ teaspoons instant coffee granules
2 teaspoons sugar
2 tablespoons hot water
1 (8-ounce) container frozen reduced-calorie whipped topping, thawed
6 reduced-fat ice cream sandwiches
4 (0.7-ounce) 33%-less-fat chocolate toffee crisp bars (such as Hershey's Sweet Escapes), coarsely chopped

1 Dissolve coffee and sugar in hot water, stirring well; cool slightly. Fold coffee mixture into whipped topping. Set aside.

2 Arrange 6 ice cream sandwiches in bottom of an 11 x 7-inch baking dish. Spread whipped topping mixture evenly over ice cream sandwiches. Sprinkle with chopped toffee bars. Cover and freeze 2 hours or until firm.

3 Cut into squares, and serve immediately.

Per Serving: Calories 152 Fat 6.1g (saturated 4.7g) Protein 2.1g
Carbohydrate 20.6g Fiber 0.5g Cholesterol 10mg Sodium 34mg
Exchanges: 1½ Starch, 1 Fat

"I like to keep this in the freezer for the times when I get a hankerin' for a decadent frozen treat."

Mocha Ice Cream Squares

Makes 9 servings (serving size: 1 square)

⅓ cup chocolate wafer crumbs
2 teaspoons light butter, melted
Cooking spray
¼ cup boiling water
2 tablespoons instant coffee granules
6 cups vanilla low-fat ice cream, softened
½ cup fat-free chocolate sundae syrup

1 Combine chocolate wafer crumbs and butter in a small bowl; stir well. Sprinkle half of crumb mixture over bottom of an 8-inch square baking pan coated with cooking spray; set aside.

2 Combine boiling water and instant coffee granules, stirring until granules dissolve.

3 Combine 2 tablespoons coffee with softened ice cream in a large bowl. Spread half of ice cream mixture into pan. Combine chocolate syrup and remaining 2 tablespoons coffee in a separate small bowl. Drizzle half of chocolate mixture over ice cream mixture; freeze 35 minutes or until firm. (Return remaining ice cream to freezer, then soften again before repeating layers.) Repeat layers with remaining ice cream mixture and chocolate mixture; sprinkle evenly with remaining crumb mixture. Freeze 35 minutes or until firm. Cut into 9 squares.

Per Serving: Calories 197 Fat 3.9g (saturated 1.8g) Protein 4.9g
Carbohydrate 35g Fiber 1.6g Cholesterol 8mg Sodium 110mg
Exchanges: 2½ Starch

"If you're a coffee drinker and have some left over from breakfast—just use ¼ cup brewed coffee instead of making coffee with the instant and water."

Tangy Fruit Cup

Makes 4 (1-cup) servings

1   tablespoon sugar
1   tablespoon lemon juice
3   tablespoons frozen orange juice concentrate, thawed
1½ cups bite-size fresh cantaloupe chunks
1½ cups bite-size fresh honeydew melon chunks
1   cup halved fresh strawberries

1 Combine first 3 ingredients in a large bowl. Add remaining ingredients; stir gently.

Per Serving: Calories 86 Fat 0.4g (saturated 0.1g) Protein 1.3g
Carbohydrate 21.2g Fiber 1.8g Cholesterol 0mg Sodium 11mg
Exchanges: 1½ Fruit

"Sweet, mouth-watering fruits are a refreshing way to end your meal. There's no better way to get a fat-free, vitamin-packed dessert!"

Mixed Berry Dessert

Makes 4 (½-cup) servings

3 tablespoons orange juice
½ teaspoon grated fresh orange rind
1 tablespoon sugar
1 cup blueberries
1 cup blackberries or raspberries
½ cup frozen reduced-calorie whipped topping, thawed

1 Combine first 3 ingredients in a medium bowl, stirring until sugar dissolves. Add blueberries and blackberries, tossing gently.

2 Spoon mixture into individual dessert dishes. Top each serving with 2 tablespoons whipped topping.

Per Serving: Calories 77 Fat 1.3g (saturated 1.0g) Protein 0.6g
Carbohydrate 16.1g Fiber 2.4g Cholesterol 0mg Sodium 2mg
Exchange: 1 Fruit

"Blueberries, blackberries, and raspberries are so good for you, it would almost be a crime to pass up dessert! And what better way to get your recommended five daily fruit and vegetable servings!"

Vanilla-Poached Peaches

Makes 4 servings

1   cup water
⅓   cup sugar
3   large ripe peaches, peeled, pitted, and quartered
1   teaspoon vanilla extract
2   tablespoons strawberry preserves
4   teaspoons chopped pistachios

1 Combine water and sugar in a medium nonaluminum saucepan; bring to a boil. Reduce heat; add peaches, and simmer 7 minutes or until tender. Remove peaches with a slotted spoon; place in a shallow dish. Bring cooking liquid to a boil, and cook until reduced to ½ cup (about 7 minutes). Remove from heat. Stir in vanilla; pour syrup over peaches. Cool to room temperature.

2 Combine strawberry preserves and 4 teaspoons peach syrup; stir with a whisk. Place 3 peach quarters and 1½ tablespoons syrup in each of 4 dishes; top each serving with 2 teaspoons strawberry mixture and 1 teaspoon pistachios.

Per Serving: Calories 132 Fat 1.4g (saturated 0.2g) Protein 1.1g
Carbohydrate 31.0g Fiber 1.5g Cholesterol 0mg Sodium 4mg
Exchanges: 1 Starch, 1 Fruit

"Here's a fancy-schmancy dessert that has less than 150 calories and is very low in fat!"

Caramelized Orange Bananas

Makes 4 servings

2   large bananas
1½ teaspoons reduced-calorie margarine
¼   cup packed brown sugar
¼   cup orange juice
¼   teaspoon vanilla extract
2   cups vanilla low-fat ice cream

1 Peel bananas, and cut each in half crosswise. Cut banana halves in half lengthwise; set aside.

2 Add margarine to a medium skillet, and place over medium heat until margarine melts. Stir in brown sugar, and cook, stirring constantly, until sugar dissolves and mixture begins to bubble. Stir in orange juice, and add bananas to pan. Increase heat to medium-high, and cook 2 minutes, stirring gently. Turn bananas, and sprinkle with vanilla extract.

3 Spoon ½ cup ice cream into each of 4 dessert bowls; spoon warm bananas evenly over ice cream. Serve immediately.

Per Serving: Calories 238 Fat 3.1g (saturated 1.3g) Protein 3.8g
Carbohydrate 50.0g Fiber 2.7g Cholesterol 5mg Sodium 68mg
Exchanges: 2 Starch, 1 Fruit

"You'll save 15 grams of fat per ½-cup serving just by switching from premium high-fat ice cream to low-fat."

Angel Food Cake with Vanilla Custard Sauce

Makes 8 servings (serving size: 1 slice cake and ¼ cup sauce)

1½   cups reduced-fat (2%) milk
¼   cup sugar
4   large egg yolks
1   tablespoon vanilla extract
8   (2-ounce) slices angel food cake

1 Place milk in a 1-quart glass measure. Microwave at HIGH 3 minutes.

2 Combine sugar and egg yolks in a bowl; stir with a whisk. Gradually add hot milk to egg mixture, stirring constantly with a whisk. Return milk mixture to glass measure. Microwave at HIGH 2½ minutes, stirring after 1½ minutes. Stir in vanilla. Cover; cool to room temperature. Serve over angel food cake slices.

Per Serving: Calories 228 Fat 3.7g (saturated 1.4g) Protein 6.4g
Carbohydrate 42.1g Fiber 0.0g Cholesterol 113mg Sodium 315mg
Exchanges: 2½ Starch, ½ Fat

"Make it easy and start with an angel food cake from the grocery store. Did you know that angel food cake is fat-free?"

Chocolate Cream Cupcakes

Makes 12 cupcakes

1   (20.5-ounce) package low-fat fudge brownie mix
⅔   cup water
Cooking spray
½   (8-ounce) package ⅓-less-fat cream cheese
3   tablespoons sugar
1   teaspoon egg substitute
2   tablespoons semisweet chocolate chips, melted

1 Preheat oven to 350°.

2 Combine brownie mix and water; stir until blended. Spoon into 12 muffin cups lined with paper liners coated with cooking spray.

3 Combine cream cheese and sugar; beat with a mixer at medium speed until light and fluffy. Add egg substitute, beating well. Stir in melted chocolate. Spoon 2 heaping teaspoons cheese mixture into center of each cupcake. Bake at 350° for 25 minutes or until centers are set. Remove from pan, and cool on a wire rack.

Per Cupcake: Calories 256 Fat 6.7g (saturated 2.5g) Protein 4.1g
Carbohydrate 44.9g Fiber 1.5g Cholesterol 7mg Sodium 203mg
Exchanges: 3 Starch, 1 Fat

"Enjoy these chocolaty treats the next time you celebrate a birthday. The low-fat brownie mix and the reduced-fat cream cheese keep the calories down."

Caramel Swirl Icebox Cake

Makes 10 servings (serving size: 1 slice)

21 cakelike ladyfingers, split and divided (see tip below)
¾ cup frozen reduced-calorie whipped topping, thawed
3½ cups vanilla low-fat frozen yogurt, softened
½ cup fat-free caramel sundae syrup, divided
1 (10-ounce) package frozen raspberries in light syrup, thawed

1 Line a 4½ x 8½-inch loaf pan with plastic wrap, smoothing plastic wrap in corners and on sides of pan. Arrange one-third of ladyfinger halves, cut sides facing in, on bottom and around sides of pan.

2 Fold whipped topping into yogurt. Spoon half of yogurt mixture into pan. Spoon ¼ cup caramel syrup over yogurt mixture. Swirl caramel syrup with a knife to create a marbled effect. Arrange half of remaining ladyfinger halves on top of caramel. Repeat layers with remaining yogurt mixture, remaining ¼ cup caramel syrup, and remaining ladyfinger halves. Cover and freeze at least 8 hours.

3 Invert dessert onto a serving plate, carefully peeling away plastic wrap. Cut into 10 slices, and top evenly with raspberries. Cover and freeze any remaining cake for up to 1 month.

Per Serving: Calories 193 Fat 2.6g (saturated 1.5g) Protein 3.8g
Carbohydrate 39.0g Fiber 2.2g Cholesterol 32mg Sodium 176mg
Exchanges: 1½ Starch, 1 Fruit, ½ Fat

Tip: Ladyfingers are light, delicate spongecakes that are very low in fat. Look for them in the bakery section or frozen dessert case of the grocery store.

Vanilla Pound Cake

Makes 16 (½-inch) slices

Butter-flavored cooking spray
- 1 **tablespoon dry breadcrumbs**
- 6 **tablespoons stick margarine, softened**
- 1½ **cups sugar**
- ¾ **cup egg substitute**
- 1 **teaspoon vanilla extract**
- ½ **teaspoon almond extract**
- ½ **teaspoon baking soda**
- ¾ **cup reduced-fat sour cream**
- 2 **cups sifted cake flour or all-purpose flour**
- ¼ **teaspoon salt**

1 Preheat oven to 325°. Coat a 4½ x 8½-inch loaf pan with cooking spray. Dust pan with breadcrumbs. Set aside.

2 Beat margarine with a mixer at medium speed until creamy; gradually add sugar, beating well. Add egg substitute and extracts; beat well.

3 Stir baking soda into sour cream. Combine flour and salt; add to margarine mixture alternately with sour cream mixture, beginning and ending with flour mixture. Mix at low speed just until blended after each addition.

4 Pour batter into prepared pan. Bake at 325° for 1 hour and 10 minutes or until a wooden toothpick inserted in center comes out clean. Cool in pan 10 minutes. Remove cake from pan, and cool completely on a wire rack.

Per Slice: Calories 183 Fat 5.7g (saturated 1.7g) Protein 2.7g
Carbohydrate 30.4g Fiber 0.4g Cholesterol 4mg Sodium 151mg
Exchanges: 2 Starch, 1 Fat

Mocha Pudding Cake

Makes 9 servings (serving size: ⅑ of cake and ¼ cup ice cream)

    1   cup all-purpose flour
    2   teaspoons baking powder
    ¼   teaspoon salt
    1   cup sugar, divided
    ¼   cup plus 2 tablespoons unsweetened cocoa, divided
  1½   tablespoons instant coffee granules
    ½   cup low-fat (1%) milk
    3   tablespoons vegetable oil
    1   teaspoon vanilla extract
Cooking spray
    1   cup boiling water
  2¼   cups vanilla low-fat ice cream

1 Preheat oven to 350°.

2 Combine flour, baking powder, salt, ⅔ cup sugar, ¼ cup cocoa, and the coffee granules in a large bowl. Combine milk, oil, and vanilla; add to dry ingredients, stirring well. Spoon batter into an 8-inch square baking pan coated with cooking spray.

3 Combine remaining ⅓ cup sugar and 2 tablespoons cocoa. Sprinkle over batter. Pour boiling water over batter. (Do not stir.) Bake at 350° for 30 minutes or until cake springs back when lightly touched in center. Serve warm, topped with ice cream.

Per Serving: Calories 247 Fat 6.8g (saturated 2.1g) Protein 4.2g
Carbohydrate 43.0g Fiber 0.4g Cholesterol 5mg Sodium 102mg
Exchanges: 2½ Starch, 1 Fat

Coconut-Date Balls

Makes 24 balls

1½ cups chopped dates
⅓ cup margarine
2 tablespoons egg substitute
1 tablespoon fat-free milk
1 teaspoon vanilla extract
¼ teaspoon salt
2 cups crisp rice cereal
⅓ cup flaked sweetened coconut

1 Combine dates and margarine in a medium saucepan. Cook over medium heat 5 minutes or until margarine melts, stirring occasionally.

2 Combine egg substitute and next 3 ingredients. Add to date mixture, and cook over medium heat 2 minutes. Remove from heat, and stir in cereal. Using 1 level tablespoonful, shape cereal mixture into balls. Lightly roll in coconut. Cover and chill at least 30 minutes.

Per Ball: Calories 69 Fat 3.1g (saturated 0.8g) Protein 0.6g
Carbohydrate 10.7g Fiber 0.9g Cholesterol 0mg Sodium 83mg
Exchanges: ½ Starch, ½ Fat

"These are great little treats to put out on a dessert table during the holidays."

Orange Oatmeal Cookies

Makes 20 cookies

2½   tablespoons stick margarine (see note below)
¼   cup sugar
2½   tablespoons light brown sugar
1   large egg white
2   teaspoons grated orange rind
⅓   cup all-purpose flour
½   cup regular oats
Cooking spray

1 Preheat oven to 350°.

2 Beat first 5 ingredients with a mixer until light and creamy. Lightly spoon flour into a dry measuring cup; level with a knife. Add flour and oats to sugar mixture and beat until well blended.

3 Drop dough by rounded teaspoonfuls 1½ inches apart onto baking sheets coated with cooking spray. Bake at 350° for 10 to 12 minutes or until edges are golden brown. Remove from oven, and let stand 3 minutes. Remove cookies from baking sheets, and cool on a wire rack.

Per Cookie: Calories 43 Fat 1.6g (saturated 0.3g) Protein 0.7g
Carbohydrate 6.6g Fiber 0.3g Cholesterol 0mg Sodium 20mg
Exchange: ½ Starch

"Be sure to use regular margarine when you make these cookies. Low-calorie margarine doesn't work too well in most cookie recipes because it contains a good bit of water."

Thumbprint Cookies

Makes 36 cookies

1 (17.5-ounce) package chocolate chip cookie mix
1 cup regular oats
⅓ cup water
1 teaspoon vanilla extract
1 egg white
Cooking spray
3 tablespoons strawberry jam

1 Preheat oven to 375°.

2 Combine first 5 ingredients in a bowl. Drop dough by 2 level teaspoonfuls 1 inch apart onto baking sheets coated with cooking spray.

3 Press center of each cookie with thumb, making an indentation; fill with ¼ teaspoon jam. Bake at 375° for 10 minutes or until golden. Cool on wire racks. Store in an airtight container.

Per Cookie: Calories 82 Fat 3.6g (saturated 1.2g) Protein 1.1g
Carbohydrate 11.7g Fiber 0.4g Cholesterol 0mg Sodium 42mg
Exchanges: 1 Starch, ½ Fat

"Don't worry about eating too many of these cookies—your kids will probably snatch 'em up before you get the chance to overindulge."

Ooey Gooey Peanut Butter-Chocolate Brownies

Makes 32 brownies

¾ cup fat-free sweetened condensed milk, divided
¼ cup butter or margarine, melted and cooled
¼ cup fat-free milk
1 (18.25-ounce) package devil's food cake mix
1 large egg, lightly beaten
Cooking spray
1 (7-ounce) jar marshmallow creme (about 1¾ cups)
½ cup peanut butter chips

1 Preheat oven to 350°.

2 Combine ¼ cup condensed milk, the butter, and next 3 ingredients in a bowl. (Batter will be very stiff.) Coat bottom of a 9 x 13-inch baking pan with cooking spray. Using a metal spreader coated with cooking spray, spread two-thirds of batter into pan; pat evenly. (Layer will be thin.)

3 Bake at 350° for 10 minutes. Combine ½ cup condensed milk and the marshmallow creme in a bowl; stir in peanut butter chips. Carefully spread marshmallow mixture evenly over brownie layer. Carefully drop remaining batter by spoonfuls over marshmallow mixture. Bake at 350° for 25 minutes. Cool completely in pan on a wire rack.

Per Brownie: Calories 138 Fat 4.4g (saturated 1.3g) Protein 2.4g
Carbohydrate 22.3g Fiber 0.6g Cholesterol 17mg Sodium 177mg
Exchanges: 1½ Starch, 1 Fat

Crunchy Oat-Apricot Bars

Makes 36 bars

  2 cups regular oats
1¾ cups all-purpose flour
  1 cup packed brown sugar
⅔ cup reduced-calorie stick margarine
1½ teaspoons vanilla extract
Cooking spray
1½ cups apricot preserves

1 Preheat oven to 350°.

2 Combine first 5 ingredients in a large bowl. Cut margarine into flour mixture with a pastry blender or 2 knives until mixture is crumbly.

3 Press half of oat mixture into bottom of a 9 x 13-inch baking pan coated with cooking spray. Spread apricot preserves over oat mixture. Sprinkle remaining oat mixture over apricot preserves, and gently press.

4 Bake at 350° for 35 minutes or until bubbly and golden brown. Cool completely in pan on a wire rack.

Per Bar: Calories 112 Fat 2.5g (saturated 0.5g) Protein 1.3g
Carbohydrate 21.9g Fiber 0.6g Cholesterol 0mg Sodium 42mg
Exchanges: 1 Starch, ½ Fruit

Butterscotch Bars

Makes 18 bars

3 tablespoons margarine
½ cup packed brown sugar
2 cups miniature marshmallows
4 cups crisp rice cereal
2 cups whole wheat flake cereal
Cooking spray

1 Melt margarine in a large saucepan over medium heat. Add sugar; stir well. Add marshmallows; cook until marshmallows melt, stirring constantly. Remove from heat; stir in cereals.

2 Press cereal mixture in bottom of a 9 x 13-inch baking pan coated with cooking spray. Cool 1 hour. Cut into bars.

Per Bar: Calories 96 Fat 2.0g (saturated 0.4g) Protein 1.0g
Carbohydrate 19.2g Fiber 0.5g Cholesterol 0mg Sodium 102mg
Exchange: 1 Starch

"The whole wheat cereal flakes add a nutty crunch to these bars, but no fat!"

French Toast-Peach Cobbler

Makes 12 servings

⅓ cup all-purpose flour
12 cups sliced fresh or frozen peaches (about 12 peaches)
1 cup plus 1 tablespoon sugar, divided
Cooking spray
1 teaspoon grated orange rind
⅓ cup fresh orange juice
3 tablespoons margarine, melted
¼ teaspoon ground cinnamon
3 large egg whites
8 (1.5-ounce) slices hearty white bread

1 Combine flour, peaches, and ¾ cup sugar in a 9 x 13-inch baking dish coated with cooking spray; let stand 30 minutes, stirring occasionally.

2 Preheat oven to 350°.

3 Combine ¼ cup sugar, orange rind, and next 4 ingredients in a shallow bowl, stirring with a whisk. Trim crusts from bread, and cut each slice in half diagonally. Dip bread in orange juice mixture; arrange on top of peach mixture. Sprinkle remaining 1 tablespoon sugar over bread. Bake at 350° for 45 minutes or until golden.

Per Serving: Calories 254 Fat 3.8g (saturated 0.5g) Protein 4.7g
Carbohydrate 54.3g Fiber 5.0g Cholesterol 0mg Sodium 189mg
Exchanges: 2½ Starch, 1 Fruit

Double Cherry Crisp

Makes 8 (¹/₂-cup) servings

2 (21-ounce) cans light cherry pie filling
¾ cup dried cherries, coarsely chopped
1 teaspoon grated lemon rind
Cooking spray
2 cups coarsely crumbled angel food cake
2 tablespoons brown sugar
2 tablespoons chopped almonds

1 Preheat oven to 375°.

2 Combine cherry pie filling, dried cherries, and lemon rind in an 8-inch square baking dish coated with cooking spray.

3 Combine cake, brown sugar, and almonds in a small bowl; sprinkle evenly over cherry mixture. Bake at 375° for 25 to 30 minutes or until topping is golden and filling is bubbly. Serve warm.

Per Serving: Calories 152 Fat 1.0g (saturated 0.1g) Protein 1.3g
Carbohydrate 33.4g Fiber 2.7g Cholesterol 0mg Sodium 68mg
Exchanges: 2 Fruit

"Did you know that eating small amounts of almonds (and other nuts) may reduce your chance of developing heart disease?"

Apple-Cranberry Crisp

Makes 8 (½-cup) servings

⅓ cup all-purpose flour
¼ cup plus 1 tablespoon granulated sugar, divided
¼ cup packed brown sugar
¼ cup butter or margarine, cut into small pieces
7 cups sliced, peeled Golden Delicious apple (about 6 large apples)
¼ cup sweetened dried cranberries
½ teaspoon ground ginger
Cooking spray

1 Preheat oven to 400°.

2 Combine flour, ¼ cup granulated sugar, and brown sugar in a small bowl; cut in butter with a pastry blender until mixture is crumbly.

3 Combine apple, cranberries, ginger, and remaining 1 table-spoon granulated sugar in a large bowl; stir gently. Spoon fruit mixture into an 8-inch square baking pan coated with cooking spray, and sprinkle with crumb mixture. Bake at 400° for 35 minutes or until golden. Serve warm.

Per Serving: Calories 189 Fat 6.2g (saturated 3.7g) Protein 0.7g
Carbohydrate 34.5g Fiber 2.2g Cholesterol 16mg Sodium 62mg
Exchanges: 1½ Starch, 1 Fruit, 1 Fat

"Any time you make a dessert with fruit you get the benefit of extra fiber plus disease-fighting vitamins and minerals."

Caramel Apple Dumplings

Makes 4 servings (serving size: 1 dumpling)

¼ cup fat-free milk
1 teaspoon ground cinnamon
8 small soft caramel candies, unwrapped
4 medium Rome apples
4 sheets fresh or frozen phyllo dough, thawed
Butter-flavored cooking spray

1 Preheat oven to 400°.

2 Combine first 3 ingredients in a medium saucepan. Place over low heat, and cook until smooth, stirring constantly. Remove from heat; set aside.

3 Core apples, cutting to, but not through, the bottom of each apple. Spoon caramel mixture evenly into centers of apples. Place apples in a 7 x 11-inch baking dish; cover and bake at 400° for 35 minutes or just until apples are tender. Remove apples from dish, and cool slightly.

4 Place 1 sheet of phyllo on a damp towel. (Keep remaining phyllo covered.) Coat phyllo sheet with cooking spray. Fold phyllo in half crosswise. Place 1 apple on phyllo rectangle. Coat edges of phyllo with cooking spray; bring corners to center, pinching phyllo to seal. Coat dumpling with cooking spray. Repeat with remaining apples and phyllo sheets.

5 Place dumplings on a baking sheet coated with cooking spray. Bake at 400° for 5 to 7 minutes or until golden.

Per Serving: Calories 236 Fat 3.4g (saturated 1.7g) Protein 3.2g
Carbohydrate 51.3g Fiber 5.2g Cholesterol 2mg Sodium 149mg
Exchanges: 2 Starch, 1½ Fruit

Banana Cream Pie

Makes 8 servings

1 (3.4-ounce) package banana cream-flavored instant pudding mix
1¼ cups low-fat (1%) milk
1¾ cups frozen reduced-calorie whipped topping, thawed and divided
1¼ cups peeled, sliced banana
1 tablespoon lemon juice
1 (6-ounce) prepared chocolate graham cracker crust (see tip below)

1 Combine pudding mix and milk in a medium bowl, stirring with a wire whisk until smooth. Gently fold 1 cup whipped topping into pudding mixture.

2 Toss banana slices with lemon juice and arrange over crust. Spoon pudding mixture over banana slices. Cover and chill 1½ hours or until set. Pipe or spoon remaining ¾ cup whipped topping around edge of pie just before serving.

Per Serving: Calories 201 Fat 7.5g (saturated 3.1g) Protein 2.2g
Carbohydrate 30.5g Fiber 0.3g Cholesterol 2mg Sodium 321mg
Exchanges: 2 Starch, 1 Fat

Tip: You can also make this pie with a regular graham cracker crust—the fat and calories in these two crusts are about the same.

Frozen Lemonade Pie

Makes 16 servings (serving size: ⅛ of pie)

1 (14-ounce) can fat-free sweetened condensed milk
1 (6-ounce) can frozen lemonade concentrate, thawed
1 (8-ounce) container frozen reduced-calorie whipped topping,
    thawed
2 (6-ounce) prepared graham cracker crusts

1 Combine condensed milk and lemonade concentrate in a bowl, stirring well. Gently fold in whipped topping. Spoon evenly into crusts.

2 Cover and freeze at least 8 hours.

Per Serving: Calories 229 Fat 7.1g (saturated 2.9g) Protein 3.1g
Carbohydrate 37.4g Fiber 0.4g Cholesterol 2mg Sodium 148mg
Exchanges: 2 Starch, ½ Fruit, 1 Fat

Tip: This recipe makes two pies that can be frozen up to a week in airtight containers.

Peaches and Cream Mousse

Makes 4 servings

1½ cups frozen unsweetened sliced peaches, thawed
 1 tablepoon unflavored gelatin
⅔ cup apricot nectar
 3 tablespoons sugar
 3 tablespoons peach schnapps (see tip below)
¼ teaspoon almond extract
 2 cups frozen reduced-calorie whipped topping, thawed and divided

1 Place peaches in a food processor or blender; process until smooth.

2 Sprinkle gelatin over apricot nectar in a small saucepan; let stand 1 minute. Stir in pureed peaches and sugar. Cook over medium heat, stirring until gelatin dissolves. Remove from heat; stir in schnapps and almond extract. Pour into a bowl; chill 1 hour or until consistency of unbeaten egg white.

3 Gently fold in 1½ cups whipped topping. Spoon mixture evenly into 4 (8-ounce) parfait glasses. Cover and chill until set. Top each parfait with 2 tablespoons whipped topping.

Per Serving: Calories 214 Fat 4.1g (saturated 4.0g) Protein 2.1g
Carbohydrate 30.5g Fiber 1.5g Cholesterol 0mg Sodium 20mg
Exchanges: 1 Starch, 1 Fruit

Tip: If you don't want to use peach schnapps, use 1½ tablespoons additional apricot nectar.

Raspberry Cheesecake Parfaits

Makes 4 servings

½ cup part-skim ricotta cheese
½ cup light cream cheese
 2 tablespoons sugar
¼ cup all-fruit raspberry spread, melted
 2 cups fresh raspberries
½ cup vanilla wafer crumbs (about 7 wafers)
¼ cup frozen reduced-calorie whipped topping, thawed

1 Combine first 3 ingredients in a food processor; process until smooth, scraping sides of processor bowl once.

2 Combine raspberry spread and raspberries, and stir gently. Spoon ¼ cup raspberry mixture into each of 4 (8-ounce) parfait glasses. Top each with 2 tablespoons cheese mixture, 2 tablespoons cookie crumbs, 2 tablespoons cheese mixture, ¼ cup raspberry mixture, and 1 tablespoon whipped topping. Chill parfaits for at least 2 hours before serving.

Per Serving: Calories 261 Fat 10.0g (saturated 6.4g) Protein 7.7g
Carbohydrate 35.3g Fiber 4.4g Cholesterol 25mg Sodium 278mg
Exchanges: 1½ Starch, 1 Fruit, 2 Fat

"The nice thing about an individually-portioned dessert is that it helps you control your serving size."

Angelic Tiramisù

Makes 12 servings (serving size: about ¾ cup)

  1   cup cold water
  1   (14-ounce) can fat-free sweetened condensed milk
  1   (3.4-ounce) package vanilla instant pudding mix
  1   (8-ounce) block ⅓-less-fat cream cheese, softened
  1   (8-ounce) container frozen reduced-calorie whipped topping,
        thawed
 24   cakelike ladyfingers (two 3-ounce packages)
  1   cup strong brewed coffee
  1   tablespoon unsweetened cocoa

1 Combine first 3 ingredients in a large bowl; stir well with a whisk. Cover and chill 30 minutes.

2 Add cream cheese; beat at medium speed of a mixer until blended. Fold in whipped topping.

3 Split ladyfingers in half lengthwise. Arrange 16 halves in a single layer in an 8-inch square baking dish. Drizzle with ⅓ cup coffee. Spread one-third of pudding mixture evenly over ladyfingers. Repeat procedure twice with remaining ladyfingers, coffee, and pudding mixture. Cover and chill 8 hours. Sprinkle with cocoa.

Per Serving: Calories 260 Fat 7.4g (saturated 5.3g) Protein 5.7g
Carbohydrate 41.7g Fiber 0.2g Cholesterol 31mg Sodium 261mg
Exchanges: 3 Starch, 1 Fat

"Instead of using the traditional super-rich mascarpone cheese in my tiramisù, I use a mixture of reduced-fat cream cheese, fat-free condensed milk, pudding mix, and whipped topping. It's almost too good to be true!"

Stirred Vanilla Custard

Makes 6 (½-cup) servings

    3 cups fat-free milk
    2 large eggs
    ½ cup sugar
1½ tablespoons all-purpose flour
    ⅛ teaspoon salt
    1 teaspoon vanilla extract

1 Heat milk in a heavy saucepan over low heat until very hot, stirring occasionally. (Do not boil.)

2 Beat eggs with a mixer at medium speed until foamy. Add sugar, flour, and salt, beating until thick. Gradually stir about 1 cup hot milk into egg mixture; add to remaining hot milk, stirring constantly.

3 Cook, stirring constantly, over medium heat 7 minutes or until thickened. Remove from heat, and stir in vanilla. Spoon ½ cup custard into individual dessert bowls. Serve custard warm or chilled.

Per Serving: Calories 141 Fat 2.0g (saturated 0.7g) Protein 6.4g
Carbohydrate 24.2g Fiber 0.1g Cholesterol 76mg Sodium 132mg
Exchanges: 1½ Starch, ½ Fat

"This creamy custard reminds me of eggnog. For a super-special treat (and to add more vitamins and fiber), I spoon it over fresh melon or mixed berries."

Microwave Chocolate Pudding

Makes 3 (½-cup) servings

6 tablespoons sugar
¼ cup unsweetened cocoa
2 tablespoons cornstarch
1½ cups reduced-fat (2%) milk
½ teaspoon vanilla extract

1 Combine sugar, cocoa, and cornstarch in a 1-quart glass measure; gradually add milk, stirring mixture with a whisk until well blended. Microwave milk mixture at HIGH 3 minutes, stirring after 1½ minutes.

2 Microwave milk mixture at MEDIUM-HIGH (70% power) 1½ minutes or until thick. Add vanilla; stir well with a whisk. Serve warm or cover and chill thoroughly.

Per Serving: Calories 212 Fat 3.3g (saturated 2.1g) Protein 6.2g
Carbohydrate 39.3g Fiber 0.0g Cholesterol 10mg Sodium 65mg
Exchanges: 2 Starch, ½ Skim Milk

"When I need a quick chocolate fix, I whip up this low-fat pudding in the microwave. It satisfies my craving, but doesn't load me up with fat grams."

Peanut Butter-Banana Pudding

Makes 16 (³⁄₄-cup) servings

 1 (3.4-ounce) package French vanilla instant pudding mix
 2 cups fat-free milk
⅓ cup reduced-fat creamy peanut butter
 1 (8-ounce) carton reduced-fat sour cream
42 vanilla wafers, divided
 6 small bananas, divided
 1 (8-ounce) carton frozen reduced-calorie whipped topping, thawed

1 Prepare pudding mix according to package directions, using a whisk and 2 cups fat-free milk. (Do not use a mixer.) Add peanut butter and sour cream, stirring well with a whisk.

2 Line bottom of a 2½-quart casserole with 14 vanilla wafers. Peel and slice 4 bananas. Top wafers with one-third each of pudding mixture, banana slices, and whipped topping. Repeat layers twice using remaining wafers, pudding mixture, banana slices, and whipped topping. Cover and chill at least 2 hours. To garnish, peel and slice remaining 2 bananas; arrange slices around outer edges of dish.

Per Serving: Calories 205 Fat 7.2g (saturated 3.6g) Protein 4.1g
Carbohydrate 31.8g Fiber 1.6g Cholesterol 9mg Sodium 176mg
Exchanges: 1 Starch, 1 Fruit, 1½ Fat

"This homestyle pudding gives you something from every food group: starch, dairy, fruit, and meat/protein."

Quick Fudge Pots

Makes 8 servings (serving size: about ⅓ cup)

1   (3.4-ounce) package chocolate-flavored pudding mix
2   cups fat-free milk
½   cup semisweet mini chocolate chips

1 Combine pudding mix and milk in a medium saucepan over medium heat. Cook, stirring constantly, until mixture comes to a boil; remove from heat.

2 Add mini chocolate chips, stirring until chocolate melts. Spoon mixture evenly into 8 custard cups. Serve warm or chilled.

Per Serving: Calories 118 Fat 3.5g (saturated 2.0g) Protein 3.2g
Carbohydrate 20.6g Fiber 0.9g Cholesterol 1mg Sodium 209mg
Exchanges: 1½ Starch

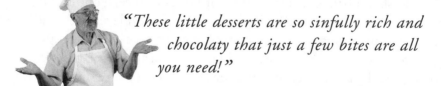

"These little desserts are so sinfully rich and chocolaty that just a few bites are all you need!"

Easy Fruited Rice Pudding

Makes 4 (⅔-cup) servings

1   **(5.5-ounce) package rice pudding mix with cinnamon and raisins**
2   **cups low-fat (1%) milk**
1   **cup diced peeled apple**

1 Prepare rice pudding according to package directions, using low-fat milk, omitting butter or margarine, and adding apple after 5 minutes of cooking. Serve warm or chilled.

Per Serving: Calories 216 Fat 1.9g (saturated 0.8g) Protein 5.9g
Carbohydrate 44.4g Fiber 1.9g Cholesterol 5mg Sodium 192mg
Exchanges: 2 Starch, 1 Fruit

"I'm always looking for ways to eat a little more fruit, so stirring apple into a pudding mix seemed like a fruitful idea!"

Easy Peanut Butter Cookies

Makes 24 cookies

1 **large egg, lightly beaten**
¾ **cup reduced-fat crunchy peanut butter (see tip below)**
¾ **cup sugar**
2 **tablespoons all-purpose flour**

1 Preheat oven to 350°.

2 Combine all ingredients; shape into ¾-inch balls. Place on an ungreased baking sheet. Bake at 350° for 10 minutes. Remove immediately to a wire rack to cool.

Per Cookie: Calories 70 Fat 2.9g (saturated 0.6g) Protein 2.5g
Carbohydrate 9.4g Fiber 0.5g Cholesterol 9mg Sodium 47mg
Exchanges: ½ Starch, ½ Fat

Tip: Reduced-fat peanut butter has about 4 grams less fat per serving than regular peanut butter. And there's no difference in fat content between creamy and crunchy.

Chapter 19

Fish & Shellfish

Cajun Catfish

Makes 4 servings

 4 teaspoons Cajun seasoning
 4 (6-ounce) farm-raised catfish fillets (1 to 1½ inch thick)
Cooking spray
 4 teaspoons fresh lemon juice
Grilled lemon slices (optional) (see note below)

1 Preheat the grill.

2 Sprinkle Cajun seasoning on both sides of fish; lightly coat fish with cooking spray. Arrange fish in a wire grilling basket coated with cooking spray. Place basket on grill rack; cover and grill 5 minutes. Turn grill basket over; drizzle lemon juice over fish. Cover and grill 5 minutes or until fish flakes easily when tested with a fork. Serve with grilled lemon slices, if desired.

Per Serving: Calories 169 Fat 4.9g (saturated 1.2g) Protein 28.1g
Carbohydrate 1.6g Fiber 0.3g Cholesterol 99mg Sodium 547mg
Exchanges: 4 Very Lean Meat

"While the fish is cooking, grill some lemon slices for 1 to 2 minutes on each side or until they're lightly browned. The lemon adds zing to the fish, but no calories!"

Tuscan Cod

Makes 2 servings (serving size: 1 fillet and ½ cup sauce)

1 teaspoon olive oil
½ cup thinly sliced onion, separated into rings
½ cup diced red bell pepper
1 garlic clove, minced
1 cup chopped tomato
1 tablespoon capers
¼ teaspoon ground cumin
⅛ teaspoon crushed red pepper
2 (6-ounce) cod fillets

1 Heat oil in a nonstick skillet over medium-high heat. Add onion, bell pepper, and garlic; sauté 2 minutes. Add tomato and next 3 ingredients; cook over medium heat 5 minutes, stirring occasionally.

2 Add fish to pan, spooning sauce over fish. Cover and cook 10 minutes or until fish flakes easily when tested with a fork.

Per Serving: Calories 214 Fat 4.1g (saturated 0.6g) Protein 32.4g
Carbohydrate 11.8g Fiber 2.7g Cholesterol 73mg Sodium 439mg
Exchanges: 2 Vegetable, 4 Very Lean Meat

"When you cook fish with high-flavor vegetables like onions, tomatoes, and peppers, you don't need much added fat. And who needs salt when you've got garlic, cumin, and ground red pepper?"

Fish in a Wrap

Makes 4 servings

2 tablespoons dried onion flakes
2 garlic cloves, crushed
1 (10-ounce) package frozen chopped spinach, thawed, drained, and squeezed dry
Cooking spray
4 (6-ounce) flounder fillets
2 teaspoons lemon juice
1 teaspoon Creole seasoning (see tip below)
¾ cup Italian-seasoned breadcrumbs
2 tablespoons light butter, melted

1 Preheat oven to 350°.

2 Stir onion flakes and garlic into chopped spinach.

3 Coat dull side of 4 (12-inch) squares of heavy-duty aluminum foil with cooking spray. Place a fillet in the center of each square; brush fish evenly with lemon juice, and sprinkle with Creole seasoning. Spoon spinach mixture evenly over fish.

4 Combine breadcrumbs and butter; spoon evenly over spinach mixture, pressing gently. Fold foil to seal. Bake at 350° for 30 minutes or until fish flakes easily when tested with a fork.

Per Serving: Calories 304 Fat 6.1g (saturated 2.7g) Protein 41.3g
Carbohydrate 20.9g Fiber 3.3g Cholesterol 100mg Sodium 971mg
Exchanges: 1 Starch, 1 Vegetable, 5 Very Lean Meat

Tip: If you need to cut down on sodium, use salt-free Creole seasoning, or use ¼ teaspoon black pepper, ¼ teaspoon red pepper and ½ teaspoon garlic powder instead of the seasoning blend.

Grilled Herbed Grouper

Makes 4 servings

1   (1½-pound) grouper fillet
2   teaspoons olive oil
½   teaspoon salt
¼   teaspoon pepper
1   cup dry breadcrumbs
⅓   cup minced fresh parsley or 3 tablespoons dried parsley flakes
1   tablespoon minced fresh or 1 teaspoon dried basil
1   tablespoon minced fresh or 1 teaspoon dried thyme
Cooking spray
Lemon slices (optional)

1 Preheat the grill.

2 Brush fish with oil; sprinkle with salt and pepper.

3 Stir together breadcrumbs and next 3 ingredients; press onto all sides of fish. Arrange fish in a wire grilling basket coated with cooking spray. Place basket on grill rack; cover and grill 6 to 7 minutes on each side or until fish flakes easily when tested with a fork. Garnish with lemon slices, if desired.

Per Serving: Calories 286 Fat 5.5g (saturated 1.0g) Protein 36.6g
Carbohydrate 20.2g Fiber 0.9g Cholesterol 63mg Sodium 619mg
Exchanges: 1½ Starch, 5 Very Lean Meat

"Fall in love with fresh herbs like I have! Just a little sprinkling of herbs adds fabulous flavor to food, but absolutely NO fat!"

Guadalajara Grouper

Makes 4 servings

1   tablespoon olive oil
3   garlic cloves, minced
1   onion, chopped
2   celery stalks, chopped
1   (8-ounce) package sliced mushrooms
2   (14½-ounce) cans Mexican-style stewed tomatoes, undrained
     (see tip below)
1   teaspoon Creole seasoning
2   teaspoons hot sauce
1½ pounds grouper or other firm white fish fillets, cut into cubes
2   cups hot cooked rice

1 Heat oil in a large nonstick skillet over medium-high heat. Add garlic and onion; sauté until tender.

2 Add celery and mushrooms, and sauté 1 minute. Add stewed tomatoes, Creole seasoning, and hot sauce; cook, stirring occasionally, 10 minutes.

3 Add fish, and cook, stirring occasionally, 6 minutes or until fish flakes easily when tested with a fork. Serve with hot cooked rice.

Per Serving: Calories 356 Fat 5.5g (saturated 0.9g) Protein 38.6g
Carbohydrate 38.5g Fiber 5.2g Cholesterol 63mg Sodium 978mg
Exchanges: 2 Starch, 2 Vegetable, 4 Very Lean Meat

Tip: If you need to cut down on sodium, use no-salt-added stewed tomatoes and a small can of chopped green chilies instead of the Mexican-style tomatoes. You can also use salt-free Creole seasoning.

Halibut with Teriyaki Sauce

Makes 4 servings (serving size: 1 fillet and 2 tablespoons sauce)

½   cup pineapple juice
3   tablespoons low-sodium teriyaki sauce
1   tablespoon honey
¾   teaspoon cornstarch
¼   teaspoon garlic powder
⅛   teaspoon ground red pepper
2   tablespoons seasoned breadcrumbs
4   (6-ounce) halibut fillets, skinned (about 1 inch thick)
    (see tip below)
1   tablespoon vegetable oil

1 Combine first 6 ingredients in a small bowl; stir well with a whisk.

2 Combine breadcrumbs and fish in a large zip-top plastic bag. Seal and shake to coat.

3 Heat oil in a large nonstick skillet over medium heat. Add fish, and cook 4 minutes on each side or until fish flakes easily when tested with a fork. Remove fish from pan; set aside, and keep warm.

4 Add teriyaki mixture to pan. Bring to a boil; cook 1 minute, stirring constantly. Pour over fish.

Per Serving: Calories 280 Fat 7.4g (saturated 1.2g) Protein 36.9g
Carbohydrate 14.1g Fiber 0.1g Cholesterol 80mg Sodium 304mg
Exchanges: 1 Starch, 5 Very Lean Meat

Tip: If you can't find halibut, use another white fish, such as grouper or haddock.

Halibut Provençal

Makes 4 servings

1   cup chopped plum tomato (about 4)
2   tablespoons sliced ripe olives
2   tablespoons chopped fresh basil or parsley
1   garlic clove, minced
¼   teaspoon salt
¼   teaspoon pepper
4   (6-ounce) halibut steaks
Olive oil-flavored cooking spray

1 Preheat the grill.

2 Combine first 4 ingredients; set aside.

3 Sprinkle salt and pepper over both sides of fish; coat with cooking spray. Arrange fish in a grill basket coated with cooking spray. Place basket on grill rack; grill, covered, 5 to 6 minutes on each side or until fish flakes easily when tested with a fork. Top fish with tomato mixture.

Per Serving: Calories 204 Fat 4.5g (saturated 0.6g) Protein 35.9g
Carbohydrate 2.8g Fiber 0.7g Cholesterol 54mg Sodium 280mg
Exchanges: ½ Vegetable, 5 Very Lean Meat

"When you see 'Provençal' in a title, it means the recipe is loaded with superfoods like garlic, tomatoes, olives, and olive oil. Tomatoes may help reduce your cancer risk, while garlic and olive oil may keep heart disease away."

Dijon Fish Fillets

Makes 2 servings

1   (8-ounce) orange roughy fillet
Butter-flavored cooking spray
1   tablespoon Dijon mustard
1½ teaspoons lemon juice
1   teaspoon reduced-sodium Worcestershire sauce
2   tablespoons Italian-seasoned breadcrumbs

1 Preheat oven to 450°.

2 Place fish in a 7 x 11-inch baking dish coated with cooking spray. Combine mustard, lemon juice, and Worcestershire sauce, stirring well; spread mixture evenly over fish. Sprinkle breadcrumbs evenly over fish.

3 Bake, uncovered, at 450° for 12 minutes or until fish flakes easily when tested with a fork.

Per Serving: Calories 115 Fat 1.8g (saturated 0.1g) Protein 17.5g
Carbohydrate 5.5g Fiber 0.0g Cholesterol 23mg Sodium 463mg
Exchanges: 3 Very Lean Meat

"What a catch! I love this fish dish because it's super simple and has a tasty breadcrumb topping that works well on any type of white fish."

Sunflower Orange Roughy

Makes 4 servings

¼ cup cornflake crumbs
2 tablespoons dry roasted sunflower kernels
1 teaspoon salt-free seasoning
4 (6-ounce) orange roughy fillets
1 tablespoon lemon juice
Cooking spray

1 Preheat oven to 425°.

2 Combine first 3 ingredients in a small bowl. Dip fish in lemon juice, and dredge in crumb mixture.

3 Place fish on rack of a broiler pan coated with cooking spray. Sprinkle any remaining crumb mixture over fish. Bake at 425° for 10 minutes or until fish flakes easily when tested with a fork.

Per Serving: Calories 162 Fat 3.2g (saturated 0.2g) Protein 26.3g
Carbohydrate 5.8g Fiber 0.4g Cholesterol 34mg Sodium 198mg
Exchanges: ½ Starch, 4 Very Lean Meat

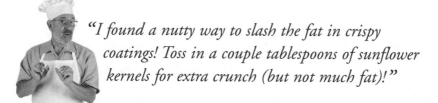

"I found a nutty way to slash the fat in crispy coatings! Toss in a couple tablespoons of sunflower kernels for extra crunch (but not much fat)!"

Glazed Salmon Steaks

Makes 8 servings

½ cup low-sodium soy sauce
⅓ cup dry sherry
1 garlic clove, crushed
8 (6-ounce) salmon steaks (½ inch thick)
⅓ cup packed brown sugar
2 tablespoons honey
2 teaspoons vegetable oil
Cooking spray

1 Combine first 3 ingredients in a large heavy-duty zip-top plastic bag. Add fish; seal bag, and shake until fish is well coated. Marinate in refrigerator 1 hour, turning occasionally.

2 Preheat the grill.

3 Remove fish from bag, reserving 3 tablespoons marinade. Discard remaining marinade. Combine reserved marinade, brown sugar, honey, and oil in a small saucepan. Bring to a boil over medium heat, stirring until sugar dissolves.

4 Place fish on grill rack coated with cooking spray; grill, covered, 4 to 5 minutes on each side or until fish flakes easily when tested with a fork, basting occasionally with brown sugar mixture.

Per Serving: Calories 321 Fat 8.7g (saturated 1.4g) Protein 43.9g
Carbohydrate 14.1g Fiber 0.1g Cholesterol 114mg Sodium 417mg
Exchanges: 1 Starch, 5 Lean Meat

"Salmon has a little more fat than some other fish, so it tastes rich and buttery! But the great news is that the fat is heart-healthy unsaturated fat."

Tortellini and Salmon Dinner

Makes 4 servings (serving size: 1 fillet and about 1 cup tortellini)

Cooking spray
1 (8-ounce) package sliced mushrooms
1½ cups low-fat marinara or pasta sauce
½ teaspoon olive oil
3 garlic cloves, thinly sliced
4 (6-ounce) skinless salmon fillets
1 (9-ounce) package refrigerated spinach- and cheese-filled
   tortellini

1 Coat a large saucepan with cooking spray; place over medium-high heat until hot. Add mushrooms; sauté 5 minutes or until tender. Stir in marinara sauce, and set aside.

2 Pour oil into a large nonstick skillet, and place over medium-high heat. Add garlic; sauté 30 seconds. Add fish, and cook 4 to 5 minutes on each side or until fish flakes easily when tested with a fork.

3 Cook pasta according to package directions, omitting salt. Drain pasta, and stir into mushroom mixture. Place over medium-high heat; cook 1 minute or until thoroughly heated, stirring often. Serve fish over pasta.

Per Serving: Calories 394 Fat 10.6g (saturated 3.5g) Protein 43.6g
Carbohydrate 29.9g Fiber 3.1g Cholesterol 103mg Sodium 779mg
Exchanges: 2 Starch, 5 Lean Meat

"Need another reason to eat salmon? The heart-healthy omega-3 fats in this fish may help prevent rheumatoid arthritis."

Sea Bass with Jalapeño-Lime Sauce

Makes 4 servings

¾ teaspoon chili powder
½ teaspoon salt
½ teaspoon dried oregano
¼ teaspoon pepper
4 (6-ounce) sea bass fillets
½ teaspoon grated lime rind
3 tablespoons fresh lime juice
2 small garlic cloves, minced
1 jalapeño pepper, seeded and minced (see tip below)
1½ tablespoons olive oil

1 Combine first 4 ingredients in a small bowl, stirring well. Rub evenly over fish. Cover and chill 10 minutes.

2 Combine lime rind and lime juice; set aside. Combine garlic and jalapeño pepper; set aside.

3 Heat oil in a large nonstick skillet over high heat. Add fish, and cook 3 minutes on each side or until fish flakes easily when tested with a fork and is brown on all sides. Remove fish from pan. Reduce heat to medium-high; add garlic mixture, and sauté 30 seconds. Remove from heat. Add lime juice mixture, stirring well; pour over fish.

Per Serving: Calories 211 Fat 8.5g (saturated 1.5g) Protein 30.4g
Carbohydrate 1.8g Fiber 0.9g Cholesterol 68mg Sodium 407mg
Exchanges: 4 Very Lean Meat, 1 Fat

Tip: When you're handling fresh jalapeño peppers, wear disposable gloves so that the peppers won't burn your hands.

Snapper with Garlic-Cilantro Sauce

Makes 4 servings

1   garlic clove
1   cup fresh cilantro
½   cup dry white wine
4   (6-ounce) red snapper or grouper fillets
½   teaspoon paprika
½   teaspoon salt
½   teaspoon grated lemon rind
Lemon wedges (optional)

1 Drop garlic through food chute with food processor on; process until minced. Add cilantro; process until finely chopped. Set aside.

2 Bring wine to a simmer over medium-high heat in a large non-stick skillet. Add fish to pan; sprinkle evenly with paprika, salt, and lemon rind. Cover, reduce heat, and simmer 8 to 10 minutes or until fish flakes easily when tested with a fork.

3 Transfer fish to a serving platter, using a large slotted spoon; cover with aluminum foil, and keep warm. Cook pan juices over medium-high heat until reduced to ⅓ cup. Add cilantro mixture to skillet; cook, stirring constantly, 1 minute. Spoon sauce evenly over fish; serve with lemon wedges, if desired.

Per Serving: Calories 175 Fat 2.3g (saturated 0.5g) Protein 35.1g
Carbohydrate 1.0g Fiber 0.1g Cholesterol 63mg Sodium 406mg
Exchanges: 5 Very Lean Meat

Red Snapper Veracruz

Makes 2 servings

1 tablespoon margarine, melted
¼ cup chopped green onions
2 cups chopped seeded tomato (about 2 large)
1 tablespoon chopped fresh cilantro or parsley
3 tablespoons fresh lime juice
2 tablespoons canned chopped green chilies
¼ teaspoon salt
⅛ teaspoon garlic powder
Dash of pepper
2 (6-ounce) red snapper fillets
Lime wedges

1 Melt margarine in a large skillet over medium-high heat. Add onions; sauté until tender. Stir in tomato and next 6 ingredients. Bring to a boil; reduce heat, and simmer, 10 minutes.

2 Place fish in pan. Spoon tomato mixture evenly over fish. Bring mixture to a boil; cover, reduce heat, and simmer 10 minutes or until fish flakes easily when tested with a fork. Serve with lime wedges.

Per Serving: Calories 260 Fat 8.4g (saturated 1.5g) Protein 36.5g
Carbohydrate 9.5g Fiber 2.0g Cholesterol 63mg Sodium 502mg
Exchanges: 2 Vegetable, 5 Very Lean Meat, 1 Fat

"Don't leave one bit of the tomato broth in the pan after you've simmered the fish. Cook some rice, and spoon the yummy broth over the fish and rice."

Tuna Pasta Primavera

Makes 6 servings

8   ounces uncooked farfalle (bow tie pasta)
1   pound asparagus
1   cup frozen green peas
¼   cup sliced green onions
½   teaspoon salt
2   teaspoons olive oil
1   cup chopped seeded tomato (about 1 large)
¼   cup lemon juice
2   (6-ounce) cans low-sodium white tuna in water, drained and
       coarsely flaked
½   teaspoon freshly ground black pepper

1 Cook pasta according to package directions, omitting any salt and oil. Drain, reserving 3 tablespoons of pasta water.

2 Snap off tough ends of asparagus. Cut asparagus into 1-inch pieces. Steam asparagus and peas, covered, 3 to 4 minutes or until asparagus is crisp-tender. Drain.

3 Combine steamed vegetables, green onions, salt, and olive oil in a large bowl. Add pasta, reserved pasta water, tomato, and lemon juice; toss well. Add tuna; toss. Sprinkle with freshly ground pepper.

Per Serving: Calories 222 Fat 2.7g (saturated 0.4g) Protein 17.4g
Carbohydrate 31.8g Fiber 3.3g Cholesterol 13mg Sodium 374mg
Exchanges: 2 Starch, 2 Very Lean Meat

Asian Tuna Steaks

Makes 4 servings

¼ cup low-sodium soy sauce
2 tablespoons dry sherry
2 teaspoons dark sesame oil or vegetable oil
1 teaspoon minced peeled fresh ginger or bottled minced ginger
½ teaspoon dried crushed red pepper
½ teaspoon minced garlic
4 (6-ounce) tuna steaks
Cooking spray

1 Combine first 6 ingredients in a large heavy-duty zip-top plastic bag. Add fish. Seal bag, and shake gently until fish is well coated. Marinate in refrigerator 10 minutes. Remove fish from marinade, reserving marinade.

2 Preheat the grill.

3 Place fish on grill rack coated with cooking spray; grill covered, 4 minutes on each side or until fish flakes easily when tested with a fork.

4 Place marinade in a small saucepan. Bring to a boil; reduce heat, and simmer, uncovered, 1 minute. Drizzle evenly over fish.

Per Serving: Calories 211 Fat 4.0g (saturated 0.9g) Protein 38.4g
Carbohydrate 1.9g Fiber 0.3g Cholesterol 80mg Sodium 597mg
Exchanges: 5 Very Lean Meat

"If you eat a 6-ounce tuna steak instead of the same size filet mignon, you'll save about 250 calories and 33 grams of fat!"

Lemon-Caper Tuna Steaks

Makes 2 servings

  1   teaspoon dried basil
  ⅛   teaspoon salt
  ⅛   teaspoon freshly ground black pepper
  1   large egg white, lightly beaten
  ¼   cup fresh breadcrumbs
  2   (6-ounce) tuna steaks (about ¾ inch thick)
Cooking spray
  1   teaspoon olive oil
  2   small garlic cloves, minced
  ¼   cup fresh lemon juice
  1   tablespoon capers
Lemon wedges (optional)

1 Combine first 4 ingredients in a shallow bowl; stir well. Place breadcrumbs in a shallow dish. Dip fish in egg white mixture, and dredge in breadcrumbs.

2 Coat a large nonstick skillet with cooking spray; add oil, and place over medium heat until hot. Add fish, and cook 2 to 3 minutes on each side or until desired degree of doneness. Place fish on individual plates; set aside, and keep warm. Add garlic to pan, and sauté 1 minute. Add lemon juice and capers, scraping pan to loosen browned bits. Pour sauce evenly over fish, and serve with lemon wedges, if desired.

Per Serving: Calories 301 Fat 11.1g (saturated 2.5g) Protein 42.3g
Carbohydrate 6.4g Fiber 0.2g Cholesterol 65mg Sodium 588mg
Exchanges: ½ Starch, 5 Lean Meat

"I like to serve tuna medium-rare because it's moister when slightly pink in the center. If tuna is overcooked, it gets too dry."

Clam Fettuccine with Mushrooms

Makes 4 (1¼-cup) servings

2   (6½-ounce) cans chopped clams, undrained
1   (1.6-ounce) envelope Alfredo pasta sauce mix
½   cup fat-free milk
1   (6-ounce) can sliced mushrooms, drained
½   cup reduced-fat sour cream
4   cups hot cooked fettuccine (about 8 ounces uncooked pasta)
¼   cup chopped fresh parsley

1 Drain clams, reserving ½ cup clam juice. Set clams aside.

2 Place pasta sauce mix in a small saucepan. Gradually add reserved clam juice and milk, stirring with a whisk until blended. Bring to a boil, and cook 1 minute or until slightly thick, stirring constantly with whisk. Stir in mushrooms and clams; cook until thoroughly heated, stirring constantly. Remove from heat; stir in sour cream.

3 Combine sauce and fettuccine in a bowl; toss well. Sprinkle with parsley. Serve immediately.

Per Serving: Calories 271 Fat 7.2g (saturated 3.6g) Protein 11.1g
Carbohydrate 42.0g Fiber 2.6g Cholesterol 23mg Sodium 1053mg
Exchanges: 3 Starch, ½ Lean Meat, 1 Fat

"If you use a packet of Alfredo sauce mix with fat-free milk and reduced-fat sour cream, you get a rich creamy flavor with a lot less fat than traditional Alfredo sauce. But remember, when you use convenience products, you're getting a lot more sodium."

Crab Cakes

Makes 4 servings (serving size: 2 crab cakes)

1	pound fresh lump crabmeat, drained
¾	cup dry breadcrumbs
¼	cup reduced-fat mayonnaise
1	tablespoon grated Parmesan cheese
1¼	teaspoons Italian seasoning
1½	teaspoons Worcestershire sauce
⅛	teaspoon salt
⅛	teaspoon freshly ground black pepper
2	to 3 green onions, thinly sliced (about ⅓ cup)
1	large egg, lightly beaten
1	medium jalapeño pepper, seeded and diced

Cooking spray
Lemon wedges (optional)
Cocktail sauce (optional)

1 Preheat oven to 400°.

2 Combine first 11 ingredients in a large bowl. Form into 8 patties, and place on a baking sheet coated with cooking spray.

3 Bake at 400° for 5 minutes on each side or until golden. If desired, serve with lemon wedges and cocktail sauce.

Per Serving: Calories 270 Fat 9.0g (saturated 1.9g) Protein 28.0g
Carbohydrate 17.6g Fiber 0.9g Cholesterol 175mg Sodium 735mg
Exchanges: 1 Starch, 3½ Lean Meat

"Instead of filling up on crab cakes as appetizers, I just make larger patties and have two cakes for my main course."

Balsamic-Glazed Scallops

Makes 4 servings
(serving size: one-fourth of scallop mixture and ¾ cup rice)

> 2 cups water
> 1 tablespoon balsamic vinegar (see note below)
> ¼ teaspoon salt
> 1 cup uncooked long-grain rice
> 1 tablespoon olive oil
> 1½ pounds sea scallops
> ¼ cup balsamic vinegar
> 1 tablespoon honey
> 1 teaspoon dried marjoram

1 Combine first 3 ingredients in a medium saucepan; bring to a boil. Add rice; cover, reduce heat, and simmer 20 minutes or until rice is tender and liquid is absorbed. Remove from heat; set aside. (Do not uncover rice.)

2 Heat oil in a large nonstick skillet over medium-high heat. Add scallops; sauté 5 minutes. Remove scallops from pan; set aside.

3 Add vinegar, honey, and marjoram to pan; bring to a boil. Reduce heat to medium; cook 3 minutes. Return scallops to pan; cook 2 minutes or until thoroughly heated. Serve scallops and sauce over rice.

Per Serving: Calories 365 Fat 5.0g (saturated 0.7g) Protein 31.9g
Carbohydrate 45.7g Fiber 0.6g Cholesterol 56mg Sodium 423mg
Exchanges: 3 Starch, 3 Very Lean Meat, ½ Fat

"Balsamic vinegar is my secret surprise ingredient. It adds a distinct tangy sweetness to foods, but, like other vinegars, it's calorie-free!"

Scallops with Lemony Spaghetti

Makes 4 servings (serving size: about 4 ounces scallops and 1 cup pasta)

1½ pounds sea scallops
½ teaspoon paprika
¼ teaspoon freshly ground pepper
2 garlic cloves, minced
2 tablespoons butter
¼ cup dry white wine
2 tablespoons fresh lemon juice
¼ teaspoon salt
2 tablespoons chopped flat leaf parsley
6 cups hot cooked spaghetti (about 16 ounces uncooked pasta)
Lemon wedges

1 Sprinkle scallops with paprika, pepper, and garlic.

2 Heat a nonstick skillet over medium-high heat until hot. Melt 1 tablespoon butter in pan; add half of scallops. Cook scallops 2 minutes on each side. Remove scallops from pan, and keep warm. Repeat with remaining butter and scallops.

3 Add wine, lemon juice, and salt to pan; simmer 30 seconds or until liquid is reduced to a glaze. Pour glaze over scallops; sprinkle with parsley. Spoon scallops over pasta, and serve with lemon wedges.

Per Serving: Calories 419 Fat 5.9g (saturated 2.7g) Protein 29.0g
Carbohydrate 60.3g Fiber 2.0g Cholesterol 48mg Sodium 326mg
Exchanges: 3 Starch, 2 Lean Meat

"I eat healthfully, but refuse to compromise on flavor. That's why I use just a bit of butter to make this sauce so-o-o yummy."

Lemon-Dill Scallops and Snow Peas

Makes 2 servings

1   teaspoon reduced-calorie margarine
8   ounces bay scallops
6   ounces fresh snow pea pods, trimmed
¾   teaspoon chopped fresh or ¼ teaspoon dried dill
⅛   teaspoon salt
1½ teaspoons fresh lemon juice

1 Melt margarine in a nonstick skillet over medium-high heat. Add scallops; sauté 2 minutes. Add snow peas and remaining ingredients; sauté 2 minutes. Serve immediately.

Per Serving: Calories 150 Fat 2.6g (saturated 0.3g) Protein 21.4g Carbohydrate 9.5g Fiber 2.2g Cholesterol 37mg Sodium 351mg
Exchanges: 1 Vegetable, 3 Very Lean Meat

"I usually buy extra snow peas so I can munch on 'em while I cook. They're oh-so-crisp and fresh-tasting!"

Shrimp with Feta

Makes 4 servings

1   teaspoon olive oil
1   pound peeled and deveined large shrimp (see tip below)
1   cup sliced green onions
4   garlic cloves, minced
1   (14.5-ounce) can diced tomatoes, undrained
1   teaspoon dried oregano
1   teaspoon dried basil
¼   teaspoon sugar
¼   teaspoon ground red pepper
¾   cup (3 ounces) crumbled feta cheese

1 Preheat broiler.

2 Heat oil in a large nonstick skillet over medium-high heat. Add shrimp; sauté 3 minutes or until done. Divide shrimp evenly among 4 individual baking dishes; set aside.

3 Return pan to medium-high heat. Add onions and garlic; sauté 1 minute. Add tomatoes and next 4 ingredients; cook 3 minutes or until liquid almost evaporates. Spoon tomato mixture evenly over shrimp, and sprinkle with cheese.

4 Broil 5 minutes or until cheese softens. (Cheese will not melt.) Serve immediately.

Per Serving: Calories 237 Fat 7.6g (saturated 3.8g) Protein 32.9g
Carbohydrate 8.8g Fiber 1.5g Cholesterol 282mg Sodium 711mg
Exchanges: 1 Vegetable, 4 Very Lean Meat

Tip: Cut down on prep time by purchasing peeled and deveined shrimp from your supermarket's seafood department.

Sweet-and-Sour Shrimp with Rice

Makes 4 servings (serving size: 1¼ cups shrimp and ¾ cup rice)

1 teaspoon vegetable oil
1 pound peeled and deveined shrimp (see tip below and on page 320)
Cooking spray
2 medium-size green bell peppers, seeded and cut into 1-inch pieces (about 3 cups)
1 medium onion, cut into wedges and separated (about 2 cups)
1 (13-ounce) can pineapple chunks in juice, drained
¾ cup sweet-and-sour sauce
3 cups hot cooked long-grain rice

1 Heat oil in a large nonstick skillet or wok over high heat. Add shrimp to pan, and stir-fry 3 minutes or until shrimp are done. Remove shrimp from pan, and keep warm.

2 Coat pan with cooking spray. Add pepper and onion; stir-fry 4 minutes. Add reserved shrimp and the pineapple chunks. Stir in sweet-and-sour sauce. Reduce heat to low, and cook, stirring constantly, 2 minutes. Serve over rice.

Per Serving: Calories 298 Fat 3.3g (saturated 0.6g) Protein 19.9g Carbohydrate 49.1g Fiber 2.9g Cholesterol 129mg Sodium 182mg
Exchanges: 2 Starch, 1 Fruit, 1 Vegetable, 2 Very Lean Meat

"Shrimp gets a bad rap because it's a little higher in sodium and cholesterol than other types of seafood. That's too bad, since it's a terrific protein source with only 1 gram of fat for a 3-ounce portion!"

Grilled Mustard-Beer Shrimp

Makes 4 servings (serving size: 2 kabobs)

48 unpeeled large shrimp (about 2 pounds)
½ teaspoon garlic powder
½ teaspoon ground red pepper
¼ cup spicy brown mustard
¼ cup light beer (see note below)
Cooking spray

1 Preheat the grill.

2 Peel and devein shrimp, leaving tails intact. Thread 6 shrimp onto each of 8 (12-inch) skewers. Sprinkle shrimp evenly with garlic powder and pepper.

3 Stir together mustard and beer.

4 Place skewers on grill rack coated with cooking spray; grill, uncovered, 5 minutes on each side, basting shrimp often with mustard mixture.

Per Serving: Calories 136 Fat 2.4g (saturated 0.3g) Protein 24.8g
Carbohydrate 1.6g Fiber 0.1g Cholesterol 221mg Sodium 400mg
Exchanges: 3 Very Lean Meat

"Beer is fantastic to cook with because the alcohol evaporates as it cooks (along with the extra calories), leaving only the wonderful flavor behind."

Chapter 20

Meatless Main Dishes

Herbed Potato Frittata

Makes 4 servings

2 cups diced red potato
1 tablespoon reduced-calorie margarine
⅓ cup sliced green onions
1 teaspoon dried basil
½ teaspoon dried marjoram
¼ teaspoon salt
¼ teaspoon black pepper
1 garlic clove, minced
2 (8-ounce) cartons egg substitute
¾ cup (3 ounces) shredded reduced-fat sharp Cheddar cheese

1 Place potatoes in a saucepan; add water to cover, and bring to a boil. Cover, reduce heat, and simmer 20 minutes or until tender; drain.

2 Melt margarine in a 10-inch cast iron skillet over medium-high heat. Add potatoes, green onions, and next 5 ingredients; sauté 2 minutes. Spread potato mixture evenly in pan.

3 Pour egg substitute over potato mixture; reduce heat to medium-low. Cook, uncovered, 8 to 10 minutes or until almost set.

4 Preheat the broiler. Broil 3 minutes; sprinkle with cheese, and broil 30 seconds or until cheese melts. Remove pan carefully from oven.

Per Serving: Calories 193 Fat 5.9g (saturated 2.7g) Protein 19.5g
Carbohydrate 15.5g Fiber 1.5g Cholesterol 14mg Sodium 507mg
Exchanges: 1 Starch, 2 Lean Meat

Confetti Cheese Omelet

Makes 2 servings

Cooking spray
- ¼ cup chopped red bell pepper
- ¼ cup chopped green bell pepper
- ¼ cup sliced green onions
- 1 cup egg substitute
- ¼ teaspoon salt
- ¼ teaspoon coarsely ground black pepper
- ½ cup (2 ounces) shredded reduced-fat Cheddar cheese

1 Coat a 10-inch nonstick skillet with cooking spray; place over medium heat until hot. Add bell peppers and green onions; cook 4 minutes, stirring occasionally.

2 Pour egg substitute into pan; sprinkle with salt and pepper. Cook, without stirring, 2 to 3 minutes or until golden brown on bottom. Sprinkle with cheese. Loosen omelet with a spatula; fold in half. Cook 2 minutes or until egg mixture is set and cheese begins to melt. Cut omelet in half. Slide halves onto serving plates.

Per Serving: Calories 159 Fat 5.9g (saturated 3.2g) Protein 20.7g
Carbohydrate 5.3g Fiber 0.7g Cholesterol 19mg Sodium 680mg
Exchanges: 1 Vegetable, 3 Lean Meat

"I like to use egg substitute for my omelets. Not only is it convenient, egg substitute is also cholesterol free and fat free!"

Cheese and Onion Quesadillas

Makes 4 servings

Butter-flavored cooking spray
1 cup chopped onion (about 1 medium)
4 (8-inch) fat-free flour tortillas
1 cup (4 ounces) shredded reduced-fat sharp Cheddar cheese
½ teaspoon ground cumin
½ cup salsa
½ cup reduced-fat sour cream

1 Coat a large nonstick skillet with cooking spray; place over medium-high heat until hot. Add onion; sauté 5 minutes or until tender. Remove from pan. Wipe pan with a paper towel.

2 Coat pan with cooking spray; place over medium heat until hot. Place one tortilla in pan. Cook 1 minute or until bottom of tortilla is golden. Sprinkle one-fourth of onion, cheese, and cumin over one side of tortilla. Fold tortilla in half. Cook tortilla 1 minute on each side or until golden and cheese melts. Repeat procedure with remaining tortillas, onion, cheese, and cumin.

3 Top each quesadilla with 2 tablespoons salsa and 2 tablespoons sour cream.

Per Serving: Calories 246 Fat 7.7g (saturated 4.4g) Protein 14.2g
Carbohydrate 29.9g Fiber 2.2g Cholesterol 24mg Sodium 639mg
Exchanges: 2 Starch, 1 High-Fat Meat

"To perk up plain ol' cheese quesadillas, I replace some of the cheese with tender sautéed onions. Not only do my quesadillas taste great—now they're lower in fat!"

Barbecued Beans 'n' Rice

Makes 8 servings (serving size: ½ cup beans and ¾ cup rice)

2 teaspoons olive oil
1 cup frozen chopped onion
1 to 2 drained canned chipotle chilies, minced
1 tablespoon bottled minced garlic
1 (16-ounce) can pinto beans, drained
1 (16-ounce) can kidney beans, drained
1 (15-ounce) can black beans, drained
1 cup hickory barbecue sauce
1 tablespoon Dijon mustard
6 cups hot cooked long-grain rice

1 Preheat oven to 350°.

2 Heat oil in a nonstick skillet over medium heat. Add onion, chilies, and garlic; sauté 5 minutes. Remove from heat. Stir in beans, barbecue sauce, and mustard. Spoon mixture into a 1½-quart casserole; cover and bake at 350° for 1 hour. Serve over rice.

Per Serving: Calories 372 Fat 2.1g (saturated 0.3g) Protein 12.2g
Carbohydrate 76.4g Fiber 5.0g Cholesterol 0mg Sodium 540mg
Exchanges: 5 Starch

Tip: If you can't find chipotle chilies, use 1 or 2 drained canned jalapeños and a few drops of mesquite-flavored barbecue smoke seasoning.

Cheesy Bean and Rice Casserole

Makes 4 servings

1 (16-ounce) package frozen rice and vegetable pilaf blend
2 tablespoons all-purpose flour
1 (12-ounce) can evaporated fat-free milk, divided
¼ teaspoon salt
¼ teaspoon coarsely ground black pepper
¼ teaspoon hot sauce
3 ounces light processed cheese, cubed (about ⅔ cup)
1 (15-ounce) can kidney beans, drained
Butter-flavored cooking spray
¼ cup dry breadcrumbs
¼ teaspoon chili powder

1 Cook rice blend according to package directions; drain.

2 Combine flour and ½ cup milk; stir until smooth. Combine flour mixture, remaining 1 cup milk, the salt, pepper, and hot sauce in a medium saucepan; stir well. Cook over medium heat, stirring constantly, until mixture is thick and bubbly. Remove from heat, and add cheese; stir until cheese melts.

3 Combine rice, cheese mixture, and beans in a microwave-safe 7 x 11-inch baking dish coated with cooking spray. Combine breadcrumbs and chili powder; sprinkle over rice mixture. Coat with cooking spray, and microwave at HIGH 9 minutes or until thoroughly heated. (See tip below.)

Per Serving: Calories 341 Fat 3.7g (saturated 1.7g) Protein 20.5g
Carbohydrate 57.8g Fiber 4.6g Cholesterol 11mg Sodium 752mg
Exchanges: 4 Starch, 1 Lean Meat

Tip: You can also bake this recipe in a regular oven at 350° for 25 minutes.

Stuffed Poblanos

Makes 5 servings (serving size: 2 stuffed peppers and ⅓ cup salsa)

1 (8-ounce) package beans and rice mix
10 large poblano peppers
1 cup frozen whole-kernel corn, thawed
1 cup (4 ounces) shredded Monterey Jack cheese
1 tablespoon 40%-less-sodium taco seasoning
1 (14.5-ounce) can no-salt-added diced tomatoes, undrained
1 (16-ounce) bottle salsa

1 Cook beans and rice mix according to package directions, omitting fat.

2 Preheat oven to 350°.

3 Cut a lengthwise strip from each pepper. Chop enough pepper strips to measure ½ cup; reserve remaining strips for another use. Remove and discard seeds from peppers. Cook peppers in boiling water to cover for 5 minutes; drain and set aside.

4 Combine chopped pepper, bean mix, corn, and next 3 ingredients. Spoon evenly into peppers; place peppers on a jelly-roll pan. Add hot water to pan to a depth of ¼ inch. Bake at 350° for 20 minutes or until thoroughly heated. Serve peppers topped with salsa.

Per Serving: Calories 370 Fat 9.4g (saturated 4.6g) Protein 18.3g
Carbohydrate 59.6g Fiber 13.8g Cholesterol 20mg Sodium 1,040mg
Exchanges: 3 Starch, 2 Vegetable, 1 High-Fat Meat

Veggie-Bean Tostadas

Makes 4 servings

Cooking spray
1½ **cups sliced mushrooms**
1½ **cups broccoli florets**
 1 **cup shredded carrot**
 ½ **cup picante sauce**
 2 **tablespoons water**
 1 **(16-ounce) can fat-free refried beans**
 4 **(6-inch) corn tortillas**
 1 **cup (4 ounces) shredded reduced-fat four-cheese Mexican cheese blend**

1 Preheat broiler.

2 Coat a large nonstick skillet with cooking spray; place over medium-high heat until hot. Add mushrooms and next 4 ingredients; cover and simmer 7 minutes or until crisp-tender. Heat beans according to label directions.

3 Place tortillas on a baking sheet; broil 1 minute on each side or until crisp and golden. Place tortillas on individual serving plates. Top with beans, vegetables, and cheese.

Per Serving: Calories 235 Fat 9.0g (saturated 5.2g) Protein 16.2g
Carbohydrate 28.6g Fiber 8.0g Cholesterol 15mg Sodium 1,004mg
Exchanges: 1 Starch, 2 Vegetable, 2 Lean Meat

"Instead of piling a lot of meat and cheese on these, I top my tostadas with fresh veggies and just a sprinkling of cheese."

Eggplant Parmigiana

Makes 6 (1-cup) servings

½ cup egg substitute
¼ cup (1 ounce) preshredded fresh Parmesan cheese, divided
¼ cup fat-free milk
1 cup Italian-seasoned breadcrumbs
1 (1-pound) eggplant, peeled and cut into ½-inch-thick slices
2 tablespoons olive oil
Cooking spray
2 cups fire-roasted tomato and garlic pasta sauce
1 cup (4 ounces) shredded part-skim mozzarella cheese

1 Preheat oven to 350°.

2 Combine egg substitute, 2 tablespoons Parmesan cheese, and the milk in a shallow bowl, stirring well. Place breadcrumbs in a shallow dish. Dip eggplant slices in egg mixture, and dredge in breadcrumbs.

3 Heat oil in a large nonstick skillet over medium-high heat. Add eggplant slices, and cook 5 minutes on each side or until golden.

4 Arrange half of eggplant slices in a 7 x 11-inch baking dish coated with cooking spray. Spoon 1 cup pasta sauce over eggplant, and sprinkle with remaining 2 tablespoons Parmesan cheese. Repeat with remaining eggplant and 1 cup sauce. Bake, uncovered, at 350° for 25 minutes. Sprinkle with mozzarella cheese; bake an additional 5 minutes or until cheese melts.

Per Serving: Calories 245 Fat 10.0g (saturated 3.4g) Protein 13.1g
Carbohydrate 25.7g Fiber 3.0g Cholesterol 14mg Sodium 977mg
Exchanges: 1 Starch, 2 Vegetable, 1 Medium-Fat Meat, 1 Fat

Smashed Potato-and-Broccoli Casserole

Makes 6 (1-cup) servings

 2 pounds baking potatoes, halved lengthwise
 1 cup chopped broccoli
 ½ cup diced onion
 ½ cup part-skim ricotta cheese
1½ teaspoons chopped fresh or ½ teaspoon dried dill
 ½ teaspoon salt
 ⅛ teaspoon ground red pepper
 1 (8-ounce) carton reduced-fat sour cream
Cooking spray
 ¾ cup (3 ounces) shredded reduced-fat sharp Cheddar cheese

1 Preheat oven to 375°.

2 Place potato halves in a large saucepan; cover with water. Bring to a boil. Reduce heat; simmer 20 minutes or until tender. Drain in a colander over a bowl, reserving 1 cup cooking liquid. Return potatoes and 1 cup liquid to pan; mash with a potato masher until slightly chunky.

3 Add broccoli and next 6 ingredients to pan; stir well. Spoon potato mixture into a 7 x 11-inch baking dish coated with cooking spray; bake at 375° for 35 minutes. Sprinkle with Cheddar cheese; bake an additional 5 minutes or until cheese melts.

Per Serving: Calories 298 Fat 6.8g (saturated 4.0g) Protein 15.0g
Carbohydrate 44.5g Fiber 3.9g Cholesterol 23mg Sodium 398mg
Exchanges: 3 Starch, 1 Medium-Fat Meat

Squash Sauté with Polenta

Makes 4 servings

1 (16-ounce) package sun-dried tomato-flavored polenta,
  cut into 12 slices
Garlic-flavored cooking spray
2 tablespoons pesto
2 tablespoons water
2 cups sliced yellow squash
2 cups sliced zucchini
1 (7-ounce) jar roasted red peppers, drained and cut into strips
½ cup (2 ounces) preshredded fresh Parmesan cheese

1 Preheat broiler.

2 Place polenta slices on a baking sheet coated with cooking spray. Broil 5 minutes on each side or until lightly browned.

3 Coat a large nonstick skillet with cooking spray; place over medium-high heat until hot. Add pesto and water, stirring well. Add yellow squash and zucchini; cover and cook 5 minutes or until vegetables are tender. Add red peppers; cook until thoroughly heated.

4 Spoon zucchini mixture evenly over polenta, and sprinkle with cheese.

Per Serving: Calories 197 Fat 5.9g (saturated 2.8g) Protein 9.9g
Carbohydrate 26.6g Fiber 3.8g Cholesterol 10mg Sodium 559mg
Exchanges: 1 Starch, 2 Vegetable, 1 Fat

Roasted Vegetable Pot Pie

Makes 6 servings

2 (16-ounce) packages frozen stew vegetables, thawed
2 tablespoons fat-free Italian dressing
1 (25¾-ounce) jar fat-free chunky spaghetti sauce with mushrooms
    and sweet peppers
1 (15-ounce) can dark red kidney beans, drained
1 (10-ounce) can refrigerated pizza crust dough
1 teaspoon fennel seeds

1 Preheat oven to 450°.

2 Combine stew vegetables and Italian dressing, tossing well; spoon onto a large baking sheet. Bake at 450° for 20 minutes or until vegetables are lightly browned, stirring once. Remove from oven. Reduce oven temperature to 375°. Combine roasted vegetable mixture, spaghetti sauce, and kidney beans, stirring well. Spoon vegetable mixture into a 9 x 13-inch baking dish.

3 Unroll dough onto a work surface; sprinkle dough with fennel seeds. Roll dough into a 10 x 14-inch rectangle; place over vegetable mixture. Bake at 375° for 30 minutes or until lightly browned.

Per Serving: Calories 297 Fat 1.9g (saturated 0.4g) Protein 12.0g
Carbohydrate 57.9g Fiber 5.1g Cholesterol 0mg Sodium 875mg
Exchanges: 4 Starch

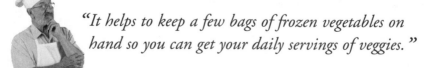

"It helps to keep a few bags of frozen vegetables on hand so you can get your daily servings of veggies."

Vegetable Fried Rice

Makes 2 (2-cup) servings

½   cup egg substitute
1¼   teaspoons dark sesame oil, divided
1⅓   cups sliced green onions
1½   cups chilled cooked instant brown rice
 2   tablespoons low-sodium soy sauce
¼   teaspoon pepper
¼   teaspoon ground ginger
1½   cups frozen baby green peas, thawed and drained

1 Cook egg substitute in ¼ teaspoon sesame oil in a large nonstick skillet or wok until set on bottom. (Do not stir.) Turn and cook an additional minute. Cut cooked egg into thin strips, and set aside.

2 Heat remaining 1 teaspoon oil in pan; add green onions, and sauté 1 minute. Add rice and next 3 ingredients; cook 2 minutes or until thoroughly heated, stirring often. Gently stir in reserved egg strips and green peas. Serve immediately.

Per Serving: Calories 336 Fat 6.8g (saturated 1.1g) Protein 16.9g
Carbohydrate 51.1g Fiber 8.9g Cholesterol 1mg Sodium 902mg
Exchanges: 3 Starch, 1 Vegetable, 1 Lean Meat, ½ Fat

Tip: If you don't have leftover rice, cook some up and chill it in the freezer for 10 minutes.

Curried
Vegetable Couscous

Makes 4 servings

1   (14½-ounce) can vegetable broth, divided
⅓   cup raisins
1   cup uncooked plain couscous
½   (16-ounce) package assorted fresh stir-fry vegetables
¼   cup water
2   teaspoons curry powder
¼   teaspoon ground red pepper
1   (15.8-ounce) can black-eyed peas, rinsed and drained

1 Combine 1¼ cups broth and the raisins in a small saucepan. Bring to a boil, and stir in couscous. Cover, remove from heat, and let stand 5 minutes.

2 Combine remaining broth, the stir-fry vegetables, and remaining 4 ingredients in a saucepan; stir well. Cover and simmer 7 minutes or until vegetables are crisp-tender. Serve over couscous mixture.

Per Serving: Calories 293 Fat 1.6g (saturated 0.2g) Protein 13.2g
Carbohydrate 58.6g Fiber 5.2g Cholesterol 0mg Sodium 364mg
Exchanges: 2 Starch, 1 Fruit, 2 Vegetable

"Couscous is made from wheat and fluffs up like rice when it's cooked. It's fat free and takes only minutes to prepare! Look for boxes of couscous in the rice and pasta section of your supermarket."

Southwestern Vegetable Bake

Makes 4 servings

2 (10-ounce) packages frozen Southwestern-style corn and roasted
   red peppers, thawed
1 (14½-ounce) can chili-style tomatoes, undrained
1 (15½-ounce) can white hominy, drained
1 (15-ounce) can no-salt-added black beans, rinsed and drained
¼ teaspoon black pepper
½ cup (2 ounces) shredded Monterey Jack cheese with jalapeño
   peppers

1 Preheat oven to 350°.

2 Combine first 5 ingredients in a 2-quart baking dish. Cover and
bake at 350° for 25 minutes or until bubbly. Uncover, sprinkle
with cheese, and bake an additional 5 minutes or until cheese melts.

Per Serving: Calories 364 Fat 6.5g (saturated 2.8g) Protein 16.6g
Carbohydrate 62.7g Fiber 8.3g Cholesterol 11mg Sodium 958mg
Exchanges: 3 Starch, 3 Vegetable

*"Meatless dishes get a nutritious boost from beans.
Dried beans have no fat and are packed with protein,
vitamins, and minerals. Plus, they're full of fiber, so
you'll feel full and satisfied."*

Spinach Pockets

Makes 4 servings (serving size: 1 pocket and ⅓ cup pasta sauce)

¾ cup 2% low-fat cottage cheese
2 tablespoons pesto
1 (10-ounce) package frozen chopped spinach, thawed, drained, and
   squeezed dry
¼ teaspoon salt
¼ teaspoon pepper
1 (10-ounce) can refrigerated pizza crust dough
Cooking spray
1 cup sliced mushrooms
½ cup (2 ounces) shredded part-skim mozzarella cheese
1⅓ cups fire-roasted tomato and garlic pasta sauce

1 Preheat oven to 425°.

2 Combine first 5 ingredients in a food processor; pulse 10 times.

3 Unroll pizza dough; cut into 4 squares. Place squares on a baking sheet coated with cooking spray. Roll out each square to ⅛-inch thickness. Spoon one-fourth of spinach mixture onto center of each square; top evenly with mushrooms and mozzarella cheese. Moisten the edges of each square with water; bring corners to center, pressing edges to seal. Bake at 425° for 12 to 14 minutes or until golden. Serve with pasta sauce.

Per Serving: Calories 365 Fat 10.5g (saturated 2.7g) Protein 20.3g
Carbohydrate 47.4g Fiber 5.0g Cholesterol 13mg Sodium 1,252mg
Exchanges: 2½ Starch, 2 Vegetable, 1 Medium-Fat Meat, 1 Fat

Grilled Portobello Pizzas

Makes 2 servings (serving size: 2 mushrooms)

½   cup finely chopped fresh basil
3   teaspoons olive oil, divided
1   tablespoon plus 1 teaspoon bottled minced roasted garlic, divided
12   plum tomatoes, seeded and chopped
1½   tablespoons minced fresh thyme
4   (4-inch) portobello mushroom caps
Cooking spray
¼   teaspoon salt
¼   teaspoon pepper
½   cup (2 ounces) shredded part-skim mozzarella cheese

1 Preheat the grill.

2 Combine basil, 2 teaspoons olive oil, and 1 teaspoon garlic; set aside. Combine remaining 1 tablespoon garlic and 1 teaspoon olive oil, the tomatoes, and thyme. Set aside.

3 Using a spoon, remove brown gills from the undersides of mushrooms; discard gills. Coat top and bottom of mushroom caps evenly with cooking spray; sprinkle with salt and pepper.

4 Place mushrooms, top side up, on grill rack coated with cooking spray; cover and grill 4 minutes. Turn mushrooms over; spoon tomato mixture evenly into caps; top each mushroom with 1 tablespoon basil mixture and 2 tablespoons cheese. Grill, covered, 4 minutes or until mushrooms are tender and cheese melts.

Per Serving: Calories 250 Fat 12.6g (saturated 4.1g) Protein 17.6g
Carbohydrate 22.8g Fiber 6.7g Cholesterol 15mg Sodium 470mg
Exchanges: 4 Vegetable, 1 Lean Meat, 2 Fat

Sweet Pepper Pizza with Three Cheeses

Makes 8 servings (serving size: 1 slice)

Olive oil-flavored cooking spray
½ (8-ounce) package sliced mushrooms
1 (10-ounce) thin-crust prepared pizza shell (such as Boboli)
3 plum tomatoes, thinly sliced
1 small onion, thinly sliced and separated into rings
1 green bell pepper, thinly sliced
2 tablespoons chopped fresh basil
3 tablespoons sliced ripe olives
1 cup (4 ounces) shredded part-skim mozzarella cheese
1 tablespoon grated Parmesan cheese
1 tablespoon grated Romano cheese

1 Preheat oven to 475°.

2 Coat a medium skillet with cooking spray. Place over medium-high heat until hot. Add mushrooms, and sauté 5 minutes or until golden.

3 Place bread shell on a baking sheet or pizza pan. Top with mushrooms, tomato, onion, pepper, basil, and olives; sprinkle with mozzarella, Parmesan, and Romano cheeses.

4 Bake at 475° for 6 to 9 minutes or until cheeses melt. Cut into 8 slices.

Per Slice: Calories 217 Fat 6.3g (saturated 2.9g) Protein 10.9g
Carbohydrate 30.2g Fiber 2.3g Cholesterol 10mg Sodium 413mg
Exchanges: 2 Starch, 1 Medium-Fat Meat

Fresh Tomato, Basil, and Cheese Pizza

Makes 6 servings (serving size: 1 slice)

1 (1-pound) cheese-flavored prepared pizza shell (such as Boboli)
2 teaspoons olive oil
½ cup (2 ounces) preshredded fresh Parmesan cheese, divided
3 tomatoes, cut into ¼-inch-thick slices (about 1½ pounds)
6 garlic cloves, thinly sliced
¼ teaspoon salt
⅛ teaspoon pepper
¼ cup fresh basil leaves

1 Preheat oven to 450°.

2 Brush crust with olive oil. Sprinkle with ¼ cup Parmesan cheese, leaving a ½-inch border. Arrange tomato slices over cheese, overlapping edges; top with garlic, remaining ¼ cup cheese, the salt, and pepper.

3 Bake pizza at 450° for 10 to 12 minutes or until crust is golden. Remove pizza to a cutting board, and top with fresh basil leaves. Let stand 5 minutes. Cut into 6 slices.

Per Slice: Calories 260 Fat 7.5g (saturated 2.7g) Protein 11.3g
Carbohydrate 38.2g Fiber 1.6g Cholesterol 4mg Sodium 611mg
Exchanges: 2 Starch, 2 Vegetable, 1 Fat

"Who says pizza isn't good for you? It is when you top it with plenty of fresh veggies and herbs and a small amount of cheese."

Fettuccine Alfredo

Makes 6 (1-cup) servings

1   (12-ounce) package spinach and egg fettuccine noodles
1   teaspoon butter
4   to 5 garlic cloves, divided
½   cup dry white wine
2   cups evaporated fat-free milk, divided
2   tablespoons all-purpose flour
½   teaspoon salt
1¼ cups (5 ounces) preshredded fresh Parmesan cheese
¼   teaspoon freshly ground black pepper

1 Cook pasta according to package directions, omitting any salt and oil; drain and keep warm.

2 Melt butter in a small saucepan over medium heat. Thinly slice 2 garlic cloves; add to butter. Sauté 2 minutes or until lightly browned. Increase heat to medium-high; add wine, and bring to a simmer. Cook 5 minutes or until mixture is reduced by half.

3 Combine 2 tablespoons milk and the flour, stirring until smooth. Add flour mixture to wine mixture; add remaining milk, stirring well. Cook, stirring constantly, 5 minutes or until thick. Stir in salt.

4 Pour sauce over noodles; toss well. Mince remaining garlic; toss with noodle mixture, and stir in cheese. Sprinkle with pepper, and serve immediately.

Per Serving: Calories 348 Fat 7.5g (saturated 3.6g) Protein 15.7g
Carbohydrate 50.5g Fiber 1.1g Cholesterol 88mg Sodium 604mg
Exchanges: 3½ Starch, 1 High-Fat Meat

Mexicali Macaroni and Cheese

Makes 6 (1-cup) servings

1   (8-ounce) package uncooked large elbow macaroni
6   ounces light processed cheese, cubed
1   teaspoon taco seasoning
½   cup salsa

1 Cook pasta according to package directions, omitting any salt and oil. Drain and return pasta to pan.

2 Add cheese and taco seasoning to pasta, stirring until cheese melts. Stir in salsa.

Per Serving: Calories 216 Fat 3.8g (saturated 2.1g) Protein 10.8g
Carbohydrate 34.4g Fiber 1.7g Cholesterol 12mg Sodium 590mg
Exchanges: 2 Starch, 1 Lean Meat

"Do you love macaroni and cheese as much as I do? Make it your main dish! And to round out the meal, simply add a tossed salad and some fresh fruit."

Vegetarian Peanut Pasta

Makes 5 servings

6   tablespoons reduced-fat peanut butter (see note below)
5   tablespoons water
3   tablespoons brown sugar
3   tablespoons low-sodium soy sauce
3   tablespoons rice vinegar
¼   to ½ teaspoon dried crushed red pepper
8   ounces uncooked spaghetti
10 ounces snow peas, trimmed
1   large carrot, shredded

1 Combine first 6 ingredients in a small saucepan. Cook over medium heat until mixture begins to boil, stirring often; remove from heat, and set sauce aside.

2 Cook pasta according to package directions, omitting any salt and oil; add snow peas to pasta for the last 3 minutes of cooking time. Drain and place in a large serving bowl. Add carrot and sauce, tossing to coat.

Per Serving: Calories 339 Fat 8.1g (saturated 0.1g) Protein 12.3g
Carbohydrate 54.2g Fiber 4.3g Cholesterol 0mg Sodium 398mg
Exchanges: 3 Starch, 1 Vegetable, 1 Medium-Fat Meat

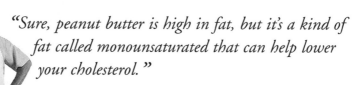

"Sure, peanut butter is high in fat, but it's a kind of fat called monounsaturated that can help lower your cholesterol."

Mostaccioli with Red Pepper Sauce

Makes 4 servings

8   ounces uncooked mostaccioli (tube-shaped pasta)
2   cups sliced zucchini (about 2 medium)
1   garlic clove
1   (7.25-ounce) jar roasted red bell peppers, drained
1   tablespoon balsamic vinegar
¼   cup low-fat mayonnaise
3   tablespoons grated Parmesan cheese

1 Cook pasta according to package directions, omitting any salt and oil. When pasta is done, add zucchini, and cook 2 minutes or until zucchini is tender.

2 Drop garlic through food chute with processor on; process until finely chopped. Add peppers and vinegar to processor; process 1 minute, stopping once to scrape down sides. Add mayonnaise and cheese; process just until combined.

3 Drain pasta-zucchini mixture; transfer to a large bowl. Add red pepper sauce to pasta, and toss gently.

Per Serving: Calories 286 Fat 3.7g (saturated 1.1g) Protein 10.9g
Carbohydrate 52.2g Fiber 2.7g Cholesterol 4mg Sodium 390mg
Exchanges: 3 Starch, 1 Vegetable

"This pasta will keep you pumpin'! It's good for your heart because the red bell peppers may help keep 'bad' cholesterol from building up in your arteries."

Vegetable Lasagna

Makes 8 servings

1	(14½-ounce) can stewed tomatoes, undrained
1½	cups pasta sauce
2	cups 1% low-fat cottage cheese
½	cup grated Parmesan cheese
¼	teaspoon freshly ground black pepper

Cooking spray

9	uncooked lasagna noodles
3	medium zucchini, trimmed and shredded
6	(1-ounce) slices provolone cheese, cut into strips

1 Preheat oven to 350°.

2 Stir together tomatoes and pasta sauce. Stir together cottage cheese, Parmesan cheese, and pepper.

3 Spoon one-third of tomato mixture into a 9 x 13-inch baking dish coated with cooking spray. Place 3 uncooked lasagna noodles over mixture; top with one-third of shredded zucchini. Spoon one-third of cottage cheese mixture evenly over zucchini; top with 2 slices provolone cheese. Repeat layers twice with remaining tomato mixture, noodles, zucchini, cheese mixture, and provolone slices.

4 Cover and bake at 350° for 35 minutes. Uncover, and bake an additional 15 minutes. Let stand 15 minutes before serving.

Per Serving: Calories 273 Fat 9.2g (saturated 5.1g) Protein 20.0g
Carbohydrate 29.1g Fiber 3.0g Cholesterol 23mg Sodium 791mg
Exchanges: 2 Starch, 2 Lean Meat

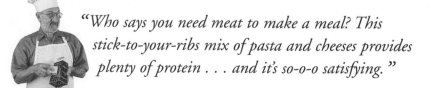

"Who says you need meat to make a meal? This stick-to-your-ribs mix of pasta and cheeses provides plenty of protein . . . and it's so-o-o satisfying."

Spinach-Stuffed Shells

Makes 5 servings (serving size: 4 shells)

½ (12-ounce) package jumbo shell pasta (20 shells)
1 (26-ounce) jar low-fat tomato and garlic pasta sauce, divided
¾ cup 1% low-fat cottage cheese
¾ cup part-skim ricotta cheese
¾ cup (3 ounces) shredded part-skim mozzarella cheese
1 (10-ounce) package frozen chopped spinach, thawed, drained, and squeezed dry
2 teaspoons dried basil
½ teaspoon ground nutmeg
⅛ teaspoon pepper
2 tablespoons grated Parmesan cheese

1 Preheat oven to 350°.

2 Cook pasta according to package directions, omitting any salt and oil. Rinse with cold water; drain.

3 Spread ¾ cup pasta sauce in a 9 x 13-inch baking dish.

4 Combine cheeses, spinach, and next 3 ingredients in a large bowl; stir well. Fill pasta shells with mixture (see tip below), and place in a single layer in the baking dish. Top shells with remaining sauce, and sprinkle with Parmesan cheese. Cover and bake at 350° for 30 minutes. Uncover and bake an additional 5 minutes.

Per Serving: Calories 348 Fat 7.9g (saturated 4.6g) Protein 23.0g Carbohydrate 46.8g Fiber 6.7g Cholesterol 24mg Sodium 820mg
Exchanges: 3 Starch, 2 Lean Meat

Tip: For a super-easy way to stuff the pasta shells, pour the spinach and cheese mixture into a heavy-duty zip-top plastic bag; cut off one corner, and squeeze the mixture into shells.

Tortellini with Pesto Sauce

Makes 4 (1¼-cup) servings

1   (9-ounce) package fresh cheese tortellini
1   (16-ounce) package frozen broccoli stir-fry vegetable mix
1   (8-ounce) carton reduced-fat sour cream
2   tablespoons pesto
¼   teaspoon salt
¼   cup (1 ounce) preshredded fresh Parmesan cheese
⅛   teaspoon coarsely ground black pepper

1 Cook tortellini and vegetables in 3 quarts boiling water 5 to 7 minutes or until vegetables and pasta are tender. Drain and return to pan.

2 Combine sour cream, pesto, and salt, stirring well. Gently stir sour cream mixture into pasta mixture. Sprinkle with Parmesan cheese and pepper. Serve immediately.

Per Serving: Calories 340 Fat 14.1g (saturated 5.7g) Protein 18.9g
Carbohydrate 36.6g Fiber 3.0g Cholesterol 37mg Sodium 648mg
Exchanges: 2 Starch, 1 Vegetable, 1 High-Fat Meat, 1 Fat

"Frozen vegetables are just as nutritious as fresh ones— just watch out for the frozen ones with high-fat cheesy or buttery sauces."

Chapter 21

Meats

Sloppy Joes

Makes 6 servings (serving size: ¾ cup meat and 1 bun)

1½ pounds ground round (see note below)
¾ cup chopped onion
1 cup chopped green bell pepper
1 (10¾-ounce) can condensed reduced-fat, reduced-sodium tomato soup, undiluted
1 (8-ounce) can tomato sauce
½ cup ketchup
1 tablespoon Worcestershire sauce
1 teaspoon prepared mustard
⅛ teaspoon garlic powder
6 (0.9-ounce) sesame seed hamburger buns, toasted

1 Cook meat, onion, and bell pepper in a large skillet over medium-high heat until browned, stirring to crumble. Drain well; return meat mixture to pan.

2 Stir in soup and next 5 ingredients; simmer 10 minutes, stirring often. Serve on toasted buns.

Per Serving: Calories 308 Fat 9.1g (saturated 3.1g) Protein 29.3g
Carbohydrate 26.0g Fiber 2.2g Cholesterol 65mg Sodium 657mg
Exchanges: 2 Starch, 3 Lean Meat

"Be sure to use ground round instead of regular ground beef—the ground round has about 15 percent fat compared to about 27 percent for ground beef."

Peppery Mushroom Burgers

Makes 4 servings

1   (8-ounce) package sliced mushrooms, divided
1   pound ground round (see note on page 350)
2   teaspoons instant minced onion
2   teaspoons low-sodium Worcestershire sauce
1   teaspoon freshly ground black pepper
Cooking spray
¼   cup dry red wine or fat-free beef broth
¼   cup water

1 Coarsely chop 1½ cups sliced mushrooms. Combine beef, chopped mushrooms, onion, and Worcestershire sauce in a bowl; shape into 4 equal patties about ¼ inch thick. Sprinkle pepper evenly on both sides of patties.

2 Coat a 12-inch nonstick skillet with cooking spray, and place over medium-high heat until hot. Add patties, and cook 5 to 6 minutes on each side or until done. Transfer to a serving platter, and keep warm.

3 Add wine, water, and remaining mushrooms to pan; cook over medium heat 3 minutes or until mushrooms are tender, stirring constantly and scraping pan to loosen browned bits. Pour mushroom mixture over patties.

Per Serving: Calories 181 Fat 6.0g (saturated 2.1g) Protein 26.3g
Carbohydrate 4.4g Fiber 0.9g Cholesterol 66mg Sodium 78mg
Exchanges: 1 Vegetable, 3 Lean Meat

Sausage-Beef Enchiladas

Makes 6 servings (serving size: 2 enchiladas)

 1 **pound ground round**
½ **pound lean turkey breakfast sausage**
½ **cup chopped onion**
 1 **tablespoon ground cumin**
 1 **tablespoon chili powder**
 1 **teaspoon pepper**
 2 **(10-ounce) cans enchilada sauce**
 1 **(11-ounce) can whole-kernel corn, drained**
12 **(6-inch) corn tortillas**
Cooking spray
¾ **cup (3 ounces) shredded reduced-fat sharp Cheddar cheese**
½ **cup thinly sliced green onions**

1 Preheat oven to 350°.

2 Combine first 6 ingredients in a large nonstick skillet; cook over medium-high heat until meat is browned, stirring to crumble. Drain. Stir in 1 can enchilada sauce and the corn. Cook over medium-high heat until thoroughly heated.

3 Stack tortillas between 2 damp paper towels. Microwave at HIGH 1 minute. Spoon meat mixture down center of each tortilla; roll up tortillas. Arrange in a 9 x 13-inch baking dish coated with cooking spray.

4 Pour remaining can of enchilada sauce over tortillas. Cover and bake at 350° for 25 minutes. Uncover, sprinkle with shredded cheese and green onions, and bake an additional 5 minutes.

Per Serving: Calories 408 Fat 14.5g (saturated 4.7g) Protein 31.9g
Carbohydrate 40.5g Fiber 4g Cholesterol 88mg Sodium 737mg
Exchanges: 2½ Starch, 3½ Lean Meat, 1 Fat

Stuffed Peppers

Makes 6 servings (serving size: 1 stuffed pepper)

6   green bell peppers (about 2 pounds)
¾   pound ground round
1¾ cups finely chopped onion (about 1 large)
1   garlic clove, minced
1   (29-ounce) can tomato sauce
1½ cups hot cooked long-grain rice
1   teaspoon dried marjoram
1   teaspoon dried oregano
⅛   teaspoon salt
¼   teaspoon black pepper
6   tablespoons reduced-fat sour cream

1 Preheat oven to 350°.

2 Cut tops off peppers. Remove and discard seeds and membranes. Finely chop pepper tops, discarding stems; set chopped pepper aside. Cook pepper cups in boiling water to cover for 5 minutes. Drain peppers; set aside.

3 Cook chopped pepper, meat, onion, and garlic in a Dutch oven over medium-high heat 5 minutes or until meat is browned and vegetables are tender, stirring to crumble meat. Add tomato sauce and next 5 ingredients. Bring to a boil; reduce heat and simmer, uncovered, 6 minutes, stirring often.

4 Spoon meat mixture evenly into pepper cups; place cups in a 7 x 11-inch baking dish. Add hot water to dish to depth of ½ inch. Bake, uncovered, at 350° for 20 to 25 minutes or until thoroughly heated. Serve each pepper topped with 1 tablespoon sour cream.

Per Serving: Calories 241 Fat 6.0g (saturated 2.6g) Protein 17.9g
Carbohydrate 31.1g Fiber 5.2g Cholesterol 40mg Sodium 922mg
Exchanges: 2 Starch, 2 Lean Meat

Quick Beef Stroganoff

Makes 5 servings (serving size: 1 cup meat mixture and ½ cup noodles)

1   pound ground round
1½ cups chopped onion (about 1 large)
1   (8-ounce) package sliced mushrooms
¼   teaspoon salt
1   (10 ¾-ounce) can condensed reduced-fat, reduced-sodium cream
     of mushroom soup
½   cup reduced-fat (2%) milk
1   (8-ounce) carton reduced-fat sour cream
3   cups hot cooked egg noodles (about 6 ounces uncooked pasta)
½   teaspoon freshly ground black pepper

1 Cook beef and onion in a large nonstick skillet over medium-high heat until browned, stirring to crumble; drain and set aside. Wipe drippings from pan with paper towels.

2 Add mushrooms to pan; place over medium-high heat and sauté 3 minutes or until browned. Add meat mixture, salt, soup and milk; cook over medium heat 5 minutes or until thoroughly heated, stirring occasionally. Stir in sour cream and cook until thoroughly heated. Serve over hot cooked egg noodles and sprinkle with freshly ground pepper.

Per Serving: Calories 400 Fat 14.2g (saturated 6.6g) Protein 30.0g
Carbohydrate 37.3g Fiber 2.4g Cholesterol 108mg Sodium 449mg
Exchanges: 2 Starch, 1 Vegetable, 3 Medium-Fat Meat

"Instead of the traditional rich cream sauce, my secret for stroganoff is a can of low-fat soup and a carton of reduced-fat sour cream."

Extra-Easy Lasagna

Makes 6 servings

1   pound ground round
1   (26-ounce) bottle tomato-basil pasta sauce
Cooking spray
6   uncooked lasagna noodles
1   (15-ounce) carton part-skim ricotta cheese
1½ cups (6 ounces) shredded part-skim mozzarella cheese
¼   cup hot water

1 Cook meat in a large nonstick skillet over medium heat until browned, stirring to crumble. Drain; wipe drippings from pan with paper towels. Return meat to pan. Stir in pasta sauce.

2 Preheat oven to 375°.

3 Spread one-third of meat mixture in bottom of a 7 x 11-inch baking dish coated with cooking spray. Arrange 3 noodles over meat mixture; top with half of ricotta cheese and half of mozzarella cheese. Repeat layers, ending with last one-third of meat mixture. Slowly pour water into dish. Tightly cover baking dish with heavy-duty foil.

4 Bake at 375° for 45 minutes. Uncover and bake an additional 10 minutes. Let stand 10 minutes before serving.

Per Serving: Calories 406 Fat 15.2g (saturated 8.1g) Protein 36.4g
Carbohydrate 29.1g Fiber 1.8g Cholesterol 81mg Sodium 650mg
Exchanges: 2 Starch, 4 Lean Meat

"Lasagna's not off limits! Just make it with lean beef and low-fat cheeses!"

Barbecue Meat Loaf

Makes 8 servings

2	slices whole wheat bread, torn into pieces
1	cup frozen chopped onion, celery, and bell pepper blend, thawed
1½	pounds ground round
½	cup low-fat (1%) milk
½	cup egg substitute
1	teaspoon bottled minced garlic
¼	teaspoon salt
¼	teaspoon black pepper

Cooking spray
½ cup barbecue sauce

1 Preheat oven to 350°.

2 Combine bread and vegetable blend in food processor; process until chopped. Add meat and next 5 ingredients. Pulse until combined.

3 Shape meat mixture into a 4 x 8-inch loaf; place on a rack in a roasting pan coated with cooking spray. Bake at 350° for 1 hour and 10 minutes. Spread barbecue sauce over meat loaf. Bake 10 minutes.

Per Serving: Calories 178 Fat 4.7g (saturated 1.7g) Protein 21.9g
Carbohydrate 11.0g Fiber 0.3g Cholesterol 50mg Sodium 383mg
Exchanges: 1 Starch, 3 Very Lean Meat

"Using a frozen vegetable blend (like the one in this recipe) is an easy way to include some vegetable servings with your meat."

Beef Fajitas

Makes 6 servings

1   pound lean flank steak
Cooking spray
½   cup bottled chili sauce
1   tablespoon salt-free Creole seasoning
3   cups onion strips
3   cups red bell pepper strips
6   (8-inch) fat-free flour tortillas

1 Cut steak diagonally across the grain into ¼-inch-thick slices. Coat a large nonstick skillet with cooking spray, and place over medium-high heat until hot. Add steak, chili sauce, and Creole seasoning; cook 4 minutes or until meat is done. Remove from pan, and set aside. Wipe drippings from pan with a paper towel.

2 Coat pan with cooking spray; place over medium-high heat until hot. Add onion and red bell pepper, and cook 7 minutes or until tender, stirring often.

3 Wrap tortillas in wax paper; microwave at HIGH 30 seconds. Spoon steak and vegetable mixture over warm tortillas; wrap or fold tortillas around mixture.

Per Serving: Calories 317 Fat 9.3g (saturated 3.8g) Protein 19.7g
Carbohydrate 38.6g Fiber 3.4g Cholesterol 41mg Sodium 697mg
Exchanges: 2 Starch, 2 Lean Meat, 1 Vegetable

Mexican Steaks

Makes 4 servings

Cooking spray
- 1   teaspoon vegetable oil
- 1   pound lean boneless sirloin steak, cut into 4 pieces
- 1   (8-ounce) jar picante sauce
- 2   tablespoons lime juice
- ¼   teaspoon pepper
- ¼   cup chopped fresh cilantro or parsley

1 Coat a large nonstick skillet with cooking spray; add oil. Place over medium-high heat until hot. Add steaks; cook 2 minutes on each side.

2 Combine picante sauce, lime juice, and pepper; pour over steaks. Cover, reduce heat, and simmer 10 minutes. Sprinkle with cilantro.

Per Serving: Calories 225 Fat 7.0g (saturated 2.3g) Protein 27.9g
Carbohydrate 12.1g Fiber 1.6g Cholesterol 69mg Sodium 929mg
Exchanges: 1 Starch, 3 Lean Meat

Tip: If you want a slightly thicker sauce, use chunky salsa instead of picante sauce.

Gingered Beef Stir-Fry

Makes 2 servings

½   cup low-salt beef broth
1   tablespoon reduced-sodium soy sauce
1   teaspoon cornstarch
1   teaspoon ground ginger
¼   to ½ teaspoon dried crushed red pepper
Cooking spray
1   teaspoon dark sesame oil
½   pound lean boneless sirloin steak, cut crosswise into ¼-inch-thick
    slices
1   (9-ounce) package frozen sugar snap peas

1 Stir together first 5 ingredients.

2 Coat a wok or large nonstick skillet with cooking spray; drizzle oil around top of wok, coating sides. Heat at medium-high (375°) until hot. Add steak, and stir-fry 2 minutes or until lightly browned. Add peas and broth mixture to wok; stir-fry 3 minutes or until broth mixture thickens.

Per Serving: Calories 249 Fat 8.7g (saturated 2.5g) Protein 28.8g
Carbohydrate 12.1g Fiber 3.7g Cholesterol 69mg Sodium 316mg
Exchanges: 1 Starch, 3 Lean Meat

"Stir-frying is one of my favorite ways to cook. It's quick and it's low-fat because you only need a bit of oil."

Slow-Cook Shredded Beef with Peppers

Makes 6 (¾-cup) servings

1½   pounds top sirloin steak
Cooking spray
   1   (16-ounce) package frozen bell pepper stir-fry
   1   (8-ounce) can tomato sauce
   ¼   cup steak sauce
   ½   cup bottled chipotle salsa
   1   tablespoon sugar
   ¼   teaspoon salt

1 Trim fat from steak. Place steak in a 4½-quart electric slow cooker coated with cooking spray. Top with pepper stir-fry. Combine tomato sauce and steak sauce; pour over peppers. Cover with lid; cook on high-heat setting for 1 hour. Reduce heat setting to low; cook 7 hours.

2 Remove steak from slow cooker with a slotted spoon. Shred steak with 2 forks. Return shredded steak to slow cooker; turn off slow cooker. Add salsa, sugar, and salt. Cover and let stand 15 minutes.

Per Serving: Calories 272 Fat 9.0g (saturated 3.4g) Protein 35.0g
Carbohydrate 11.5g Fiber 1.8g Cholesterol 101mg Sodium 647mg
Exchanges: 2 Vegetable, 3 Lean Meat

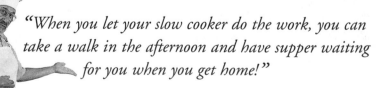

"When you let your slow cooker do the work, you can take a walk in the afternoon and have supper waiting for you when you get home!"

All-American Grilled Steak

Makes 6 servings

1   cup dry red wine
¼   cup ketchup
3   tablespoons Dijon mustard
2   tablespoons red wine vinegar
½   teaspoon salt
½   teaspoon dried thyme
½   teaspoon pepper
2   garlic cloves, minced
1   bay leaf
1   (1½-pound) lean boneless top round steak (about 1½ inches thick)
Cooking spray

1 Combine first 9 ingredients in a large heavy-duty zip-top plastic bag; add steak, and seal bag. Marinate in refrigerator 8 hours or overnight, turning occasionally.

2 Preheat the grill.

3 Remove steak from bag, reserving marinade; discard bay leaf. Place marinade in a saucepan. Bring to a boil; remove from heat. Place steak on grill rack coated with cooking spray; grill 5 minutes on each side or until desired degree of doneness, basting with reserved marinade. Slice steak diagonally across grain into thin slices.

Per Serving: Calories 177 Fat 5.2g (saturated 1.7g) Protein 26.2g
Carbohydrate 4.5g Fiber 0.2g Cholesterol 65mg Sodium 599mg
Exchanges: 3½ Lean Meat

Garlic-Herb Steaks

Makes 4 servings

¼ cup minced garlic
1 tablespoon minced fresh rosemary
¼ teaspoon salt
¼ teaspoon freshly ground black pepper
4 (4-ounce) beef tenderloin steaks
Cooking spray

1 Combine first 4 ingredients; sprinkle mixture evenly on meat. Cover and chill 1 hour.

2 Preheat the grill.

3 Place meat on grill rack coated with cooking spray; grill, covered, 10 minutes on each side or until desired degree of doneness.

Per Serving: Calories 192 Fat 8.5g (saturated 3.2g) Protein 24.3g
Carbohydrate 3.1g Fiber 0.2g Cholesterol 70mg Sodium 201mg
Exchanges: 3½ Lean Meat

"The combination of garlic and fresh rosemary adds out-of-this-world flavor to the steaks, so there's no need to cook them with any extra fat."

Beef Brisket in Beer

Makes 11 servings (serving size: 3 ounces brisket and 3 tablespoons gravy)

1	(4-pound) beef brisket
½	teaspoon black pepper
1	cup sliced onion, separated into rings
½	cup chili sauce
3	tablespoons brown sugar
2	garlic cloves, crushed
1	(12-ounce) bottle beer
2½	tablespoons all-purpose flour
¼	teaspoon salt
½	cup plus 2 tablespoons water

1 Preheat oven to 350°.

2 Trim fat from brisket; place in a 9 x 13-inch baking dish. Sprinkle top of brisket with pepper; arrange onion rings over brisket.

3 Combine chili sauce and next 3 ingredients; pour over brisket. Cover, and bake at 350° for 3 hours. Uncover, and bake an additional 20 minutes or until brisket is tender. Place brisket on a serving platter, reserving cooking liquid. Set brisket aside, and keep warm.

4 Pour 1½ cups cooking liquid into a small saucepan. Place flour and salt in a bowl. Gradually add water, blending with a whisk; add to saucepan. Bring to a boil, and cook 2 minutes or until gravy thickens, stirring constantly. Serve gravy with brisket.

Per Serving: Calories 229 Fat 6.9g (saturated 2.3g) Protein 30.7g
Carbohydrate 9.7g Fiber 0.5g Cholesterol 82mg Sodium 326mg
Exchanges: 1 Starch, 4 Very Lean Meat

Roast with Peppered Gravy

Makes 8 servings

1   (2-pound) lean boneless eye of round roast
Cooking spray
1   medium onion, cut into wedges
1¼ cups low-salt beef broth
¼   cup red wine vinegar
1   teaspoon dried crushed red pepper
½   teaspoon salt
¼   teaspoon pepper
2   large garlic cloves, crushed
3   tablespoons all-purpose flour
2   tablespoons water

1 Trim fat from roast. Heat a 4-quart pressure cooker coated with cooking spray over medium-high heat. Add roast; cook until browned on all sides. Add onion and next 6 ingredients. Following manufacturer's instructions, close lid securely; bring to high pressure over high heat. Adjust heat to medium; cook 40 minutes.

2 Remove pressure cooker from heat; place under cold running water. Remove lid. Transfer roast to a serving platter; set aside, and keep warm.

3 Skim fat from pan juices. Combine flour and water, stirring until smooth; add flour mixture to juices in pan. Cook over medium heat, stirring constantly, until thick. Serve gravy with roast.

Per Serving: Calories 176 Fat 5.5g (saturated 2.0g) Protein 24.4g
Carbohydrate 5.2g Fiber 0.6g Cholesterol 56mg Sodium 200mg
Exchanges: 3 Lean Meat

Veal Marsala

Makes 4 servings

Cooking spray
  2 (8-ounce) packages sliced mushrooms
 ½ cup all-purpose flour
 ½ teaspoon salt
 ¼ teaspoon cracked black pepper
  1 pound veal scallopine or very thin veal cutlets
  1 tablespoon margarine
  1 cup Marsala wine

1 Coat a large nonstick skillet with cooking spray; place over medium-high heat until hot. Add mushrooms, and sauté 5 minutes or until tender. Set aside; keep warm.

2 Place flour, salt, and pepper in a large heavy-duty zip-top plastic bag. Seal bag; shake to mix. Add veal; seal bag, and shake to coat veal. Remove veal from flour mixture, reserving 2 tablespoons flour mixture; discard remaining flour mixture.

3 Melt margarine in pan over medium-high heat. Add veal, and cook 3 minutes on each side or until browned. Transfer veal to a serving platter, and keep warm.

4 Combine wine and reserved 2 tablespoons flour mixture, stirring well with a whisk; add to pan. Bring to a boil, scraping browned particles that cling to bottom of pan. Spoon mushroom mixture and wine mixture over veal.

Per Serving: Calories 253 Fat 7.0g (saturated 1.6g) Protein 27.0g
Carbohydrate 19.7g Fiber 1.9g Cholesterol 94mg Sodium 434mg
Exchanges: 1 Starch, 1 Vegetable, 3 Lean Meat

"Serve the veal the traditional Italian way—over pasta! Use 8 ounces of dry pasta to get 4 cups cooked."

Rosemary-Grilled Veal Chops

Makes 4 servings

4   (6-ounce) lean veal loin chops (¾ inch thick)
Olive oil-flavored cooking spray
1½   teaspoons dried rosemary, crushed
¾   teaspoon lemon-pepper seasoning

1 Preheat the grill.

2 Trim fat from veal. Coat both sides of veal with cooking spray. Combine rosemary and lemon-pepper seasoning; rub evenly over veal.

3 Place veal on grill rack coated with cooking spray; grill, covered, 5 to 6 minutes on each side or until done.

Per Serving: Calories 187 Fat 10.7g (saturated 4.5g) Protein 21.1g
Carbohydrate 0.3g Fiber 0.1g Cholesterol 88mg Sodium 140mg
Exchanges: 3 Lean Meat

"To get a bigger flavor punch from dried herbs, crush them between your fingers."

Osso Buco

Makes 4 servings

4 (5-ounce) veal shanks
2 tablespoons all-purpose flour
Olive oil-flavored cooking spray
½ cup chopped onion
½ cup chopped carrot
2 (14½-ounce) cans no-salt-added diced tomatoes, undrained
½ cup dry white wine
½ cup low-salt beef broth
½ teaspoon salt
¼ teaspoon freshly ground black pepper

1 Trim fat from veal; dredge shanks in flour. Coat a Dutch oven with cooking spray; place over medium-high heat until hot. Add veal; cook until browned on all sides. Remove veal; set aside, and keep warm. Wipe drippings from pan with a paper towel.

2 Coat pan with cooking spray; place over medium-high heat until hot. Add onion and carrot, and sauté until tender. Stir in tomatoes and next 4 ingredients; add veal. Bring to a boil; cover, reduce heat, and simmer 20 minutes. Uncover and simmer 30 minutes or until veal is tender.

3 Transfer each veal shank to an individual soup bowl; spoon vegetable mixture over veal.

Per Serving: Calories 220 Fat 3.8g (saturated 1.0g) Protein 25.6g
Carbohydrate 20.4g Fiber 2.4g Cholesterol 98mg Sodium 443mg
Exchanges: 1 Starch, 1 Vegetable, 3 Very Lean Meat

"Osso buco is a classic Italian dish of veal shanks and tomatoes. Its traditional garnish is gremolata—a mixture of equal parts minced parsley, lemon rind, and minced garlic."

Moussaka

Makes 6 servings

2 small eggplants (about ¾ pound each)
Olive-oil flavored cooking spray
1 pound lean ground lamb or ground round
1 (27½-ounce) jar fat-free chunky spaghetti sauce with mushrooms
1 teaspoon ground cinnamon
½ teaspoon pepper
1 (10¾-ounce) can condensed reduced-fat, reduced-sodium cream of mushroom soup, undiluted
⅓ cup water
2 tablespoons dry breadcrumbs
2 tablespoons preshredded fresh Parmesan cheese

1 Preheat oven to 375°. Peel eggplants; cut crosswise into ¼-inch-thick slices. Place on a baking sheet coated with cooking spray. Coat slices with cooking spray. Bake at 375° for 25 minutes or until tender and lightly browned, turning once. Cool slightly.

2 Cook meat in a large nonstick skillet over medium-high heat until browned; stir to crumble. Drain. Wipe drippings from pan.

3 Return meat to pan; add spaghetti sauce, cinnamon, and pepper. Bring to a boil; reduce heat, and simmer, uncovered, 5 minutes or until thick, stirring occasionally.

4 Coat a 7 x 11-inch baking dish with cooking spray; place half of eggplant in dish; top with half of meat. Repeat layers with remaining eggplant and remaining meat. Combine soup and water, stirring until smooth; pour over meat. Combine breadcrumbs and cheese; sprinkle over soup mixture. Bake, uncovered, at 375° for 25 minutes or until browned and bubbly.

Per Serving: Calories 248 Fat 7.8g (saturated 2.7g) Protein 22.0g
Carbohydrate 23.3g Fiber 4.2g Cholesterol 59mg Sodium 685mg
Exchanges: 1 Starch, 1 Vegetable, 2 Medium-Fat Meat

Lamb Shish Kabob

Makes 6 servings (serving size: 2 kabobs)

¼   cup dry red wine
1½ tablespoons dried oregano
1½ tablespoons dried mint flakes
2   tablespoons lemon juice
2   teaspoons olive oil
4   garlic cloves, minced
1½ pounds lean cubed boned leg of lamb
12 (1-inch) squares green bell pepper (about 2 large)
12 large cherry tomatoes
1   large onion, cut into 12 wedges
Cooking spray

1 Combine first 6 ingredients in a large heavy-duty zip-top plastic bag; add lamb, and seal bag. Marinate lamb in refrigerator 12 to 24 hours.

2 Preheat the grill.

3 Remove lamb from bag, reserving marinade. Place marinade in a saucepan. Bring to a boil; remove from heat. Thread lamb, peppers, tomatoes, and onion alternately onto 12 (10-inch) skewers. Place kabobs on grill rack coated with cooking spray; grill, covered, 5 minutes on each side or until desired degree of doneness, turning and basting frequently with marinade.

Per Serving: Calories 195 Fat 7.1g (saturated 2.1g) Protein 24.6g
Carbohydrate 8.3g Fiber 1.8g Cholesterol 73mg Sodium 78mg
Exchanges: 1 Vegetable, 3 Lean Meat

Chili-Style Lamb Chops

Makes 6 servings

6 (5-ounce) lean lamb loin chops (¾ inch thick)
Cooking spray
⅔ cup chili sauce
¼ cup low-sugar orange marmalade
2 teaspoons dark brown sugar
½ teaspoon coarse-grained mustard
¼ teaspoon salt
¼ teaspoon chili powder
⅛ teaspoon pepper

1 Preheat oven to 350°.

2 Trim fat from chops; place chops in a 7 x 11-inch baking dish coated with cooking spray.

3 Combine chili sauce and remaining ingredients in a small saucepan; cook over medium heat, stirring constantly, until marmalade melts and brown sugar dissolves.

4 Pour chili sauce mixture evenly over chops. Bake, uncovered, at 350° for 50 minutes or to desired degree of doneness.

Per Serving: Calories 200 Fat 6.2g (saturated 2.2g) Protein 19.0g
Carbohydrate 16.0g Fiber 0.4g Cholesterol 60mg Sodium 917mg
Exchanges: 1 Starch, 2 Lean Meat

Tip: Even though the mustard and chili sauce have practically no fat, they do add a good bit of sodium to the recipe. If you need to cut back on sodium, leave out the ¼ teaspoon of salt, and decrease the chili sauce to ½ cup.

Mint-Grilled Lamb Chops

Makes 4 servings

⅓ cup chopped fresh mint leaves
2 tablespoons plain low-fat yogurt
2 garlic cloves, crushed
4 (5-ounce) lean lamb loin chops (1 inch thick)
1 small lemon, cut in half
Cooking spray
Fresh mint sprigs (optional)

1 Preheat the grill.

2 Combine first 3 ingredients in a small bowl.

3 Trim fat from lamb. Rub lemon halves on both sides of lamb. Place lamb on grill rack coated with cooking spray; grill, covered, 5 minutes. Turn lamb; spread mint mixture evenly over lamb. Grill 5 additional minutes or to desired degree of doneness. Garnish with mint sprigs, if desired.

Per Serving: Calories 173 Fat 7.9g (saturated 2.9g) Protein 23.0g
Carbohydrate 1.2g Fiber 0.1g Cholesterol 74mg Sodium 66mg
Exchanges: 3 Lean Meat

Tip: Look for the words "loin" and "leg" on meat package labels when you're trying to pick out the leanest cuts of lamb and pork.

Cowboy Pork Chops and Pinto Beans

Makes 4 servings

4   (6-ounce) bone-in center-cut loin pork chops
2   teaspoons ground cumin, divided
½   teaspoon garlic powder
¼   teaspoon ground red pepper
¼   teaspoon salt
Cooking spray
1   (16-ounce) can pinto beans, undrained
½   cup salsa
¼   cup barbecue sauce
2   green onions, sliced

1 Preheat broiler.

2 Trim fat from chops. Sprinkle both sides of pork with 1 teaspoon cumin, the garlic powder, ground red pepper, and salt.

3 Place pork on rack of a broiler pan coated with cooking spray; broil 5 minutes on each side or until pork is done.

4 Combine remaining 1 teaspoon cumin, the beans, and remaining 3 ingredients in a medium saucepan. Bring to a boil; reduce heat, and simmer, uncovered, 8 minutes, stirring occasionally. Serve pork with beans.

Per Serving: Calories 317 Fat 12.1g (saturated 3.7g) Protein 28.6g
Carbohydrate 22.6g Fiber 1.0g Cholesterol 72mg Sodium 415mg
Exchanges: 1 Starch, 1 Vegetable, 3 Medium-Fat Meat

Picante Pork Chops

Makes 8 servings

8 (6-ounce) bone-in center-cut pork loin chops
Cooking spray
1 (16-ounce) jar thick-and-chunky picante sauce

1 Trim fat from pork chops. Coat a large skillet with cooking spray, and place over medium-high heat until hot. Add pork; cook until browned on both sides.

2 Pour one-fourth of picante sauce into a 3½- to 4-quart electric slow cooker coated with cooking spray; add pork. Top with remaining picante sauce. Cover with lid; cook on high-heat setting 1 hour. Reduce heat setting to low; cook 8 hours. Or cover and cook on high-heat setting 4 hours. Reserve 1 cup sauce. Serve 2 tablespoons sauce over each chop.

Per Serving: Calories 119 Fat 4.7g (saturated 1.6g) Protein 15.2g
Carbohydrate 3.0g Fiber 0.4g Cholesterol 41mg Sodium 273mg
Exchanges: 2 Lean Meat

"To get the extra fat out of the sauce in the slow cooker, plop an ice cube into the sauce, and scoop out the ice with a slotted spoon. The hardened fat will magically stick on the ice cube."

Marmalade Pork Chops

Makes 4 servings

Cooking spray
1 teaspoon olive oil
4 (4-ounce) lean boneless pork loin chops, trimmed
2 teaspoons lemon-pepper seasoning
2 tablespoons cider vinegar
¼ cup low-sugar orange marmalade

1 Coat a large nonstick skillet with cooking spray; add oil, and place over medium-high heat until hot. Sprinkle pork on both sides with seasoning; add pork to pan, and cook 5 minutes on each side or until done. Remove from pan, and keep warm.

2 Add vinegar to pan; stir in marmalade. Return pork to pan, turning once to coat; cook 1 minute or until thoroughly heated. Serve immediately.

Per Serving: Calories 221 Fat 9.4g (saturated 3.0g) Protein 25.1g
Carbohydrate 7.1g Fiber 0.0g Cholesterol 71mg Sodium 245mg
Exchanges: ½ Starch, 3 Lean Meat

"Think pork is fatty? Compared to 20 years ago, today's pork loin has 77% less fat and 53% fewer calories! The amount of fat in many cuts of pork is similar to that in lean beef and chicken."

Pork Chops with Dijon Cream Sauce

Makes 4 servings

4 (4-ounce) boneless center-cut pork loin chops (½ inch thick)
½ teaspoon salt
½ teaspoon coarsely ground black pepper
Cooking spray
⅓ cup fat-free, less-sodium chicken broth
1½ tablespoons Dijon mustard
⅓ cup fat-free half-and-half or evaporated fat-free milk

1 Trim fat from chops. Sprinkle both sides of pork evenly with salt and pepper. Coat a large nonstick skillet with cooking spray; place over medium-high heat until hot. Add pork to pan, and cook 3 to 4 minutes on each side or until browned. Remove pork from pan, and keep warm.

2 Add chicken broth to pan, stirring to loosen browned bits. Combine mustard and half-and-half; add to pan. Reduce heat, and simmer 7 minutes or until sauce thickens slightly. Spoon sauce over pork.

Per Serving: Calories 201 Fat 9.0g (saturated 3.0g) Protein 23.5g
Carbohydrate 2.7g Fiber 0.1g Cholesterol 68mg Sodium 567mg
Exchanges: 3 Lean Meat

"You can save yourself a lot of calories just by trimming the fat from chops before you cook 'em."

Corn Bread-Crusted Pork Cutlets

Makes 4 servings

¾ cup low-fat buttermilk
1 tablespoon Dijon mustard
1 tablespoon grated onion
½ teaspoon poultry seasoning
4 (4-ounce) pork cutlets (about ½ inch thick)
1 (6-ounce) box seasoned corn bread stuffing mix, coarsely crushed
Cooking spray

1 Combine first 4 ingredients in a large baking dish. Add pork, turning to coat. Marinate in refrigerator 30 minutes, turning pork occasionally.

2 Preheat oven to 425°.

3 Place stuffing mix into a shallow dish or pie plate. Remove pork from baking dish, and discard marinade. Dredge both sides of pork cutlets in stuffing mix, pressing to coat thoroughly. Place pork cutlets on a baking sheet coated with cooking spray, and bake at 425° for 15 to 20 minutes or until done.

Per Serving: Calories 284 Fat 8.0g (saturated 2.3g) Protein 27.6g
Carbohydrate 23.4g Fiber 1.4g Cholesterol 67mg Sodium 427mg
Exchanges: 1½ Starch, 3 Lean Meat

Bourbon Pork Tenderloin with Peach Chutney

Makes 4 servings

1   (1-pound) pork tenderloin
½   cup bourbon (see tip below)
2   tablespoons coarse-ground mustard
1   tablespoon chopped fresh thyme leaves or 1 teaspoon dried thyme
Cooking spray
2   cups coarsely chopped peeled fresh or frozen peaches, thawed
¼   cup hot mango chutney
1   tablespoon sliced green onions

1 Trim fat from pork. Combine bourbon, mustard, and thyme in a large heavy-duty zip-top plastic bag. Add pork; marinate in refrigerator 8 hours.

2 Preheat the grill.

3 Remove pork from bag, reserving marinade. Place pork on grill rack coated with cooking spray; grill, covered, 9 minutes. Turn, and brush with marinade. Cover and grill 7 to 9 minutes or until meat thermometer inserted into thickest part of pork registers 160°.

4 Stir together peaches, chutney, and onions. Cut pork into thin slices, and spoon chutney mixture over slices.

Per Serving: Calories 250 Fat 4.7g (saturated 1.4g) Protein 25.2g
Carbohydrate 24.6g Fiber 1.8g Cholesterol 79mg Sodium 453mg
Exchanges: ½ Starch, 1 Fruit, 3 Lean Meat

Tip: The bourbon gives the pork a slightly sweet taste, and when the pork is cooked, most of the calories in the alcohol evaporate.

Indonesian Pork Tenderloin

Makes 4 servings

1   (1-pound) pork tenderloin
2   tablespoons low-sodium soy sauce
2   tablespoons reduced-fat creamy peanut butter
1   teaspoon dried crushed red pepper
2   garlic cloves, minced
Cooking spray
¼   cup pineapple preserves or orange marmalade

1 Preheat oven to 375°.

2 Trim fat from pork. Combine soy sauce and next 3 ingredients. Spread soy sauce mixture over pork.

3 Place pork on a rack in a roasting pan coated with cooking spray. Insert meat thermometer into thickest part of pork. Bake, uncovered, at 375° for 30 minutes. Brush pork with pineapple preserves. Bake an additional 10 minutes or until meat thermometer registers 160°, basting often with preserves. Let stand 10 minutes before slicing.

Per Serving: Calories 247 Fat 7.3g (saturated 2.0g) Protein 26.7g
Carbohydrate 17.5g Fiber 3.2g Cholesterol 79mg Sodium 327mg
Exchanges: 1 Starch, 3 Lean Meat

"Good news for all you pork fans: The amount of fat in pork tenderloin is about the same as that in a skinless chicken breast."

Garlic-Studded Pork Loin Roast

Makes 8 servings

1 (2¼-pound) boned pork loin roast
1 tablespoon white vinegar
2 large garlic cloves, thinly sliced
½ teaspoon salt
½ teaspoon cracked black pepper
Cooking spray
Sage, oregano, and rosemary sprigs (optional)

1 Preheat oven to 350°.

2 Trim fat from meat. Rub surface of roast with vinegar. Make several 1-inch-deep slits in meat, and stuff with garlic slices. Sprinkle ½ teaspoon salt and ½ teaspoon pepper over meat.

3 Place roast on a broiler pan coated with cooking spray. Insert meat thermometer into thickest portion of meat. Bake at 350° for 1 hour and 40 minutes or until thermometer registers 160° (slightly pink). Garnish with herb sprigs, if desired.

Per Serving: Calories 185 Fat 10.6g (saturated 3.7g) Protein 20.4g
Carbohydrate 0.4g Fiber 0.0g Cholesterol 69mg Sodium 199mg
Exchanges: 3 Lean Meat

Spinach Fettuccine with Bacon-Cheese Sauce

Makes 6 (1-cup) servings

1	tablespoon margarine
2	teaspoons minced garlic
4	slices Canadian bacon, diced
5	tablespoons all-purpose flour
1½	cups low-fat (1%) milk
3	tablespoons light cream cheese
½	teaspoon freshly ground black pepper
¾	cup grated Parmesan cheese
6	cups hot cooked spinach fettuccine (about 12 ounces uncooked pasta)

1 Melt margarine in a large nonstick skillet over medium-high heat. Add garlic and bacon; cook until bacon begins to brown. Reduce heat to medium; stir in flour. Gradually add milk, stirring with a whisk until blended. Cook, stirring constantly, until thick and bubbly. Stir in cream cheese and pepper; cook, stirring constantly, until blended. Add Parmesan cheese; cook, stirring often, until cheese melts.

2 Add sauce to hot pasta; toss. Serve immediately.

Per Serving: Calories 355 Fat 10.0g (saturated 4.6g) Protein 19.2g
Carbohydrate 45.9g Fiber 2.4g Cholesterol 27mg Sodium 610mg
Exchanges: 3 Starch, 1½ Lean Meat

"Canadian bacon is a good substitute for regular pork bacon because it has 11 grams less fat per ounce."

Ham and Hash Brown Casserole

Makes 8 servings (serving size: one-eighth of casserole)

1¾ cups evaporated fat-free milk, divided
3 tablespoons all-purpose flour
¾ teaspoon dry mustard
¼ teaspoon pepper
⅛ teaspoon salt
4 ounces light processed cheese, cubed
1 (8-ounce) carton reduced-fat sour cream
8 ounces reduced-fat, 33%-less-sodium ham, chopped
1 (32-ounce) package frozen cubed hash brown potatoes with onions and peppers, thawed
Cooking spray

1 Preheat oven to 350°.

2 Combine ½ cup milk and the flour, stirring until smooth. Combine flour mixture, remaining 1¼ cups milk, the mustard, pepper, and salt in a medium saucepan, stirring well. Cook over medium heat, stirring constantly, until thick and bubbly. Remove from heat; add cheese, stirring until cheese melts. Stir in sour cream.

3 Combine cheese mixture, ham, and potatoes in a large bowl, stirring well. Spoon potato mixture into a 9 x 13-inch baking dish coated with cooking spray. Cover and bake at 350° for 30 minutes. Uncover and bake an additional 30 to 35 minutes or until golden.

Per Serving: Calories 254 Fat 6.6g (saturated 1.5g) Protein 16.1g
Carbohydrate 33.3g Fiber 1.7g Cholesterol 35mg Sodium 570mg
Exchanges: 2 Starch, ½ Very Lean Meat, 1 Fat

Maple-Glazed Ham

Makes 3 servings

1 (8-ounce) slice lean cooked ham (about ¼ inch thick)
　　(see tip below)
⅛ teaspoon ground black pepper
Cooking spray
2 tablespoons maple syrup
1 teaspoon Dijon mustard
2 teaspoons cider vinegar

1 Cut ham slice into 3 pieces; sprinkle with pepper.

2 Coat a large nonstick skillet with cooking spray; place over medium-high heat until hot. Add ham to pan, and cook 3 minutes on each side. Transfer ham to a serving platter, and keep warm.

3 Combine maple syrup, mustard, and vinegar in pan. Cook over medium heat, stirring constantly, 1 minute or until mixture is smooth and bubbly. Spoon glaze over ham.

Per Serving: Calories 147　Fat 4.4g　(saturated 1.4g)　Protein 15.9g
Carbohydrate 10.5g　Fiber 0.0g　Cholesterol 40mg　Sodium 953mg
Exchanges: ½ Starch, 2 Lean Meat

Tip: Even though lean ham is very low in fat, it's high in sodium. If you need to cut down on sodium, look for reduced-sodium ham at the grocery store meat counter or deli.

Chapter 22

Poultry

Southwestern Chicken Casserole

Makes 8 servings

¾ cup chopped green bell pepper (about 1 large)
1½ cups chopped onion (about 1 large)
Cooking spray
3 cups frozen cooked diced chicken breast, thawed (about 1 pound)
1 (10-ounce) can diced tomatoes and green chilies
1 (14-ounce) can no-salt-added diced tomatoes
1 (10¾-ounce) can condensed reduced-fat, reduced-sodium cream of chicken soup, undiluted
1 (10¾-ounce) can condensed reduced-fat, reduced-sodium cream of mushroom soup, undiluted
12 (6-inch) corn tortillas, cut into quarters
1½ cups (6 ounces) shredded reduced-fat sharp Cheddar cheese

1 Preheat oven to 325°. Place a large nonstick skillet over medium-high heat until hot. Coat bell pepper and onion with cooking spray; add to pan. Sauté 4 minutes or until tender. Add chicken and cook until thoroughly heated. Remove from heat; stir in tomatoes and soups.

2 Place one-third of tortillas in a 9 x 13-inch baking dish coated with cooking spray. Top with one-third of chicken mixture; sprinkle with ¼ cup cheese. Repeat layers twice, reserving ½ cup cheese for topping.

3 Bake, uncovered, at 325° for 35 minutes. Sprinkle with remaining ½ cup cheese, and bake an additional 5 minutes. Let stand 5 minutes before serving.

Per Serving: Calories 265 Fat 4.7g (saturated 1.9g) Protein 22.7g
Carbohydrate 33.1g Fiber 3.8g Cholesterol 44mg Sodium 673mg
Exchanges: 2 Starch, 1 Vegetable, 2 Lean Meat

Barbecued Chicken Pizza

Makes 6 servings (serving size: 1 slice)

Cooking spray
  1 (10-ounce) package refrigerated pizza crust
  ¾ cup chopped green bell pepper (about 1 large)
  ¾ cup thinly sliced red onion wedges (about 1 small)
  ½ cup honey barbecue sauce
1½ cups shredded cooked chicken breast (see note below)
  1 cup (4 ounces) shredded part-skim mozzarella cheese

1 Preheat oven to 425°.

2 Coat a 12-inch pizza pan or large baking sheet with cooking spray. Unroll dough, and press into pan. Bake at 425° for 5 minutes or until crust begins to brown.

3 Meanwhile, coat a medium nonstick skillet with cooking spray; place over medium-high heat until hot. Add green pepper and onion; sauté 5 minutes or until vegetables are tender.

4 Spread barbecue sauce evenly over baked crust; top evenly with shredded chicken. Arrange vegetable mixture evenly over chicken; sprinkle with cheese. Bake 8 minutes or until crust is golden and cheese melts.

Per Serving: Calories 238 Fat 5.5g (saturated 2.2g) Protein 16.2g
Carbohydrate 21.3g Fiber 0.9g Cholesterol 35mg Sodium 889mg
Exchanges: 1 Starch, 1 Vegetable, 2 Lean Meat

"For pizza pronto, use roasted chicken breasts from the deli. But first be sure to remove the skin—that's where the fat is!"

Chicken Pot Pie

Makes 6 servings

  1 (10¾-ounce) can condensed reduced-fat, reduced-sodium cream of
       mushroom soup, undiluted
  ½ cup fat-free milk
  ½ teaspoon salt
  ¼ teaspoon pepper
  3 cups chopped cooked chicken breast
  2 cups frozen peas and carrots, thawed
  ½ cup chopped onion (about 1 small)
  ½ cup thinly sliced celery
  1 (2-ounce) jar sliced pimiento, drained
1½ cups low-fat biscuit mix
  ¾ cup fat-free milk
  1 large egg, lightly beaten
Butter-flavored cooking spray
  1 tablespoon preshredded fresh Parmesan cheese

1 Preheat oven to 375°.

2 Combine soup and next 3 ingredients in saucepan; bring to a
boil. Reduce heat, and simmer, uncovered, 1 minute, stirring
constantly until smooth. Add chicken, peas and carrots, and next 3
ingredients, stirring well. Bring to a boil; cover, reduce heat, and
simmer 5 minutes. Pour mixture into a 7 x 11-inch baking dish.

3 Combine biscuit mix, ¾ cup milk, and egg; stir until smooth.
Spread evenly over chicken mixture; coat with cooking spray.
Sprinkle with cheese. Bake, uncovered, at 375° for 30 to 35 minutes
or until golden.

Per Serving: Calories 293 Fat 5.3g (saturated 1.6g) Protein 25.2g
Carbohydrate 35.0g Fiber 2.3g Cholesterol 85mg Sodium 883mg
Exchanges: 2 Starch, 1 Vegetable, 2½ Very Lean Meat, ½ Fat

Quick Curried Chicken

Makes 4 servings (serving size: 1 cup chicken mixture and ½ cup rice)

 2   tablespoons light butter
 1   pound skinless, boneless chicken breasts, cut into bite-size pieces
1½   cups chopped onion (about 1 large)
 1   (10¾-ounce) can condensed reduced-fat, reduced-sodium cream
        of chicken soup, undiluted
 2   teaspoons curry powder
 ¼   teaspoon salt
 ¾   cup reduced-fat sour cream
 3   cups hot cooked rice
 2   tablespoons chopped green onions (optional)
 1   tablespoon raisins (optional)

1 Melt butter in a large skillet over medium-high heat. Add chicken and onion; sauté 8 minutes or until chicken is done and onion is tender.

2 Stir in soup, curry powder, and salt; bring to a boil, stirring constantly. Stir in sour cream.

3 Serve chicken over rice. If desired, top with green onions or raisins.

Per Serving: Calories 384 Fat 11.6g (saturated 6.6g) Protein 32.8g
Carbohydrate 35.4g Fiber 2.3g Cholesterol 105mg Sodium 583mg
Exchanges: 2½ Starch, 3 Lean Meat

Creamy Poblano Chicken

Makes 5 (1-cup) servings

1   teaspoon light butter
2   cups chopped sweet onion (about 2 medium)
2   poblano chilies, seeded and diced (about 1⅓ cups)
3   garlic cloves, minced
1   pound skinless, boneless chicken breast halves, cut into bite-sized
      pieces
¼   teaspoon salt
½   teaspoon pepper
1   (10¾-ounce) can condensed reduced-fat, reduced-sodium cream
      of mushroom or chicken soup, undiluted
1   (8-ounce) container reduced-fat sour cream
¾   cup (3 ounces) shredded reduced-fat sharp Cheddar cheese

1 Melt butter in a Dutch oven over medium-high heat. Add onion, chili peppers, and garlic; sauté 5 to 7 minutes or until onion is tender. Add chicken, salt, and pepper; cook, stirring frequently, 10 to 12 minutes or until chicken is done.

2 Stir in soup and sour cream until smooth. Add cheese, and cook 7 to 8 minutes or until cheese melts.

Per Serving: Calories 309 Fat 11.9g (saturated 6.7g) Protein 30.9g
Carbohydrate 19.4g Fiber 3.1g Cholesterol 94mg Sodium 583mg
Exchanges: 1 Starch, 4 Lean Meat

"Substituting a can of reduced-fat, reduced-sodium soup for regular soup is a great way to cut the fat but keep the creaminess and flavor."

Chicken-Almond Stir-Fry

Makes 5 servings (serving size: 1 cup chicken mixture and ½ cup rice)

- 2   teaspoons vegetable oil
- 4   (4-ounce) skinless, boneless chicken breast halves, cut into thin strips
- ¼   cup sliced almonds
- 1   (16-ounce) package frozen broccoli, carrots, and water chestnuts, thawed and drained
- ½   cup low-sodium soy sauce
- ⅓   cup pineapple juice
- 1   tablespoon cornstarch
- 1   tablespoon brown sugar
- ½   teaspoon ground ginger
- 2½   cups hot cooked long-grain rice

1 Heat oil over medium-high heat in a large nonstick skillet. Add chicken and almonds; sauté 5 minutes. Stir in vegetables; cover and cook 8 minutes, stirring once.

2 Combine soy sauce and next 4 ingredients; add to chicken, stirring gently. Cook, stirring constantly, 3 to 4 minutes or until mixture thickens slightly. Serve over rice.

Per Serving: Calories 299 Fat 6.5g (saturated 0.8g) Protein 27.4g
Carbohydrate 32.5g Fiber 4.0g Cholesterol 53mg Sodium 1054mg
Exchanges: 2 Starch, 3 Lean Meat

"If you don't have time to chop fresh vegetables, use frozen! You'll still get all those veggie benefits: fiber, vitamins, and minerals."

Chicken Parmesan Tenders

Makes 4 servings

¼   cup all-purpose flour
⅛   teaspoon pepper
1   pound chicken tenders
1   large egg, lightly beaten
⅓   cup fat-free milk
½   cup Italian-seasoned breadcrumbs
2   tablespoons grated Parmesan cheese
Cooking spray
1   cup pasta sauce

1 Preheat oven to 425°.

2 Combine flour and pepper in a heavy-duty zip-top plastic bag. Add chicken; seal bag, and shake well to coat.

3 Combine egg and milk in a shallow bowl. Combine breadcrumbs and Parmesan cheese in a separate bowl. Dip chicken in egg mixture; dredge in breadcrumb mixture.

4 Place chicken on a large baking sheet coated with cooking spray. Lightly coat chicken with cooking spray; bake, covered, at 425° for 20 minutes. Uncover and bake an additional 10 minutes or until done. Heat pasta sauce, and serve with chicken.

Per Serving: Calories 285 Fat 5.5g (saturated 1.7g) Protein 33.6g
Carbohydrate 23.0g Fiber 1.9g Cholesterol 122mg Sodium 813mg
Exchanges: 1½ Starch, 4 Very Lean Meat

Jalapeño-Peach Chicken

Makes 6 servings (serving size: 1 chicken breast half)

6   (4-ounce) skinless, boneless chicken breast halves
½   teaspoon salt
½   teaspoon black pepper
Cooking spray
½   cup peach preserves
1   large jalapeño pepper, seeded and minced (see note below)
2   tablespoons balsamic vinegar

1 Preheat oven to 350°.

2 Sprinkle chicken with salt and black pepper. Place in a 9 x 13-inch baking dish coated with cooking spray. Combine peach preserves, jalapeño pepper, and vinegar, stirring with a whisk. Spoon mixture over chicken. Bake at 350° for 50 minutes or until done.

Per Serving: Calories 267 Fat 10.6g (saturated 3.0g) Protein 23.7g
Carbohydrate 19.9g Fiber 0.1g Cholesterol 73mg Sodium 282mg
Exchanges: 1 Starch, 3 Lean Meat

"Be sure to wear some type of gloves when you're handling fresh jalapeños or you'll get burned."

Garlic Chicken

Makes 4 servings
(serving size: 1 chicken breast half and 2 tablespoons sauce)

4   (4-ounce) skinless, boneless chicken breast halves
¼   cup water
½   cup all-purpose flour
¼   teaspoon salt
¼   cup light butter
2   tablespoons minced garlic
1   cup apple juice
3   tablespoons fresh lemon juice
½   teaspoon pepper

1 Place 1 chicken breast in a heavy-duty zip-top plastic bag with 1 tablespoon water; seal bag. Flatten chicken to ¼-inch thickness, using a meat mallet or rolling pin. Repeat procedure with remaining chicken breast halves.

2 Place flour in a shallow bowl. Sprinkle chicken with salt. Dredge chicken in flour.

3 Melt 2 tablespoons butter in a large nonstick skillet over medium-high heat; add half of chicken. Cook 4 to 5 minutes on each side or until chicken is done. Remove chicken from pan, and keep warm. Repeat procedure with remaining 2 tablespoons butter and the chicken.

4 Add garlic, apple juice, lemon juice, and pepper to pan, scraping pan to loosen browned bits. Bring to a boil; cook 6 to 8 minutes or until reduced to ½ cup. Serve immediately over chicken.

Per Serving: Calories 322 Fat 16.7g (saturated 7.1g) Protein 26.1g
Carbohydrate 17.8g Fiber 0.6g Cholesterol 93mg Sodium 291mg
Exchanges: 1 Starch, 3 Lean Meat, 1 Fat

Oven-Fried Chicken

Makes 4 servings

½ cup all-purpose flour
½ teaspoon black pepper
½ teaspoon ground red pepper
½ teaspoon garlic powder
½ cup low-fat buttermilk
1 large egg, lightly beaten
1½ cups saltine crackers, coarsely crushed (about 35 crackers)
2 teaspoons paprika
¼ teaspoon salt
4 (4-ounce) skinless, boneless chicken breast halves
Cooking spray
1 tablespoon vegetable oil

1 Preheat oven to 450°.

2 Combine first 4 ingredients in a shallow bowl. Combine buttermilk and egg in another shallow bowl; stir well with a whisk. Combine cracker crumbs, paprika, and salt; pour into a shallow bowl.

3 Dredge chicken breasts, one at a time, in flour mixture; dip in buttermilk mixture, and dredge in crumb mixture.

4 Coat a baking sheet with cooking spray. Pour oil in center of baking sheet; heat oil at 450° for 3 minutes. Remove pan from oven; reduce heat to 400°. Spread hot oil with a spatula over an area just large enough to accommodate chicken. Quickly place chicken in oil on pan. Bake at 400° for 10 minutes; turn, and bake an additional 10 minutes or until done.

Per Serving: Calories 266 Fat 8.2g (saturated 1.8g) Protein 30.4g
Carbohydrate 15.9g Fiber 1.0g Cholesterol 120mg Sodium 448mg
Exchanges: 1 Starch, 3 Lean Meat

Praline Chicken

Makes 6 servings

6 (4-ounce) skinless, boneless chicken breast halves
2 teaspoons Creole seasoning
2 tablespoons light butter
⅓ cup maple syrup
2 tablespoons brown sugar
⅓ cup chopped pecans, toasted

1 Sprinkle chicken evenly with Creole seasoning.

2 Melt butter in a large nonstick skillet over medium heat. Add chicken; cook 4 minutes on each side or until browned. Remove chicken from pan; set aside, and keep warm.

3 Add maple syrup and sugar to drippings in pan; bring to a boil. Stir in pecans; cook 1 minute. Spoon pecan mixture over chicken.

Per Serving: Calories 315 Fat 17.3g (saturated 4.8g) Protein 24.6g Carbohydrate 15.8g Fiber 0.6g Cholesterol 79mg Sodium 298mg
Exchanges: 1 Starch, 3 Lean Meat, 1 Fat

"Have you heard the news? You need to have a little bit of fat in your diet, and it needs to be the 'good-for-you' kind of fat found in nuts."

Grilled Tomato-Basil Chicken

Makes 4 servings

½   teaspoon minced garlic
 4   plum tomatoes, quartered
¾   cup balsamic vinegar
¼   cup fresh basil leaves
½   teaspoon pepper
¼   teaspoon salt
 4   (4-ounce) skinless, boneless chicken breast halves
 4   plum tomatoes, halved
Cooking spray

1 Combine first 6 ingredients in a food processor; process until smooth. Set aside ¼ cup tomato mixture; cover and chill.

2 Place chicken in a large heavy-duty zip-top plastic bag. Pour remaining tomato mixture over chicken. Seal bag; turn bag to coat chicken. Marinate in refrigerator 8 hours.

3 Preheat the grill.

4 Remove chicken from marinade, discarding marinade. Coat tomato halves with cooking spray. Place chicken and tomato halves on grill rack coated with cooking spray; grill, covered, 5 to 6 minutes on each side or until chicken is done and tomato is cooked but still slightly firm. Place chicken on 4 individual serving plates; top each chicken breast half with 1 tablespoon reserved tomato mixture. Arrange 2 grilled tomato halves on each plate with chicken.

Per Serving: Calories 160 Fat 3.6g (saturated 0.9g) Protein 26.5g
Carbohydrate 4.7g Fiber 1.2g Cholesterol 70mg Sodium 143mg
Exchanges: 1 Vegetable, 3½ Very Lean Meat

Citrus Chicken with Roasted Corn Relish

Makes 4 servings

4 (6-ounce) skinless bone-in chicken breast halves
⅔ cup fresh lime juice, divided
½ teaspoon ground cumin
½ teaspoon chili powder
¼ teaspoon salt
¼ teaspoon ground red pepper, divided
Olive oil-flavored cooking spray
1 (16-ounce) package frozen corn with peppers and onions, thawed
2 tablespoons chopped fresh cilantro

1 Place chicken in a heavy-duty zip-top plastic bag. Reserve 1 tablespoon lime juice; pour remaining juice over chicken. Seal bag, and shake until chicken is well coated. Marinate in refrigerator 1 hour, turning bag occasionally.

2 Preheat broiler.

3 Combine cumin, chili powder, salt, and ⅛ teaspoon red pepper. Remove chicken from marinade; discard marinade. Sprinkle chicken with cumin mixture. Place on rack; broil 25 minutes. Turn and broil 15 minutes or until done. Set aside; keep warm.

4 Coat a large nonstick skillet with cooking spray. Place pan over medium-high heat until hot. Add corn and ⅛ teaspoon red pepper; sauté until corn is lightly browned and tender. Spoon corn evenly onto individual plates; top with chicken. Drizzle evenly with reserved 1 tablespoon lime juice; sprinkle with chopped cilantro.

Per Serving: Calories 237 Fat 4.1g (saturated 0.9g) Protein 29.1g
Carbohydrate 20.2g Fiber 1.5g Cholesterol 72mg Sodium 226mg
Exchanges: 1 Starch, 1 Vegetable, 3 Very Lean Meat

Baked Buffalo Chicken

Makes 2 servings (serving size: 2 thighs and 2 tablespoons dressing)

Cooking spray
1½ teaspoons vegetable oil
  4 small chicken thighs (about 1½ pounds), skinned
  ¼ cup hot sauce
  2 tablespoons reduced-calorie margarine, melted
  2 tablespoons water
  1 tablespoon white vinegar
  1 teaspoon celery seeds
  ⅛ teaspoon pepper
  ¼ cup reduced-fat blue cheese dressing

1 Preheat oven to 400°.

2 Coat a nonstick skillet with cooking spray; add oil. Place over medium-high heat until hot. Add chicken; cook 4 minutes on each side. Transfer chicken to a 7 x 11-inch baking dish coated with cooking spray.

3 Combine hot sauce and next 5 ingredients; pour over chicken. Bake, uncovered, at 400° for 25 minutes. Serve with blue cheese dressing.

Per Serving: Calories 310 Fat 17.2g (saturated 3.8g) Protein 30.1g Carbohydrate 7.7g Fiber 0.4g Cholesterol 118mg Sodium 811mg
Exchanges: ½ Starch, 4 Lean Meat, 1 Fat

"These chicken thighs may remind you of the spicy wings served at your local sports grill. But instead of being fried, these are quickly browned in a skillet and baked in a tangy hot sauce mixture."

Moroccan Chicken

Makes 4 servings

4 (4-ounce) skinless, boneless chicken thighs
1½ teaspoons ground cumin
2 teaspoons grated lemon rind
½ teaspoon ground ginger
½ teaspoon salt
¼ teaspoon ground cinnamon
2 garlic cloves, minced
2 teaspoons olive oil
Cooking spray

1 Trim fat from chicken.

2 Combine cumin and next 5 ingredients in a large bowl. Brush olive oil evenly over chicken. Add chicken to bowl, and toss well to coat chicken with spice mixture. Let stand 10 minutes.

3 Preheat the grill.

4 Place chicken on grill rack coated with cooking spray. Cover; grill 6 minutes on each side or until done.

Per Serving: Calories 161 Fat 6.9g (saturated 1.5g) Protein 22.5g
Carbohydrate 1.3g Fiber 0.2g Cholesterol 94mg Sodium 392mg
Exchanges: 3 Lean Meat

"Whether you call it grilling or barbecuing, it's a great low-fat way to cook because you're not cooking the food in fat."

"The Works" Deep-Pan Pizza

Makes 6 servings (serving size: 1 slice)

1 (6.5-ounce) package pizza crust mix
⅓ cup yellow cornmeal
⅔ cup hot water
Cooking spray
1 (8-ounce) can no-salt-added tomato sauce
1 teaspoon dried Italian seasoning
6 ounces turkey breakfast sausage, cooked and crumbled
1 (6-ounce) can sliced mushrooms, drained
⅓ cup drained peperoncini pepper rings
1 cup (4 ounces) shredded part-skim mozzarella cheese

1 Preheat oven to 425°.

2 Combine first 3 ingredients in a bowl; stir with a fork until well blended. Shape dough into a ball; coat with cooking spray. Cover and let stand 5 minutes. Press dough in bottom and 1 inch up sides of a 10-inch cast iron skillet coated with cooking spray; prick several times with a fork. Bake at 425° for 5 minutes.

3 Combine tomato sauce and Italian seasoning; spread over crust. Top with sausage, mushrooms, peppers, and cheese. Bake at 425° for 20 minutes or until cheese melts and crust is golden. Let stand 10 minutes before serving.

Per Serving: Calories 279 Fat 9.6g (saturated 3.9g) Protein 14.5g
Carbohydrate 33.2g Fiber 1.9g Cholesterol 33mg Sodium 582mg
Exchanges: 2 Starch, 1 Medium-Fat Meat, 1 Fat

Red Beans and Rice

Makes 4 servings (serving size: 1 cup rice and 1 cup bean mixture)

1   **family-size bag quick-cooking boil-in-bag rice**
1   **slice turkey bacon, diced**
1   **large onion, minced**
4   **garlic cloves, minced**
1   **(16-ounce) can red kidney beans, rinsed and drained**
1   **(14.5-ounce) can no-salt-added stewed tomatoes, undrained**
4   **ounces low-fat smoked turkey sausage, cut into bite-size pieces**
1   **teaspoon hot sauce**
½   **teaspoon freshly ground black pepper**
2   **bay leaves**

1 Cook boil-in-bag rice according to package directions, omitting salt and fat.

2 Cook bacon in a 3-quart saucepan over medium heat until browned. Add onion and garlic; cook until crisp-tender, stirring often. Stir in beans and remaining 5 ingredients. Bring to a boil; cover, reduce heat, and simmer 20 minutes, stirring occasionally.

3 Remove and discard bay leaves. Spoon rice into individual bowls; top evenly with bean mixture.

Per Serving: Calories 409 Fat 4.8g (saturated 1.3g) Protein 15.5g
Carbohydrate 74.4g Fiber 8.3g Cholesterol 26mg Sodium 601mg
Exchanges: 4½ Starch, 1 Vegetable, ½ High-Fat Meat

"Low-fat smoked turkey sausage has the same great smoky flavor as pork sausage, but a whole lot less fat."

Southwestern-Style Spaghetti

Makes 3 servings

  4   ounces uncooked spaghetti
  8   ounces freshly ground raw turkey breast (see tip below)
  ½   cup frozen chopped onion
1½   teaspoons bottled minced garlic
  1   teaspoon ground cumin
  1   (14½-ounce) can salsa-style tomatoes, undrained
  ½   cup picante sauce
  ¼   cup chopped fresh cilantro
  2   tablespoons shredded part-skim mozzarella cheese

1 Cook spaghetti according to package directions, omitting salt and fat. Drain well.

2 Cook turkey and next 3 ingredients in a large saucepan over medium heat until browned, stirring to crumble turkey. Add tomatoes and picante sauce; simmer, uncovered, 10 minutes or until mixture thickens slightly. Spoon over spaghetti; sprinkle with cilantro and cheese.

Per Serving: Calories 305 Fat 2.7g (saturated 1.0g) Protein 27.1g
Carbohydrate 43.6g Fiber 4.0g Cholesterol 48mg Sodium 917mg
Exchanges: 2 Starch, 2 Vegetable, 3 Very Lean Meat

Tip: Be sure to check the ground turkey label to see that you're getting white meat only. If the label only states "ground turkey," you're getting white and dark meat, plus skin, so the fat content may end up being higher than ground beef.

Old-Fashioned Turkey Hash

Makes 4 servings (serving size: about 1 cup hash and 1 slice toast)

Cooking spray
1 teaspoon vegetable oil
2 cups cubed cooked turkey breast (see note below)
1 cup chopped onion (about 1 large)
1 (15-ounce) can sliced cooked potatoes, drained
⅔ cup fat-free milk
½ cup fat-free, less-sodium chicken broth
¼ teaspoon freshly ground black pepper
¼ teaspoon ground thyme
4 (¾-ounce) slices light wheat sandwich bread, toasted
Additional freshly ground black pepper (optional)

1 Coat a large nonstick skillet with cooking spray; add oil, and place over medium-high heat until hot. Add turkey, chopped onion, and potatoes; cook 10 minutes or until onion is tender and potatoes are browned, stirring occasionally.

2 Add milk and next 3 ingredients to turkey mixture; bring to a boil. Reduce heat, and simmer, uncovered, 8 to 10 minutes or until desired consistency, stirring occasionally.

3 Cut slices of toast in half diagonally, and place on 4 individual serving plates. Spoon hash mixture evenly over toast. Sprinkle with additional pepper, if desired.

Per Serving: Calories 224 Fat 4.4g (saturated 1.1g) Protein 25.3g
Carbohydrate 21.4g Fiber 4.9g Cholesterol 27mg Sodium 1054mg
Exchanges: 1½ Starch, 3 Very Lean Meat

"Here's a great way to use your leftover holiday turkey! To keep your hash as low-fat as possible, be sure to use the white meat instead of the dark."

Cranberry-Ginger Grilled Turkey

Makes 4 servings

1 (8-ounce) can whole-berry cranberry sauce
1 teaspoon ground ginger
1½ teaspoons brown sugar
½ teaspoon dry mustard
¼ teaspoon pepper
2 (8-ounce) turkey tenderloins
Cooking spray

1 Preheat the grill.

2 Combine first 5 ingredients, stirring well. Reserve ½ cup cranberry mixture to heat and serve with turkey. Use remaining cranberry mixture for basting.

3 Place tenderloins on grill rack coated with cooking spray; grill, uncovered, 8 to 10 minutes on each side or until meat thermometer registers 170°, basting often with cranberry mixture.

4 Slice tenderloins diagonally across grain into thin slices. Bring reserved ½ cup cranberry mixture to a boil in a small saucepan. Serve with turkey.

Per Serving: Calories 226 Fat 3.1g (saturated 0.9g) Protein 25.1g
Carbohydrate 23.6g Fiber 0.2g Cholesterol 58mg Sodium 71mg
Exchanges: 1 Starch, ½ Fruit, 3 Very Lean Meat

"I like this recipe so much that I also make it with boneless chicken breast halves. I cook the chicken for about 5 minutes on each side."

Turkey Cutlets in Orange Sauce

Makes 4 servings

2   teaspoons vegetable oil
1   pound turkey cutlets
2   tablespoons all-purpose flour
⅓   cup sliced green onions (about 2)
⅛   teaspoon garlic powder
¾   cup orange juice
1   tablespoon reduced-sodium soy sauce
Orange slices (optional)

1 Heat oil over high heat in a large nonstick skillet. Dredge turkey cutlets in flour. Add turkey to hot pan, and cook 3 minutes or until browned, turning once. Remove turkey from pan.

2 Reduce heat to medium-high; add green onions and garlic powder; sauté 30 seconds. Add orange juice and soy sauce to pan; bring to a boil. Cook, stirring constantly, 2 minutes or until mixture thickens slightly.

3 Return turkey to pan; simmer 2 minutes or until turkey is thoroughly heated. Transfer to a serving platter; garnish with orange slices, if desired.

Per Serving: Calories 190 Fat 4.1g (saturated 1.0g) Protein 27.7g
Carbohydrate 8.8g Fiber 0.3g Cholesterol 68mg Sodium 194mg
Exchanges: ½ Fruit, 4 Very Lean Meat

"This zesty orange sauce is really good on other low-fat meats like pork tenderloin or chicken breast halves."

Chapter 23

Salads

Melon Wedges with Raspberry Dressing

Makes 5 servings

1   honeydew or cantaloupe (about 3 pounds)
2   tablespoons no-sugar-added raspberry spreadable fruit
2   tablespoons vanilla low-fat yogurt
2   tablespoons raspberry vinegar
½   cup raspberries

1 Peel and seed melon, and cut into 20 wedges. Arrange 4 wedges on each of 5 individual salad plates. Set aside.

2 Combine spreadable fruit, yogurt, and vinegar in a small bowl; stir with a wire whisk until smooth. Spoon dressing over wedges; sprinkle with raspberries.

Per Serving: Calories 126 Fat 0.9g (saturated 0.5g) Protein 2.8g
Carbohydrate 29.9g Fiber 4.3g Cholesterol 0mg Sodium 29mg
Exchanges: 2 Fruit

"Yogurt is full of bone-protecting calcium, so it's a great thing to keep in the fridge for a snack or a low-fat dessert topping."

Cantaloupe Salad

Makes 7 (¾-cup) servings

¼ cup low-fat mayonnaise
2 tablespoons thawed orange juice concentrate
4 cups cubed cantaloupe
⅓ cup seedless green or red grapes

1 Combine mayonnaise and orange juice concentrate, stirring well. Combine cantaloupe and grapes. Add mayonnaise mixture to fruit; stir well.

Per Serving: Calories 75 Fat 1.0g (saturated 0.1g) Protein 1.1g
Carbohydrate 17.2g Fiber 1.1g Cholesterol 0mg Sodium 89mg
Exchange: 1 Fruit

"Cantaloupe is a super melon! One-fourth of a cantaloupe has as much vitamin A and vitamin C as most people need in a day—these are the vitamins that can help you reduce the risk of heart disease and certain cancers."

Refreshing Melon Duo

Makes 4 (1-cup) servings

2 cups cubed honeydew melon
2 cups cubed cantaloupe
¼ cup white balsamic vinegar (see tip below)
1 teaspoon brown sugar

1 Combine honeydew and cantaloupe in a bowl.

2 Combine vinegar and brown sugar, stirring until sugar dissolves.

3 Pour vinegar mixture over melon, and stir gently to coat. Cover and chill.

Per Serving: Calories 62 Fat 0.3g (saturated 0.2g) Protein 1.1g
Carbohydrate 15.9g Fiber 1.7g Cholesterol 0mg Sodium 16mg
Exchange: 1 Fruit

Tip: Make sure to use white balsamic vinegar because the brown balsamic will discolor the fruit.

Autumn Fruit Salad

Makes 7 (1-cup) servings

1 (8-ounce) carton low-fat sour cream
¼ cup packed brown sugar
½ teaspoon ground cinnamon
1¾ cups sliced banana
1½ cups chopped apple
1½ cups chopped pear
1¼ cups orange sections

1 Combine first 3 ingredients, stirring well.

2 Combine banana and remaining 3 ingredients in a large bowl; toss well. Spoon sour cream mixture evenly over fruit.

Per Serving: Calories 171 Fat 4.4g (saturated 2.5g) Protein 2.0g
Carbohydrate 34.0g Fiber 4.9g Cholesterol 12mg Sodium 16mg
Exchanges: ½ Starch, 1½ Fruit, 1 Fat

"Sometimes I make this sweet fruit salad for dessert. And the creamy dressing is fantastic on any kind of fresh fruit!"

Cranberry Waldorf Salad

Makes 6 servings (serving size: about ½ cup)

2 Red Delicious apples, cored and chopped
¼ cup chopped celery
1½ tablespoons chopped walnuts (see note below)
⅓ cup cranberry-orange relish

1 Combine all ingredients in a medium bowl; toss well.

2 Cover and chill for at least 30 minutes before serving.

Per Serving: Calories 67 Fat 1.3g (saturated 0.1g) Protein 0.6g
Carbohydrate 14.0g Fiber 1.7g Cholesterol 0mg Sodium 6mg
Exchange: 1 Fruit

"If you're nuts about nuts (like I am!), you'll be happy to hear that walnuts, peanuts, and almonds contain compounds that not only protect against heart disease, but also help lower cholesterol."

Mandarin Salad

Makes 4 (1¼-cup) servings

6 cups torn romaine lettuce
1 (11-ounce) can mandarin oranges in light syrup, drained
¼ cup coarsely chopped pecans, toasted
2 thinly sliced green onions
Freshly ground black pepper
⅓ cup reduced-fat Italian dressing

1 Combine first 5 ingredients in a large bowl. Add dressing just before serving, and toss gently.

Per Serving: Calories 118 Fat 7.5g (saturated 0.8g) Protein 2.3g
Carbohydrate 12.6g Fiber 3.0g Cholesterol 1mg Sodium 169mg
Exchanges: ½ Fruit, 1 Vegetable, 1½ Fat

"Just a small sprinkling of toasted nuts can add crunch and flavor to a salad."

Corn Bread Salad

Makes 12 (1-cup) servings

1 (7.5-ounce) package corn muffin mix
6 cups torn romaine lettuce
1 cup chopped seeded tomato
1 cup chopped green bell pepper
¾ cup chopped red onion
3 turkey bacon slices, cooked and crumbled
⅔ cup light ranch dressing

1 Preheat oven, and prepare muffin mix according to package directions using an 8-inch square baking pan and water instead of milk. Cool 10 minutes.

2 Remove corn bread from pan, reserving half of corn bread for another use. Cut remaining corn bread into cubes. Place cubes on a baking sheet; bake at 400° for 10 minutes or until crisp and lightly browned. Place in a large bowl.

3 Add lettuce and next 4 ingredients to bowl; toss well. Pour dressing over salad, and toss well. Serve immediately.

Per Serving: Calories 131 Fat 5.7g (saturated 1.2g) Protein 2.4g
Carbohydrate 17.5g Fiber 1.6g Cholesterol 7mg Sodium 334mg
Exchanges: 1 Starch, 1 Fruit

"I slashed the calories and fat in these yummy corn bread croutons by baking, not frying them!"

Classic Layered Salad

Makes 7 (1-cup) servings

½   cup light mayonnaise
2   tablespoons grated Parmesan cheese
2   teaspoons sugar
⅛   teaspoon salt
⅛   teaspoon black pepper
1   large ripe tomato, cut into 8 wedges
4   cups torn iceberg lettuce
2   cups small cauliflower florets
½   cup thinly sliced red onion (about 1 small)
1   tablespoon bottled real bacon bits

1 Combine first 5 ingredients; stir well with a whisk. Arrange tomato wedges in bottom of a 2-quart serving bowl. Top with lettuce and cauliflower. Spread mayonnaise mixture over cauliflower. Top with onion and bacon bits. Cover with plastic wrap, and chill 8 hours or overnight before serving.

Per Serving: Calories 65 Fat 2.4g (saturated 0.8g) Protein 2.1g
Carbohydrate 9.5g Fiber 1.3g Cholesterol 2mg Sodium 261mg
Exchanges: 2 Vegetable

"Cauliflower is in the cruciferous clan of vegetables, and this clan helps fight against cancer and protect against strokes."

Mediterranean Tossed Salad

Makes 4 (1½-cup) servings

6 cups torn leaf lettuce
½ cup thinly sliced red onion (about 1 small)
¼ cup sliced ripe olives
½ cup (2 ounces) crumbled feta cheese with basil and sun-dried tomatoes
1 teaspoon dried oregano
⅓ cup low-fat balsamic vinaigrette

1 Combine first 5 ingredients in a large bowl; pour vinaigrette over salad, and toss gently. Serve immediately.

Per Serving: Calories 86 Fat 4.1g (saturated 2.3g) Protein 3.3g
Carbohydrate 9.7g Fiber 2.0g Cholesterol 13mg Sodium 507mg
Exchanges: 2 Vegetable, 1 Fat

"I've found that when I fill up on a simple green salad before my main course, I'm not as likely to overeat."

Succotash Slaw

Makes 5 (¾-cup) servings

1 cup frozen baby lima beans
2 cups shredded cabbage
1 cup frozen whole-kernel corn, thawed
½ cup chopped red bell pepper
¼ cup sliced green onions
¼ cup light ranch dressing
2 tablespoons reduced-fat sour cream

1 Cook lima beans according to package directions, omitting salt. Drain; rinse with cold water, and drain again.

2 Combine lima beans, cabbage, and next 3 ingredients in a large bowl. Combine dressing and sour cream. Pour dressing mixture over cabbage mixture; toss well.

Per Serving: Calories 128 Fat 4.1g (saturated 0.8g) Protein 4.5g
Carbohydrate 20.1g Fiber 4.4g Cholesterol 6mg Sodium 148mg
Exchanges: 1 Starch, 1 Vegetable, 1 Fat

"In my neck of the woods, succotash is a side dish made from lima beans, corn, and red or green bell peppers. Since I'm trying to eat more vegetables, I thought I'd add some cabbage to the mix."

Hot Bacon Slaw

Makes 3 (1-cup) servings

2 bacon slices (see tip below)
1 (16-ounce) package ready-to-eat coleslaw
¼ cup balsamic vinegar
1½ tablespoons brown sugar
3 tablespoons water
½ teaspoon seasoned salt
¼ teaspoon ground red pepper

1 Cook bacon in a large nonstick skillet over medium-high heat until crisp; remove bacon from pan, reserving drippings in pan. Set bacon aside.

2 Add coleslaw to drippings; sauté over medium-high heat 3 minutes. Add vinegar and remaining 4 ingredients; cook 1 minute, stirring constantly. Remove from heat; crumble bacon, and stir into coleslaw. Serve warm.

Per Serving: Calories 94 Fat 2.3g (saturated 0.8g) Protein 3.4g
Carbohydrate 16.4g Fiber 6.7g Cholesterol 5mg Sodium 172mg
Exchange: 1 Starch

Tip: Used in small quantities, bacon isn't a "no-no" when you're losing weight. One slice of regular bacon has only about 35 calories and 3 grams of fat.

Garden Potato Salad

Makes 6 (⅔-cup) servings

3 medium-sized round red potatoes (about 1 pound)
1 cup frozen cut green beans
1 cup frozen whole-kernel corn
⅓ cup chopped red bell pepper
⅓ cup thinly sliced green onions
½ cup reduced-fat sour cream
2 tablespoons low-fat mayonnaise
½ teaspoon salt
½ teaspoon black pepper
½ teaspoon dried oregano
¼ teaspoon ground cumin

1 Peel potatoes, and cut into cubes. Place in saucepan; add water to cover. Bring to a boil; cover, reduce heat, and simmer 15 minutes or until tender. Drain and place in large bowl to cool.

2 Place green beans and corn in the same saucepan; add water to cover. Bring to a boil; cover, reduce heat, and simmer 5 minutes or until beans are crisp-tender. Drain and cool.

3 Add green beans and corn, red pepper, and green onions to potatoes in bowl. Combine sour cream and remaining 5 ingredients. Pour sour cream mixture over potato mixture and toss well. Cover and chill at least 2 hours before serving.

Per Serving: Calories 123 Fat 3.0g (saturated 1.6g) Protein 4.1g
Carbohydrate 23.6g Fiber 3.2g Cholesterol 10mg Sodium 259mg
Exchanges: 1½ Starch

"Adding all these vegetables to plain ol' potato salad kind of 'bulks up' the salad, so you fill up without filling out!"

Black Bean-Rice Salad

Makes 4 (1-cup) servings

1   (16-ounce) package frozen rice pilaf with vegetables
1   (15-ounce) can black beans, rinsed and drained
3   tablespoons reduced-fat olive oil vinaigrette
1   tablespoon lemon juice
¼   teaspoon salt
¼   teaspoon hot sauce
⅛   teaspoon pepper

1 Cook rice pilaf according to package directions, omitting any salt and fat.

2 Transfer rice pilaf to a large bowl. Add beans and remaining ingredients; toss mixture well. Cover and chill at least 30 minutes before serving.

Per Serving: Calories 205 Fat 3.2g (saturated 0.1g) Protein 7.9g
Carbohydrate 38.4g Fiber 4.3g Cholesterol 0mg Sodium 397mg
Exchanges: 2 Starch, 1 Vegetable, ½ Fat

Presto Pasta Salad

Makes 7 (1-cup) servings

- 8 ounces uncooked rotini (corkscrew pasta)
- 1½ cups broccoli florets
- 1 large red bell pepper, cut into 1-inch pieces (about 2 cups)
- ¾ cup reduced-fat Caesar dressing
- 2 tablespoons preshredded fresh Parmesan cheese

1 Cook pasta according to package directions, omitting any salt and oil. Drain. Rinse with cold water; drain and place in a large bowl.

2 Add broccoli, bell pepper, and dressing; toss well. Cover and chill, if desired. Sprinkle with Parmesan cheese just before serving.

Per Serving: Calories 197 Fat 2.0g (saturated 0.6g) Protein 9.7g
Carbohydrate 35g Fiber 2.1g Cholesterol 2mg Sodium 320mg
Exchanges: 2 Starch, 1 Vegetable

"I now have a chilled pasta salad for lunch with my sandwiches instead of high-fat potato chips."

Caesar Tortellini Salad

Makes 4 servings (serving size: 2½ cups pasta mix and 2 cups lettuce)

1   (9-ounce) package fresh cheese tortellini
2   cups halved cherry tomatoes
½   cup thinly sliced red onion (about 1 small)
¼   cup sliced ripe olives
¼   cup (2 ounces) preshredded fresh Parmesan cheese
½   teaspoon pepper
1   thinly sliced cucumber
½   cup reduced-fat Caesar dressing
1   (10-ounce) package romaine salad

1 Cook pasta according to package directions, omitting any salt and oil. Rinse with cold water; drain again.

2 Combine pasta and next 7 ingredients; toss well. Cover and chill. Serve over romaine salad.

Per Serving: Calories 317 Fat 8.8g (saturated 4.0g) Protein 14.4g
Carbohydrate 45.7g Fiber 4.3g Cholesterol 28mg Sodium 676mg
Exchanges: 3 Starch, 1 Lean Meat, 1 Fat

"Go for the green! The darker the green of the lettuce, the more nutrients it contains."

Roast Beef and Blue Cheese Salad

Makes 4 servings

8   cups packed European-style mixed salad greens
8   ounces thinly sliced, well-trimmed deli roast beef
20 cherry tomatoes
¼   cup (1 ounce) crumbled blue cheese
⅓   cup fat-free raspberry vinaigrette

1 Arrange salad greens evenly on each of 4 plates.

2 Divide roast beef slices into 2 stacks; roll each stack, jelly-roll fashion, and cut crosswise into 1-inch slices.

3 Arrange beef, tomatoes, and cheese over greens. Drizzle evenly with vinaigrette.

Per Serving: Calories 171 Fat 7.4g (saturated 1.4g) Protein 14.9g Carbohydrate 12.9g Fiber 2.9g Cholesterol 5mg Sodium 579mg
Exchanges: 2 Vegetable, 2 Lean Meat

"It only takes about 7 minutes to throw together this no-cook salad. So no excuses for not having time to go for a walk!"

Taco Salad

Makes 4 servings

¾ pound ground round
1 cup chopped onion (about 1 large)
½ teaspoon minced garlic
1 teaspoon salt-free Mexican seasoning
1 (10-ounce) can enchilada sauce
1 (8-ounce) can no-salt-added whole-kernel corn, drained
8 cups shredded iceberg lettuce
1½ cups chopped tomato (about 2 medium)
¾ cup coarsely crushed baked tortilla chips

1 Cook beef, onion, and garlic in a large nonstick skillet over medium-high heat until browned; stir to crumble.

2 Add Mexican seasoning to beef mixture in pan; cook 1 minute. Stir in enchilada sauce and corn. Reduce heat to low, and simmer, uncovered, 5 minutes.

3 Arrange lettuce on 4 individual salad plates. Spoon beef mixture evenly over lettuce; top with tomato and chips.

Per Serving: Calories 310 Fat 8.2g (saturated 1.9g) Protein 22.3g
Carbohydrate 37.5g Fiber 3.9g Cholesterol 52mg Sodium 420mg
Exchanges: 2 Starch, 1 Vegetable, 2 Medium-Fat Meat

Tijuana Chicken Salad

Makes 4 servings

6 cups ready-to-eat garden salad
2 cups shredded roasted chicken breast
½ cup salsa
½ cup reduced-fat sour cream
2 tablespoons lime juice
36 baked tortilla chips (about 4 ounces)

1 Combine garden salad and chicken in a large bowl. Combine salsa, sour cream, and lime juice in a small bowl, stirring well. Pour salsa mixture over salad mixture, and toss gently.

2 Place 9 tortilla chips on each of 4 serving plates. Spoon salad mixture evenly over tortilla chips. Serve immediately.

Per Serving: Calories 299 Fat 7.5g (saturated 3.1g) Protein 26.9g
Carbohydrate 31.5g Fiber 4.4g Cholesterol 75mg Sodium 434mg
Exchanges: 2 Starch, 3 Lean Meat

"When it's time for tortilla chips, grab the bag of low-fat chips. They have 83 percent less fat than regular tortilla chips."

Fruited Chicken Salad

Makes 6 (1-cup) servings

3   cups chopped cooked chicken breast
¾   cup chopped celery
⅓   cup seedless red grapes, halved
1   (20-ounce) can pineapple chunks in juice, drained
¼   cup chopped pecans
½   cup light mayonnaise
¼   teaspoon salt
Lettuce leaves (optional)
Freshly ground black pepper (optional)

1 Combine first 5 ingredients in a large bowl, tossing well. Add mayonnaise and salt, stirring gently until well blended. Cover and chill for at least 30 minutes before serving. If desired, serve on lettuce-lined plates, and sprinkle with pepper.

Per Serving: Calories 248 Fat 11.1g (saturated 1.9g) Protein 21.6g
Carbohydrate 14.7g Fiber 0.8g Cholesterol 64mg Sodium 275mg
Exchanges: 1 Fruit, 3 Lean Meat, ½ Fat

"When you stir juicy fruit like grapes and pineapple into your chicken salad, you can use less mayonnaise and still get a moist, creamy salad."

Chapter 24

Side Dishes

Apple Cider Applesauce

Makes 6 (½-cup) servings

8   cups peeled, sliced cooking apple (about 2½ pounds)
½   cup apple cider or apple juice
¼   cup sugar
⅛   teaspoon ground nutmeg
¼   teaspoon ground cinnamon

1 Combine apple and apple cider in a large saucepan. Bring to a boil, stirring frequently; cover, reduce heat, and simmer 20 minutes or until apple is tender, stirring occasionally.

2 Add sugar and nutmeg to apple mixture; stir. Cook until sugar dissolves, stirring constantly. Mash apple mixture slightly with a potato masher until mixture is chunky. Cover and chill thoroughly. Sprinkle evenly with cinnamon before serving.

Per Serving: Calories 117 Fat 0.5g (saturated 0.1g) Protein 0.3g
Carbohydrate 30.2g Fiber 3.5g Cholesterol 0mg Sodium 1mg
Exchanges: 2 Fruit

"I usually use Rome Beauty, Cortland, or Winesap apples to get the best texture for this applesauce."

Curried Baked Pineapple

Makes 8 servings (serving size: about ⅔ cup)

2   (20-ounce) cans pineapple chunks in juice, drained
15 reduced-fat round buttery crackers, crushed
¼   cup packed brown sugar
¼   cup (1 ounce) shredded reduced-fat sharp Cheddar cheese
½   teaspoon curry powder
Fat-free butter spray

1 Preheat oven to 450°.

2 Place pineapple chunks in a 7 x 11-inch baking dish; set aside.

3 Combine cracker crumbs and next 3 ingredients. Sprinkle cracker mixture over pineapple. Coat cracker mixture with butter spray (about 5 sprays). Bake at 450° for 10 minutes or until lightly browned.

Per Serving: Calories 118 Fat 1.4g (saturated 0.4g) Protein 1.4g
Carbohydrate 24.6g Fiber 0.0g Cholesterol 2mg Sodium 82mg
Exchanges: ½ Starch, 1 Fruit

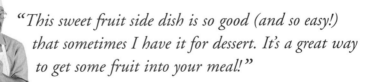

"This sweet fruit side dish is so good (and so easy!) that sometimes I have it for dessert. It's a great way to get some fruit into your meal!"

Asparagus with Cheese Sauce

Makes 6 servings

1½	pounds asparagus spears
1	teaspoon reduced-calorie margarine
½	tablespoon all-purpose flour
½	cup evaporated fat-free milk
¼	cup (1 ounce) finely shredded provolone cheese
⅛	teaspoon salt

Paprika (optional)

1 Snap off tough ends of asparagus. Steam asparagus, covered, 6 to 8 minutes or until crisp-tender.

2 Melt margarine in a small heavy saucepan over medium heat; add flour. Cook, stirring constantly with a whisk, 1 minute. Gradually add milk, stirring constantly until mixture is thick and bubbly. Add cheese and salt, stirring until cheese melts. Arrange asparagus on a serving platter; pour cheese sauce over asparagus. Sprinkle with paprika, if desired.

Per Serving: Calories 50 Fat 1.8g (saturated 0.9g) Protein 4.0g
Carbohydrate 5.2g Fiber 1.0g Cholesterol 4mg Sodium 122mg
Exchange: 1 Vegetable

"The fat-free evaporated milk is the secret ingredient in this creamy, low-fat cheese sauce!"

Creamy
Broccoli Casserole

Makes 8 (½-cup) servings

2   (10-ounce) packages frozen chopped broccoli
½   cup water
1   (10¾-ounce) can condensed reduced-fat, reduced-sodium cream
     of mushroom soup, undiluted
1   (8-ounce) can sliced water chestnuts, drained
⅓   cup minced onion
¼   teaspoon salt
Cooking spray
⅔   cup (2.6 ounces) shredded reduced-fat Cheddar cheese

1 Preheat oven to 350°.

2 Combine broccoli and water in a 1½-quart glass baking dish.
Cover with heavy-duty plastic wrap, and vent. Microwave at
HIGH 7 to 9 minutes or until tender. Drain broccoli, and place in a
medium bowl.

3 Add soup and next 3 ingredients to broccoli in bowl; stir. Coat
same baking dish with cooking spray; spoon broccoli mixture into
dish. Cover and bake at 350° for 20 minutes or until bubbly. Uncover and sprinkle with cheese; bake 2 to 3 minutes or until cheese
melts.

Per Serving: Calories 80 Fat 2.8g (saturated 1.4g) Protein 5.3g
Carbohydrate 9.4g Fiber 2.3g Cholesterol 7mg Sodium 304mg
Exchanges: 2 Vegetable, ½ Fat

*"Vegetable casseroles can trip you up when you're losing
weight because they're usually full of high-fat cheese
and rich sauces. Not this one! But you'd never know
that it's low fat by the taste!"*

Carrots and Zucchini in Browned Pecan Butter

Makes 8 (¹/₃-cup) servings

2   tablespoons butter
½   pound carrots, peeled and thinly sliced
¼   cup finely chopped pecans
½   pound zucchini, trimmed and thinly sliced
¼   teaspoon salt
⅛   teaspoon freshly ground black pepper

1 Melt butter in a large skillet over medium-high heat. Add carrots and pecans; sauté 3 minutes or until pecans are toasted and butter is lightly browned.

2 Add zucchini; sauté 5 minutes or until crisp-tender. Stir in salt and pepper. Serve immediately.

Per Serving: Calories 67 Fat 5.6g (saturated 2.0g) Protein 1.0g
Carbohydrate 4.2g Fiber 1.4g Cholesterol 8mg Sodium 118mg
Exchanges: 1 Vegetable, 1 Fat

"Just a little bit of butter and a little sprinkling of nuts give these vegetables a BIG flavor boost without adding too much fat."

Green Beans with Onion and Garlic

Makes 4 servings

2 cups fresh green beans, trimmed
1 cup water
Cooking spray
2 teaspoons margarine
1 medium onion, thinly sliced
2 garlic cloves, minced

1 Place beans in a large saucepan; add water, and bring to a boil. Cover, reduce heat, and simmer 12 to 15 minutes or until beans are tender. Drain.

2 Coat a large skillet with cooking spray, and add margarine; place over medium-high heat until margarine melts. Add onion and garlic, and cook 5 to 7 minutes or until onion is tender, stirring often. Add green beans to pan, and cook 1 minute or until beans are thoroughly heated, stirring often.

Per Serving: Calories 51 Fat 2.2g (saturated 0.4g) Protein 1.5g
Carbohydrate 7.5g Fiber 1.8g Cholesterol 0mg Sodium 27mg
Exchanges: 1 Vegetable, 1 Fat

"It may be that garlic can actually help fight cancer and heart disease. And we know for sure how good it makes food taste!"

Grilled Eggplant

Makes 4 servings

½ teaspoon dried thyme
¼ teaspoon salt
¼ teaspoon dried rosemary, crushed
¼ teaspoon pepper
1 medium eggplant, unpeeled (about 1¼ pounds)
¼ cup reduced-fat Italian dressing
Cooking spray

1 Preheat the grill.

2 Combine first 4 ingredients. Cut eggplant into ½-inch-thick slices. Brush both sides of each slice with dressing, and sprinkle evenly with herb mixture.

3 Place eggplant on grill rack coated with cooking spray; grill, covered, 5 minutes on each side or until eggplant is tender.

Per Serving: Calories 54 Fat 1.8g (saturated 0.3g) Protein 1.5g
Carbohydrate 9.6g Fiber 3.7g Cholesterol 1mg Sodium 269mg
Exchanges: 2 Vegetable

"Grilling adds a whole new flavor dimension to fresh vegetables! And since grilling doesn't require much extra fat, it's a very healthy way to cook veggies."

Stewed Okra, Corn, and Tomatoes

Makes 4 (¾-cup) servings

1½ cups frozen sliced okra
1 cup frozen whole-kernel corn
¼ cup chopped reduced-fat, 33%-less-sodium ham
1 (14½-ounce) can no-salt-added stewed tomatoes, undrained
1 teaspoon dried basil
¼ teaspoon salt
¼ teaspoon pepper
Cooking spray

1 Combine first 7 ingredients in a large saucepan coated with cooking spray. Bring to a boil; cover, reduce heat, and simmer 15 minutes, stirring occasionally.

Per Serving: Calories 88 Fat 0.8g (saturated 0.2g) Protein 4.7g
Carbohydrate 17.7g Fiber 2.1g Cholesterol 4mg Sodium 238mg
Exchange: 1 Starch

"When fresh veggies aren't in season, get your fill of vitamins and minerals with convenient frozen vegetables."

Sugar Snap Peas
with Cashews

Makes 4 servings

¼ cup orange juice

2 tablespoons reduced-sodium soy sauce

1½ teaspoons cornstarch

Cooking spray

1 (16-ounce) package frozen sugar snap peas

½ cup thinly sliced green onions (about 4 large)

2 tablespoons chopped salted cashews

Orange slices (optional)

1 Combine first 3 ingredients. Set aside.

2 Coat a large nonstick skillet with cooking spray; place over medium-high heat until hot. Add peas and green onions, and cook 4 minutes, stirring often. Add orange juice mixture to pan. Cook, stirring constantly, 1 to 2 minutes or until mixture thickens. Transfer to a serving bowl; sprinkle with cashews. Garnish with orange slices, if desired.

Per Serving: Calories 97 Fat 2.9g (saturated 0.5g) Protein 3.5g
Carbohydrate 14.2g Fiber 3.5g Cholesterol 0mg Sodium 282mg
Exchanges: 1 Starch, ½ Fat

"A little splash of orange juice adds natural sweetness to these crisp and crunchy peas."

Spinach-Artichoke Bake

Makes 6 servings

2   (10-ounce) packages frozen chopped spinach
1   (14½-ounce) can artichoke hearts, undrained
2   teaspoons margarine
½   cup finely chopped onion (about 1 small)
1   (8-ounce) carton reduced-fat sour cream
¼   teaspoon pepper
⅛   teaspoon salt
½   cup (2 ounces) preshredded fresh Parmesan cheese, divided
Cooking spray

1 Cook spinach according to package directions. Drain well, pressing between layers of paper towels to remove excess moisture; set aside.

2 Preheat oven to 350°.

3 Drain artichoke hearts, reserving ¼ cup liquid. Chop artichoke hearts.

4 Melt margarine over medium heat in a large nonstick skillet. Add onion, and sauté until tender. Gently stir in spinach, artichoke hearts, reserved liquid, the sour cream, pepper, salt, and ¼ cup Parmesan cheese.

5 Spoon into a 1½-quart casserole coated with cooking spray; sprinkle with remaining ¼ cup Parmesan cheese. Bake, uncovered, at 350° for 25 to 30 minutes.

Per Serving: Calories 153 Fat 8.0g (saturated 4.3g) Protein 9.0g
Carbohydrate 12.6g Fiber 3.1g Cholesterol 24mg Sodium 441mg
Exchanges: 2 Vegetable, ½ Medium-Fat Meat, 1 Fat

Baked Tomatoes

Makes 5 servings (serving size: 2 slices)

2 large tomatoes, cut into 10 slices
Olive oil-flavored cooking spray
⅓ cup sliced green onions
1½ teaspoons bottled minced garlic
¾ teaspoon dried Italian seasoning
¼ teaspoon salt
¼ teaspoon pepper
¼ cup (1 ounce) preshredded fresh Parmesan cheese

1 Preheat oven to 350°.

2 Arrange tomato slices in a single layer in a 9 x 13-inch baking dish coated with cooking spray.

3 Sprinkle green onions and remaining ingredients over tomato slices. Bake, uncovered, at 350° for 10 to 12 minutes or until thoroughly heated. Serve warm.

Per Serving: Calories 47 Fat 1.6g (saturated 0.8g) Protein 2.7g
Carbohydrate 6.9g Fiber 1.6g Cholesterol 3mg Sodium 193mg
Exchange: 1 Vegetable

"Tomatoes have vitamin C and lycopene—both of which help stop healthy cells from breaking down. So arm yourself with tomatoes in the fight against everything from wrinkles to heart disease!"

Cheese Fries

Makes 6 servings

1½ pounds baking potatoes, unpeeled and cut into thin strips (about 3 potatoes)
Cooking spray
¼ cup grated Parmesan cheese
¼ teaspoon salt
¼ teaspoon pepper
¼ teaspoon paprika

1 Preheat oven to 450°.

2 Coat potato strips with cooking spray, and place in a large heavy-duty zip-top plastic bag.

3 Combine cheese and remaining 3 ingredients; sprinkle over potato strips in bag. Seal bag, and turn to coat.

4 Arrange potato strips in a single layer on a large baking sheet coated with cooking spray. Bake at 450° for 15 minutes, turning once. Serve immediately.

Per Serving: Calories 147 Fat 1.7g (saturated 0.9g) Protein 4.4g
Carbohydrate 28.9g Fiber 2.1g Cholesterol 4mg Sodium 190mg
Exchanges: 2 Starch

"For all you folks who can't give up French fries (like me!), here's the recipe for you. I never crave fast-food fries anymore!"

Feta Mashed Potatoes

Makes 8 (½-cup) servings

2 pounds baking potatoes, peeled and cubed (about 5¼ cups)
¼ cup fat-free milk
3 tablespoons crumbled feta cheese
2 tablespoons reduced-fat sour cream
½ teaspoon salt
½ teaspoon dried oregano
¼ teaspoon pepper

1 Place potatoes in a large saucepan; cover with water, and bring to a boil. Cover, reduce heat, and simmer 20 minutes or until potatoes are very tender.

2 Drain potatoes; return to pan. Beat with a mixer at high speed until smooth. Add milk and remaining ingredients; beat well.

Per Serving: Calories 93 Fat 1.3g (saturated 0.9g) Protein 2.5g
Carbohydrate 18.1g Fiber 1.3g Cholesterol 5mg Sodium 196mg
Exchange: 1 Starch

"When you use a sharp-flavored cheese such as feta, you need only a small amount to get a big bang of flavor!"

Sweet Potatoes in Orange Syrup

Makes 8 (½-cup) servings

2¼ pounds sweet potatoes, peeled and cut into ¼-inch-thick slices
Butter-flavored cooking spray
 ¼ cup reduced-calorie maple syrup
  1 tablespoon frozen orange juice concentrate
  2 tablespoons coarsely chopped pecans, toasted

1 Preheat oven to 375°.

2 Place potato slices, overlapping slightly, on a jelly-roll pan coated with cooking spray. Coat potato with cooking spray. Bake, uncovered, at 375° for 30 minutes or until tender, turning once. Transfer to a bowl.

3 Combine syrup, juice concentrate, and pecans in a glass measure. Microwave at HIGH 30 seconds; drizzle over potato slices.

Per Serving: Calories 141 Fat 2.0g (saturated 0.2g) Protein 2.0g
Carbohydrate 29.7g Fiber 3.5g Cholesterol 0mg Sodium 17mg
Exchanges: 2 Starch

"Sweet potatoes are one holiday food you don't need to give up because they're packed with fiber, iron, and vitamins A, E, and C."

Garlic-Herb Cheese Grits

Makes 6 (¾-cup) servings

2 (16-ounce) cans fat-free, less-sodium chicken broth
1 cup uncooked quick-cooking grits
1 (6-ounce) package garlic-and-spices light cream cheese
    (see tip below)
¼ teaspoon pepper

1 Bring broth to a boil in a medium saucepan over high heat; gradually stir in grits. Cook, stirring constantly, 5 to 7 minutes or until thick.

2 Remove grits from heat, and stir in cream cheese and pepper. Serve immediately.

Per Serving: Calories 170 Fat 5.2g (saturated 3.0g) Protein 6.8g
Carbohydrate 23.5g Fiber 1.3g Cholesterol 20mg Sodium 182mg
Exchanges: 1½ Starch, 1 Fat

Tip: If you can't find garlic-and-spices cream cheese, use light cream cheese and stir in 1 or 2 teaspoons of a garlic-and-herb seasoning blend.

Microwave Risotto

Makes 6 (¹⁄₂-cup) servings

2 tablespoons light butter
¹⁄₂ cup fresh or frozen chopped onion
1 cup uncooked Arborio or other short-grain rice
3 cups fat-free, less-sodium chicken broth
¹⁄₄ teaspoon salt
¹⁄₄ teaspoon freshly ground black pepper
¹⁄₄ cup (1 ounce) preshredded fresh Parmesan cheese

1 Heat butter in a 1¹⁄₂-quart microwave-safe dish, uncovered, at HIGH 30 seconds or until melted. Add onion and rice, stirring to coat. Cook, uncovered, at HIGH 4 minutes.

2 Stir in chicken broth; cook, uncovered, at HIGH 9 minutes. Stir well, and cook, uncovered, at HIGH 9 minutes. Remove from microwave, and let stand 5 minutes or until all liquid is absorbed. Stir in salt, pepper, and cheese.

Per Serving: Calories 186 Fat 3.3g (saturated 2.1g) Protein 6.0g
Carbohydrate 31.3g Fiber 0.9g Cholesterol 10mg Sodium 509mg
Exchanges: 2 Starch, ¹⁄₂ Fat

"You may never make risotto the traditional way again (with constant stirring) after you see what creamy results you can get from the microwave."

Spanish Rice

Makes 6 (½-cup) servings

Cooking spray
- 1   cup chopped onion
- ⅔   cup diced green bell pepper
- 1   cup uncooked instant rice
- ½   teaspoon prepared mustard
- ¼   teaspoon black pepper
- 1   (14.5-ounce) can whole tomatoes, undrained and chopped (see note below)
- 1   (5.5-ounce) can tomato juice

1 Coat a large nonstick skillet with cooking spray; place over medium-high heat until hot. Add onion and bell pepper; sauté 2 minutes or until tender.

2 Add rice, and sauté 5 minutes. Add mustard and remaining ingredients; reduce heat, and simmer, uncovered, 8 minutes or until liquid is absorbed.

Per Serving: Calories 90 Fat 0.3g (saturated 0.1g) Protein 2.4g
Carbohydrate 19.9g Fiber 1.4g Cholesterol 0mg Sodium 352mg
Exchanges: 1 Starch, 1 Vegetable

"If you're trying to cut down on sodium, use no-salt-added canned tomatoes and low-sodium tomato juice."

Garlic and Lemon Linguine

Makes 5 (½-cup) servings

1½   tablespoons reduced-calorie margarine
¼   cup grated Parmesan cheese
2   tablespoons lemon juice
½   teaspoon pepper
2   garlic cloves, crushed
2½   cups hot cooked linguine (about 6 ounces uncooked pasta)

1 Melt margarine in a small saucepan over medium heat; stir in Parmesan cheese and next 3 ingredients.

2 Pour cheese mixture over pasta; toss gently. Serve immediately.

Per Serving: Calories 80 Fat 3.6g (saturated 1.1g) Protein 3.1g
Carbohydrate 9.2g Fiber 0.5g Cholesterol 3mg Sodium 108mg
Exchanges: ½ Starch, 1 Fat

"It's not that you have to give up pasta to lose weight—you just don't need to eat a whole platter of noodles to be satisfied."

Macaroni and Cheese

Makes 11 (½-cup) servings

1 (8-ounce) package elbow macaroni
2 tablespoons reduced-calorie margarine
2 tablespoons all-purpose flour
2 cups fat-free milk
1½ cups (6 ounces) shredded reduced-fat sharp Cheddar cheese
½ teaspoon salt
3 tablespoons egg substitute
Cooking spray
¼ teaspoon paprika

1 Preheat oven to 350°.

2 Cook pasta according to package directions, omitting any salt and oil. Drain.

3 Melt margarine in a heavy saucepan over low heat; add flour, stirring until smooth. Cook, stirring constantly, 1 minute. Gradually add milk; cook over medium heat, stirring constantly, until thick and bubbly. Add cheese and salt, stirring until cheese melts. Gradually stir about one-fourth of hot mixture into egg substitute. Add to remaining hot mixture, stirring constantly.

4 Combine cheese sauce and pasta; pour into a 2-quart baking dish coated with cooking spray. Sprinkle with paprika. Bake at 350° for 25 to 30 minutes or until thoroughly heated.

Per Serving: Calories 111 Fat 4.6g (saturated 2.0g) Protein 7.6g
Carbohydrate 9.8g Fiber 0.4g Cholesterol 11mg Sodium 268mg
Exchanges: 1 Starch, 1 Fat

Chapter 25

Soups & Sandwiches

Chilled Strawberry-Ginger Soup

Makes 6 (¾-cup) servings

1   (16-ounce) package frozen unsweetened strawberries, partially
      thawed
1   (15-ounce) can pear halves in juice, undrained
½   cup thawed orange juice concentrate, undiluted
¼   cup honey
1   tablespoon grated peeled fresh ginger or bottled minced ginger

1 Combine all ingredients in a blender; process until smooth,
stopping once to scrape down sides. Cover and chill at least 1
hour before serving.

Per Serving: Calories 143 Fat 0.2g (saturated 0.0g) Protein 1.2g
Carbohydrate 36.8g Fiber 1.4g Cholesterol 0mg Sodium 6mg
Exchanges: ½ Starch, 2 Fruit

*"When you don't have time to peel, chop, or slice raw
fruit, frozen is fine. You can enjoy this quick soup
year-round with convenient frozen and canned
fruit."*

Tropical Melon Soup

Makes 4 (1-cup) servings

2 cups chopped cantaloupe (about 1 large)
1½ cups chopped mango (about 2)
1 tablespoon lemon juice
½ teaspoon almond extract
1 cup fat-free half-and-half
¼ cup cream of coconut (see note below)
4 teaspoons flaked sweetened coconut, toasted

1 Combine first 6 ingredients in a blender; process until smooth, stopping once to scrape down sides. Cover and chill 1 hour.

2 Ladle soup into serving bowls; sprinkle each with 1 teaspoon toasted coconut.

Per Serving: Calories 143 Fat 4.2g (saturated 3.5g) Protein 1.7g
Carbohydrate 25.3g Fiber 2.3g Cholesterol 0mg Sodium 53mg
Exchanges: 1½ Fruit, 1 Fat

"Coconut and cream of coconut both have saturated fat—but a little coconut goes a long way in blending up a taste of the tropics."

Gazpacho

Makes 4 (1-cup) servings

1 (14.5-ounce) can diced tomatoes with garlic and onions,
   undrained and chilled
1 cup vegetable juice, chilled
¾ cup seeded peeled cucumber, coarsely chopped
½ cup chopped green bell pepper
⅓ cup chopped green onions
1 tablespoon red wine vinegar
1 teaspoon olive oil
¼ teaspoon salt
⅛ teaspoon freshly ground black pepper
⅛ teaspoon hot sauce
1 garlic clove, minced
12 fat-free herb-seasoned croutons

1 Combine all ingredients except croutons in a large bowl. Cover and chill at least 1 hour.

2 Ladle soup into individual serving bowls. Top each serving with 3 croutons.

Per Serving: Calories 83 Fat 1.5g (saturated 0.2g) Protein 2.6g
Carbohydrate 15.3g Fiber 1.3g Cholesterol 0mg Sodium 804mg
Exchanges: 3 Vegetable

"This refreshing chilled soup is loaded with good-for-you foods such as canned tomatoes and tomato juice. Tomato products contain the nutrient lycopene, which may help fight certain types of cancer."

French Onion Soup

Makes 4 (1¾-cup) servings

 1 teaspoon olive oil
2½ pounds sweet onions, sliced and separated into rings
 2 (14½-ounce) cans fat-free, less-sodium beef broth
 2 teaspoons dry sherry
 2 teaspoons low-sodium Worcestershire sauce
 4 (½-inch-thick) slices French bread baguette
 ½ cup (2 ounces) shredded Swiss cheese
Freshly ground black pepper (optional)

1 Heat oil in a Dutch oven over medium-high heat 1 minute. Add onion. Cook 12 minutes or until tender and golden, stirring often.

2 Stir in broth; bring to a boil. Cover, reduce heat, and simmer 20 minutes. Stir in sherry and Worcestershire sauce.

3 Preheat broiler.

4 Place bread slices on a baking sheet, and broil 1 minute or until lightly browned. Turn bread; sprinkle evenly with cheese. Broil an additional 1 minute or until cheese melts.

5 Ladle 1¾ cups soup into serving bowls. Top each serving with a cheese-topped bread slice, and sprinkle with freshly ground pepper, if desired. Serve immediately.

Per Serving: Calories 254 Fat 6.9g (saturated 3.0g) Protein 9.8g
Carbohydrate 37.0g Fiber 5.4g Cholesterol 16mg Sodium 287mg
Exchanges: 2 Starch, 1 Vegetable, 1 Fat

Minestrone

Makes 10 (1-cup) servings

 2 teaspoons olive oil
 2 garlic cloves, minced
 3 (14½-ounce) cans fat-free, less-sodium chicken broth
 1 (16-ounce) package frozen Italian-style vegetables
 1 (16-ounce) can pinto beans, rinsed and drained
 1 (14.5-ounce) can diced Italian-style tomatoes, undrained
¾ cup (3 ounces) uncooked tubetti (small tubular pasta)
1½ teaspoons dried Italian seasoning
10 teaspoons preshredded fresh Parmesan cheese

1 Heat oil in a large saucepan over medium heat. Add garlic, and sauté 1 minute or until lightly browned. Stir in chicken broth and next 5 ingredients. Bring to a boil; reduce heat, and simmer, uncovered, 15 minutes or until pasta is tender.

2 Ladle into individual serving bowls, and sprinkle each serving with 1 teaspoon Parmesan cheese.

Per Serving: Calories 143 Fat 1.9g (saturated 0.5g) Protein 6.2g
Carbohydrate 23.9g Fiber 3.3g Cholesterol 1mg Sodium 509mg
Exchanges: 1 Starch, 2 Vegetable

"This hearty soup has a lot of fiber from the vegetables and the pinto beans, so it really fills me up."

Potato-Broccoli Soup

Makes 7 (1-cup) servings

3 cups cubed peeled potato (about 1 pound)
1 cup frozen chopped broccoli, thawed
½ cup chopped carrot
½ cup water
¼ teaspoon salt
1 (14½-ounce) can fat-free, less-sodium chicken broth
1½ cups low-fat (1%) milk
3 tablespoons all-purpose flour
6 ounces light processed cheese, cubed

1 Combine first 6 ingredients in a large Dutch oven. Bring to a boil; cover, reduce heat, and simmer 20 minutes.

2 Combine milk and flour, stirring until smooth. Add milk mixture and cheese to vegetable mixture in pan. Cook over medium heat, stirring constantly, until cheese melts and mixture thickens.

Per Serving: Calories 153 Fat 3.3g (saturated 2.1g) Protein 9.4g
Carbohydrate 22.0g Fiber 2.0g Cholesterol 11mg Sodium 484mg
Exchanges: 1 Starch, 1 Vegetable, 1 Lean Meat

"What better way to eat your vegetables than in a creamy, cheesy soup?"

Southwestern Vegetable Soup

Makes 8 (1-cup) servings

2 cups chopped onion
½ cup water
2 garlic cloves, minced
1 tablespoon ground cumin
1 tablespoon ground coriander
1 cup bottled salsa
¾ cup chopped red bell pepper (about 1)
¾ cup chopped green bell pepper (about 1)
2 (15-ounce) cans black beans, rinsed and drained
2 (14.5-ounce) cans stewed tomatoes, undrained
2 cups frozen whole-kernel corn
3 tablespoons chopped fresh or 1 tablespoon dried cilantro leaves

1 Combine first 3 ingredients in a large Dutch oven; cook over medium-high heat 3 to 5 minutes or until onion is tender, stirring often. Add cumin and coriander; cook 1 minute, stirring constantly. Stir in salsa and peppers. Cover, reduce heat, and simmer 5 minutes, stirring occasionally.

2 Add black beans and tomatoes; cover and simmer 10 minutes. Add corn; cook 5 minutes. Stir in cilantro just before serving.

Per Serving: Calories 194 Fat 1.4g (saturated 0.2g) Protein 10.1g
Carbohydrate 39.3g Fiber 6.2g Cholesterol 0mg Sodium 576mg
Exchanges: 2 Starch, 2 Vegetable

New England Clam Chowder

Makes 7 (1-cup) servings

2 teaspoons light butter
3 small red potatoes, diced
1 onion, chopped
1 cup chopped celery
1 cup chopped carrot
¼ teaspoon pepper
3 (8-ounce) bottles clam juice, divided
2 tablespoons all-purpose flour
2 (6.5-ounce) cans minced clams, undrained
¾ cup fat-free half-and-half

1 Melt butter in a Dutch oven over medium heat. Add potatoes and next 4 ingredients. Cover and cook over medium heat 10 minutes, stirring occasionally. (Do not brown.)

2 Combine ½ cup clam juice and the flour; add to vegetables, stirring gently. Stir in remaining clam juice. Bring to a boil; reduce heat, and simmer, uncovered, 25 minutes or until vegetables are tender. Stir in clams and half-and-half, and serve immediately.

Per Serving: Calories 143 Fat 0.8g (saturated 0.4g) Protein 7.0g Carbohydrate 25.8g Fiber 2.7g Cholesterol 18mg Sodium 509mg
Exchanges: ½ Starch, ½ Vegetable, ½ Very Lean Meat

Sausage and Tortellini Soup

Makes 8 (1-cup) servings

½   pound turkey Italian sausage
¾   cup chopped onion
2   garlic cloves, minced
2   (14½-ounce) cans diced tomatoes with basil, garlic, and oregano, undrained (see tip below)
2   (14½-ounce) cans fat-free, less-sodium chicken broth
½   teaspoon fennel seeds
½   teaspoon coarsely ground black pepper
1   (9-ounce) package fresh cheese tortellini
2   cups torn fresh spinach

1 Remove casings from sausage. Cook sausage, onion, and garlic in a large Dutch oven over medium heat until sausage is browned, stirring to crumble. Drain well; return to pan.

2 Add tomatoes and next 3 ingredients; bring to a boil. Cover, reduce heat, and simmer 15 minutes. Add tortellini; cover and simmer 6 minutes, stirring occasionally. Stir in spinach, and cook 2 minutes.

Per Serving: Calories 198 Fat 5.5g (saturated 2.1g) Protein 14.0g
Carbohydrate 27.0g Fiber 2.3g Cholesterol 47mg Sodium 1,192mg
Exchanges: 1½ Starch, 1 Vegetable, 1 Medium-Fat Meat

Tip: If you need to reduce the sodium, use no-salt-added tomatoes and low-sodium chicken broth.

Vegetable-Beef Soup

Makes 6 (2-cup) servings

1   pound lean beef tips (see note below)
2   (14½-ounce) cans low-salt beef broth
2   (14½-ounce) cans no-salt-added stewed tomatoes, undrained
2   (16-ounce) packages frozen mixed vegetables
1   cup frozen whole-kernel corn
½   teaspoon salt
½   teaspoon pepper
1½ teaspoons minced fresh or ½ teaspoon dried thyme

1 Cook meat in a Dutch oven over medium-high heat until browned, stirring frequently. Add broth and remaining ingredients, stirring well. Bring to a boil; cover, reduce heat, and simmer 20 minutes.

Per Serving: Calories 286 Fat 3.8g (saturated 1.3g) Protein 25.0g
Carbohydrate 37.2g Fiber 7.6g Cholesterol 43mg Sodium 378mg
Exchanges: 2 Starch, 1 Vegetable, 2 Lean Meat

"If you have leftover lean roast beef, you can cut it into bite-sized pieces and use it in the soup instead of beef tips."

Cheesy Chicken-Corn Soup

Makes 12 (1-cup) servings

3   (10¾-ounce) cans condensed reduced-fat, reduced-sodium cream
      of chicken soup, undiluted
1   (14½-ounce) can fat-free, less-sodium chicken broth
2   cups chopped cooked chicken breast
8   ounces light processed cheese, cubed
¼   teaspoon pepper
1   (16-ounce) package frozen whole-kernel corn
1   (10-ounce) can diced tomatoes and green chilies, undrained
1   (8½-ounce) can cream-style corn
1   garlic clove, minced

1 Combine soup and broth in a large Dutch oven, stirring well
with a whisk; add chicken and remaining ingredients. Bring to
a boil over medium heat. Reduce heat, and simmer, uncovered, 30
minutes, stirring often.

Per Serving: Calories 184 Fat 4.5g (saturated 2.3g) Protein 14.3g
Carbohydrate 22.2g Fiber 1.4g Cholesterol 34mg Sodium 855mg
Exchanges: 1½ Starch, 2 Very Lean Meat

Tip: If you can't use 12 cups of soup all at one time, you can freeze
some of this in an airtight container for up to a month.

Quick Chicken Gumbo

Makes 5 (1-cup) servings

1 teaspoon olive oil
1 (10-ounce) package frozen chopped onion, celery and pepper blend
2 tablespoons all-purpose flour
1 cup fat-free, less-sodium chicken broth
¼ teaspoon hot sauce
1 (14½-ounce) can Cajun-style stewed tomatoes, undrained
1 (10-ounce) package frozen sliced okra
1½ cups frozen diced cooked chicken breast

1 Heat olive oil in a large nonstick skillet over medium-high heat. Add vegetable blend; sauté 3 minutes. Add flour, stirring well.

2 Add chicken broth, hot sauce, and tomatoes to pan; cook 3 minutes or until mixture thickens slightly. Add okra and chicken; cover and cook 8 minutes or until okra is tender.

Per Serving: Calories 164 Fat 3.1g (saturated 0.6g) Protein 16.8g
Carbohydrate 16.8g Fiber 2.0g Cholesterol 33mg Sodium 462mg
Exchanges: 3 Vegetable, 2 Very Lean Meat

"I keep frozen diced or chopped cooked chicken in my freezer all the time so I'll always have some ready to stir into soups or stuff into a sandwich."

Dump-and-Stir Chili

Makes 11 (1-cup) servings

2   (15-ounce) cans 99% fat-free turkey chili without beans
2   (15-ounce) cans no-salt-added pinto beans, undrained
2   (14½-ounce) cans no-salt-added diced tomatoes, undrained
1   (10-ounce) can diced tomatoes and green chilies, undrained
3   tablespoons instant minced onion
1   tablespoon chili powder

1 Combine all ingredients in a large Dutch oven; bring to a boil. Cover, reduce heat, and simmer 10 minutes. Uncover and simmer 10 minutes, stirring occasionally.

Per Serving: Calories 170 Fat 1.2g (saturated 0.4g) Protein 14.1g Carbohydrate 25.6g Fiber 7.3g Cholesterol 0mg Sodium 591mg
Exchanges: 1½ Starch, ½ Vegetable, 1 Very Lean Meat

"My favorite toppings for a bowl of chili are shredded cheese, sour cream, and crushed tortilla chips. Look at the differences in fat between the regular and reduced-fat versions."

TOPPING	FAT (GRAMS)
Shredded Cheddar (2 tablespoons)	4.7
Reduced-fat shredded Cheddar (2 tablespoons)	2.5
Sour cream (1 tablespoon)	3.0
Reduced-fat sour cream (1 tablespoon)	1.9
Tortilla chips (1 ounce)	6.1
Low-fat baked tortilla chips (1 ounce)	1.0

Breakfast Bagel Stack-Ups

Makes 4 sandwiches

½ (8-ounce) tub light cream cheese, softened
1 tablespoon brown sugar
4 (2.8-ounce) plain bagels, split
¼ cup sliced strawberries
4 (¼-inch-thick) slices pineapple

1 Combine cream cheese and brown sugar in a small bowl, stirring well.

2 Spread cheese mixture evenly over cut sides of 4 bagel halves. Place strawberry slices evenly over cheese mixture; top each serving with a pineapple slice. Top with remaining bagel halves.

Per Sandwich: Calories 388 Fat 7.0g (saturated 2.9g) Protein 14.2g
Carbohydrate 70.0g Fiber 4.0g Cholesterol 16mg Sodium 612mg
Exchanges: 2 Starch, 2 Fruit, 1 High-Fat Meat

For Blueberry Bagel Stack-Ups, substitute ¼ cup fresh blueberries for the strawberries, and use blueberry bagels instead of plain.

"This grab-it-and-go breakfast will keep the mid-morning hunger pangs away. And when you've had breakfast, you're less likely to overeat at lunch."

Garden Vegetable Wraps

Makes 4 wraps

2   turkey bacon slices
¼   cup roasted garlic-flavored light cream cheese
4   (10-inch) flour tortillas
20   fresh basil or spinach leaves, cut into thin strips
2½   cups coarsely chopped tomato (about 2 large)
¾   cup chopped red bell pepper (about 1 small)
¼   teaspoon freshly ground black pepper

1 Microwave bacon at HIGH 2 minutes or until crisp; crumble and set aside.

2 Spread 1 tablespoon cream cheese over each tortilla. Layer bacon, basil, tomato, and red bell pepper evenly over cream cheese; sprinkle evenly with black pepper.

3 Roll up tortillas, jelly-roll fashion; wrap sandwiches with parchment paper or aluminum foil. Cover and chill for at least 15 minutes before serving.

Per Wrap: Calories 194 Fat 6.1g (saturated 2.1g) Protein 6.0g
Carbohydrate 24.2g Fiber 2.9g Cholesterol 13mg Sodium 461mg
Exchanges: 1½ Starch, 1 Fat

"Pack this veggie-filled sandwich in your brown bag so you don't have to resort to the vending machine for lunch."

Cajun Catfish Sandwiches

Makes 4 sandwiches

¼ cup Italian-seasoned breadcrumbs
1 tablespoon salt-free Cajun or Creole seasoning
2 teaspoons dried parsley flakes
4 (4-ounce) farm-raised catfish fillets
3 tablespoons fresh lemon juice (about 1 lemon)
Cooking spray
½ cup reduced-fat sour cream
4 (2-ounce) hamburger buns, toasted
4 green leaf lettuce leaves
¼ cup bottled salsa

1 Combine first 3 ingredients in a small bowl. Dip fish in lemon juice, and dredge in breadcrumb mixture.

2 Coat a large nonstick skillet with cooking spray. Place over medium-high heat until hot. Add fish, and cook 4 to 5 minutes on each side or until fish flakes easily when tested with a fork.

3 Spread sour cream evenly on bottom halves of rolls. Top evenly with lettuce, fish, and salsa; cover with tops of rolls.

Per Sandwich: Calories 372 Fat 9.2g (saturated 2.6g) Protein 28.9g
Carbohydrate 40.6g Fiber 2.0g Cholesterol 71mg Sodium 765mg
Exchanges: 2½ Starch, 3 Lean Meat

"When you eat this fish sandwich instead of a fast-food fried fish sandwich, you save about 15 grams of fat!"

Shrimp Rémoulade Loaf

Makes 6 servings

3   cups water
1   pound peeled and deveined medium shrimp
1   (8-ounce) loaf French bread
¼   cup Creole mustard
3   tablespoons light mayonnaise
3   tablespoons dill pickle relish
¼   teaspoon pepper
6   green leaf lettuce leaves

1 Preheat oven to 425°.

2 Bring water to a boil in a medium saucepan; add shrimp, and cook 3 to 5 minutes or until shrimp are done.

3 Split bread loaf in half horizontally; place halves back together, and wrap loaf in aluminum foil. Bake at 425° for 5 minutes or until heated.

4 Combine mustard and next 3 ingredients. Drain shrimp well; rinse with cold water. Coarsely chop shrimp; add to mustard mixture, stirring well.

5 Line each cut half of bread loaf with 3 lettuce leaves. Spoon shrimp mixture evenly over lettuce. Cut each half diagonally into 3 slices.

Per Serving: Calories 202 Fat 4.2g (saturated 0.4g) Protein 16.8g
Carbohydrate 22.6g Fiber 1.1g Cholesterol 120mg Sodium 610mg
Exchanges: 1½ Starch, 2 Lean Meat

French Dip Sandwiches

Makes 4 sandwiches

4   small soft hoagie rolls, split lengthwise and toasted
4   teaspoons Dijon mustard
1   (14½-ounce) can fat-free beef broth
2   teaspoons dried onion flakes
½   pound 98% fat-free thinly sliced deli roast beef

1 Spread bottom half of each roll with 1 teaspoon mustard. Set aside.

2 Place broth and onion flakes in a small saucepan; bring to a boil.

3 Using tongs, dip one-fourth of beef into broth for 30 seconds and place on bottom half of a roll. Cover with top half of roll. Repeat procedure with remaining roast beef and rolls. Pour remaining broth into ramekins; serve with sandwiches.

Per Sandwich: Calories 279 Fat 5.9g (saturated 3.0g) Protein 17.3g
Carbohydrate 34.9g Fiber 2.1g Cholesterol 20mg Sodium 1,053mg
Exchanges: 2 Starch, 1½ Lean Meat

"The basic sandwich—bread, lunch meats, cheese, and mustard—can pile on the sodium. Fat-free meats and reduced-calorie condiments can help slash fat and calories, but not sodium. So choose low-sodium accompaniments such as carrot and celery sticks rather than chips or pickles."

Hot Beef and Pepper Rolls

Makes 4 sandwiches

Olive oil-flavored cooking spray
½ pound thinly sliced lean roast beef, cut into strips
1 large red bell pepper, seeded and thinly sliced
1 large green bell pepper, seeded and thinly sliced
1 large onion, thinly sliced
4 (2.8-ounce) steak or hoagie rolls, split and warmed
Dried oregano (optional)

1 Coat a large nonstick skillet with cooking spray; place over medium-high heat until hot. Add meat, peppers, and onion; sauté until meat is hot and vegetables are tender.

2 Spoon meat mixture evenly onto bottom halves of rolls. Sprinkle with oregano, if desired, and top with remaining roll halves.

Per Sandwich: Calories 373 Fat 8.0g (sat 2.3g) Protein 21.8g
Carbohydrate 56.1g Fiber 5.0g Cholesterol 66mg Sodium 821mg
Exchanges: 3 Starch, 2 Vegetable, 1 Lean Meat, 1 Fat

"Did you know that one red bell pepper has more vitamin C than a cup of orange juice? And eating foods with vitamin C can reduce our risk of heart disease and even some cancers."

Grilled New Yorker

Makes 2 sandwiches

1   tablespoon low-fat mayonnaise
1   teaspoon Dijon mustard
4   (1-ounce) slices rye bread
2   (¾-ounce) slices low-fat processed Swiss cheese
4   ounces thinly sliced lean 33%-less-sodium ham
1   cup thinly sliced green cabbage
Cooking spray

1 Combine mayonnaise and mustard. Spread mayonnaise mixture on 2 bread slices; top each with 1 cheese slice, 1 ounce ham, ½ cup cabbage, and another 1 ounce ham. Top with remaining 2 bread slices.

2 Coat a nonstick skillet with cooking spray, and place over medium heat until hot. Add sandwiches, and cook 3 minutes on each side or until golden.

Per Sandwich: Calories 276 Fat 6.6g (saturated 2.0g) Protein 20.5g
Carbohydrate 33.8g Fiber 4.3g Cholesterol 34mg Sodium 1,258mg
Exchanges: 2 Starch, 1 Vegetable, 2 Lean Meat

"To reduce the fat in your sandwiches, go easy on the mayo, and switch to a low-fat variety. Small changes can make a big difference when you're on the weight-loss trail!"

Dagwood Sandwich

Makes 4 sandwiches

3   tablespoons low-fat mayonnaise
4   (2½-ounce) submarine rolls
2   tablespoons spicy hot mustard
8   small green leaf lettuce leaves
4   (1-ounce) slices turkey breast, cut in half diagonally
4   (¾-ounce) slices low-fat Swiss cheese, cut in half diagonally
4   slices small red onion
4   (1-ounce) slices turkey ham, cut in half diagonally
4   (¾-ounce) slices low-fat sharp Cheddar cheese, cut in half diagonally

1 Spread mayonnaise evenly on top half of each roll. Spread mustard evenly on bottom half of each roll. Place 1 lettuce leaf on bottom of each roll; top evenly with turkey, Swiss cheese, onion, remaining lettuce, the turkey ham, and Cheddar cheese. Place top of roll over cheese.

Per Sandwich: Calories 415 Fat 12.3g (saturated 4.2g) Protein 30.0g
Carbohydrate 43.7g Fiber 3.0g Cholesterol 51mg Sodium 1,416mg
Exchanges: 3 Starch, 3 Lean Meat

"If you're not a milk drinker, adding cheese to your sandwiches can help boost your calcium intake. And make no bones about it, this is one mineral that most of us don't get enough of, especially when we're cutting calories."

Barbecued Pork Sandwiches

Makes 4 sandwiches

2 (½-pound) pork tenderloins
1 teaspoon vegetable oil
½ cup no-salt-added tomato sauce
2 tablespoons brown sugar
2 tablespoons water
2 tablespoons vinegar
2 tablespoons Worcestershire sauce
¼ teaspoon garlic powder
¼ teaspoon dry mustard
Dash of hot sauce
4 reduced-calorie whole wheat hamburger buns

1 Slice pork; flatten, using a meat mallet. Heat oil in a large non-stick skillet over medium-high heat. Add pork, and cook 3 minutes on each side or until browned.

2 Drain and coarsely chop pork. Wipe drippings from pan; add tomato sauce and next 7 ingredients. Bring to a boil; add pork. Cover, reduce heat, and simmer 20 minutes, stirring often. Spoon ¾ cup pork mixture onto each bun. Serve warm.

Per Sandwich: Calories 269 Fat 6.2g (saturated 1.6g) Protein 27.6g
Carbohydrate 26.5g Fiber 2.9g Cholesterol 67mg Sodium 334mg
Exchanges: 2 Starch, 3 Very Lean Meat

"Starting with lean pork tenderloin is the way to get low-fat barbecued pork!"

Apple-Chicken Salad Sandwich

Makes 4 servings (serving size: ½ pita)

1½   cups chopped cooked chicken breast
 2   cups chopped Red Delicious apple (about 2 large)
¼   cup minced red onion
¼   cup low-fat mayonnaise
½   teaspoon curry powder
¼   teaspoon salt
⅛   teaspoon black pepper
½   cup chopped red bell pepper
 2   (8-inch) pita bread rounds, cut in half crosswise

1 Combine all ingredients except pita bread.

2 Spoon chicken mixture evenly into pita halves.

Per Serving: Calories 364 Fat 10.4g (saturated 1.6g) Protein 26.2g
Carbohydrate 43.6g Fiber 8.4g Cholesterol 53mg Sodium 601mg
Exchanges: 2½ Starch, ½ Fruit, 2½ Very Lean Meat

"This traditional chicken salad sandwich gets a nutritious boost with the addition of fiber-rich chopped apple and bell pepper. And when you increase your fiber, you just may help decrease your risk of developing diabetes."

Oriental Chicken Wraps

Makes 4 wraps

1   teaspoon vegetable oil
2   cups broccoli slaw
1   cup sliced mushrooms
1   (9-ounce) package frozen cooked diced chicken
⅓   cup fat-free, less-sodium chicken broth
½   teaspoon garlic-pepper seasoning
1   tablespoon low-sodium soy sauce
1½   teaspoons cornstarch
4   (6-inch) flour tortillas

1 Heat oil in a large nonstick skillet over medium-high heat. Add broccoli slaw and mushrooms; cook 3 to 4 minutes or until crisp-tender, stirring occasionally.

2 Stir in chicken, broth, and garlic-pepper seasoning. Cover and cook over medium heat 3 minutes or until thoroughly heated.

3 Combine soy sauce and cornstarch, stirring until smooth. Add to pan; cook, stirring constantly, 1 minute or until slightly thick. Spoon one-fourth of chicken mixture down center of each tortilla. Roll up tortillas; serve immediately.

Per Wrap: Calories 256 Fat 6.2g (saturated 1.3g) Protein 24.9g
Carbohydrate 23.8g Fiber 2.8g Cholesterol 54mg Sodium 451mg
Exchanges: 1 Starch, 2 Vegetable, 2 Lean Meat

"Have a little fun with your sandwich fixins' and wrap 'em up in a flour tortilla! (Tortillas just happen to be very low in fat, too.)"

Turkey Pepperoni-Stuffed Pitas

Makes 4 servings (serving size: 2 pita halves)

4   cups torn romaine leaves
½   cup thinly sliced red onion
2   tablespoons light ranch dressing
32 slices turkey pepperoni, cut in half
1   small zucchini, cut into 2-inch strips
½   cup (2 ounces) crumbled tomato-basil feta cheese
4   whole wheat pita bread rounds, cut in half crosswise
¼   teaspoon pepper

1 Combine first 5 ingredients in a large bowl. Stir in feta cheese.

2 Wrap pita halves in damp paper towels, and microwave at HIGH 20 seconds. Spoon about ¾ cup lettuce mixture into each pita half; sprinkle with pepper.

Per Serving: Calories 282 Fat 7.8g (saturated 3.3g) Protein 14.5g
Carbohydrate 40.5g Fiber 6.2g Cholesterol 32mg Sodium 813mg
Exchanges: 2 Starch, 1 Vegetable, 1 High-Fat Meat

"For added protein, omit the zucchini, and add 1 (15-ounce) can drained garbanzo beans."

Recipe Index

Subject Index

p. 359

p. 462

p. 400

p. 460

p. 333

p. 351

p. 395

p. 378

p. 451

p. 464

p. 346

p. 375

p. 371

p. 266

p. 221

p. 367

p. 228

p. 402

p. 289

p. 469